A Process Theory of Organization

A Process Theory of Organization

Tor Hernes

UNIVERSITY PRESS

OXFORD
UNIVERSITY PRESS

Great Clarendon Street, Oxford, OX2 6DP,
United Kingdom

Oxford University Press is a department of the University of Oxford.
It furthers the University's objective of excellence in research, scholarship,
and education by publishing worldwide. Oxford is a registered trade mark of
Oxford University Press in the UK and in certain other countries

© Tor Hernes 2014

The moral rights of the author have been asserted

First Edition published in 2014

Impression: 2

All rights reserved. No part of this publication may be reproduced, stored in
a retrieval system, or transmitted, in any form or by any means, without the
prior permission in writing of Oxford University Press, or as expressly permitted
by law, by licence or under terms agreed with the appropriate reprographics
rights organization. Enquiries concerning reproduction outside the scope of the
above should be sent to the Rights Department, Oxford University Press, at the
address above

You must not circulate this work in any other form
and you must impose this same condition on any acquirer

Published in the United States of America by Oxford University Press
198 Madison Avenue, New York, NY 10016, United States of America

British Library Cataloguing in Publication Data

Data available

Library of Congress Control Number: 2014933811

ISBN 978–0–19–969507–2 (hbk.)
ISBN 978–0–19–969508–9 (pbk.)

Printed and bound by
CPI Group (UK) Ltd, Croydon, CR0 4YY

Links to third party websites are provided by Oxford in good faith and
for information only. Oxford disclaims any responsibility for the materials
contained in any third party website referenced in this work.

For Maya and Tania

PREFACE

At the closing session of the First Organization Studies Summer Workshop in Santorini, Greece in 2005, which was dedicated to process thinking and organization studies, one of the panellists suggested that after having debated process for several days, the time had now come to develop a theory of processes. The proposal drew acclaim from some participants, but created consternation in others. The difference in people's reactions, in fact, reflected a divide between world views that could be sensed throughout the conference. The researchers who felt dismayed thought that if a theory of process could be developed, it would signify a view of process as something that can be observed or measured at a distance. It would, they argued, imply the submission of processes to an interpretation framework hovering somewhere above the processes to be studied. They would rather see process as constitutive *of* the world—including theories about the world. Somewhat in line with Whitehead (1920: 53) they would reject that process can be subject to explanation, and instead see process as an invitation to use speculative language for demonstrating the processual nature of things.

This book is an attempt at theorizing organization on the assumption that process is constitutive of the world. It suggests a vocabulary derived from process philosophy not commonly applied in organization studies. The vocabulary may therefore seem unfamiliar, and perhaps even awkward, to readers schooled primarily by the organizational literature. One reason for proposing a different vocabulary is nevertheless to try to address the ongoing work of organizing as the connecting of heterogeneous actors. I regard any attempt at stabilizing the connecting between actors to be acts of organizing, which is why it is important to understand how various kinds of actors in the making interact in time and space to form an organization, however provisional it may be. For this reason the reader will find, alongside examples from 'normal' organizational life, many examples that would normally not be associated with the organizational literature, such as shepherding, the sinking of a passenger ship, the experience of a sex change, a conversation in a laboratory, and several others.

The book is the result of a journey of puzzling questions that I have asked myself about what happens in time and space in organizational life as the trajectories represented by actors' histories and projections become entangled. Just such a moment of perplexity occurred when I was hospitalized in a large public hospital in Geneva some years ago and was struck by the combined vastness, complexity, and fluidity of its organizational life. To keep boredom at bay I spent some time ruminating about how various theories of organization could be applied to make sense of what was going on around me. Obviously, most theories can be used for explaining parts of what is going on in organizations, and it would be equally trite to say that no theory will ever be able to explain everything that goes on. Still, I was left with a feeling of theoretical inadequacy as I attempted to apply various theories to separate segments and levels of the organizational life that I was witnessing. In particular, I discerned that there was little in the way of theory that could access the situated nature of what I observed while not losing sight of the more general picture. That gnawing feeling of inadequacy, combined with extensive reading of relevant philosophical and sociological literature in subsequent years, has resulted in this book, which makes an attempt to connect the fluidity of day-to-day organizational life with the structures it articulates.

When I use the expression 'organizational life' I do not mean 'life in organizations'. What I mean by organizational life is the ongoing process of making, remaking, unmaking, and relating of organizational actors of all sorts: humans, technologies, concepts, groups, and the like, into meaningful wholes. These meaningful wholes can be a Twitter community, an emerging interest group, an entrepreneur with an idea, a think tank, a fashion show, sporadic interactions among scattered actors around a concept, or the spread of a technology, as well as any form of formalized organization or institution. Meaningful wholes are not entities as such, but may be temporarily experienced as entities.

A bit like Friedman's (2010) description of the lean start-up company EndoStim,[1] the view is of a flat world, where connectedness prevails over size, flow prevails over stability, and temporality prevails over spatiality. A 'flat world' is not meant as a description of a world of endless possibilities, but as a convenient analytical assumption for the appreciation of the emergence of various types of actors, including bureaucracies, entrepreneurs, designers, firms, institutions, brands, concepts, and technologies, and their interconnectedness. Organizational life needs more and better models for explaining the temporal dynamics that arise in the meeting between actors, where they bring different histories with them while shaping futures in which they share. In a previous book (Hernes 2008), using the idea of tangledness to reflect a process-based view of organization, I tentatively regarded process as the becoming of entangled actors. This book, on the other hand, explicitly focuses on the role of time and temporality in the making of actors, which raises a number of issues, such as what we mean by present, past, and future, and how we deal with the notions of continuity and change.

If there is one main message conveyed by this book, it is that 'time matters', and this in a dual sense. Time matters because it is important, and perhaps more important than ever, as the world is apparently continually being sucked into a whirl of crises and events, while uncertainty grows about how to project past experience on future possibilities, and even about whether the past should weigh in at all. Time is also of significance because it gives meaning to *matter*.

The passing of time and the way actors deal with being in time shape and reshape how individuals, groups, organizations, markets, and technologies are understood, and consequently how interaction between dispersed entities of different kinds is undertaken and how the interaction is given meaning and, hence, agency with the passing of time. Of interest is the meaning of being as defined by temporality, which refers to the carving out of temporal existence (present, past, and future) from the passing of time. It invites the study of the impact on things by the passing of time.

The book has theoretical precedents from within organization theory, particularly represented by works by March and colleagues, for whom the connecting of streams of actions, actors, feelings, beliefs, and problems constitutes organizations. While March and colleagues have contributed considerably to better process understanding of organizations, there is a need to extend from their work, notably by focusing more explicitly on time and temporality, which remain distinctly underexamined in organization studies (Langley et al. 2013).[2] Process philosophers hold a key to furthering the field of organization studies precisely by enabling better understanding of the workings of time and temporality. While the book is by no means the first to bring process philosophy to organization studies, its emphasis on time and temporality is distinctly novel.

Until now organization studies has been somewhat complacent about the effects of time on the experience of organizing. Writers have been inclined to seek refuge in spatial representations of reality, while tending to relegate time and temporality to static representations against which space has been understood. Process philosophers, however, invite us to afford time and temporality an active role in organizational life. Bluntly speaking, they invite us to explore the 'work' performed by time and temporality on spatial representations of organizational life. What tends to be forgotten in organizational theorizing is that actors act upon a future state of affairs based on their histories, even if those same histories may be faked, forgotten, or rejected by those actors.

Giving an active role to time and temporality seems particularly important given the present evolution of organizational life. Some years ago a manufacturing company, for example, might employ thousands of people and carry out virtually all related functions, whereas today that same company might consist of a brand and core technology managed by only a handful of people, with the related functions being carried out in various parts of the world. Moreover, those various functions come into being and are upheld through their relations with other entities, each of which brings their own histories to the interactions. In other words, we are looking at a distributed system of actors mutually constituted by temporally ordered acts, rather than a hierarchically ordered monolithic system. Therefore time and temporality typically play a different role in a distributed view than in a hierarchical one. In a hierarchical system time is seen as a scarce resource endowed from the apex, whereas in a distributed system of actors' time becomes the resource from which reality is carved out. The traditional view of an organizational apex that wields authority over a range of in-house functions is badly in need of revision, not least because a distributed rather than a hierarchical view of organizations forces consideration of how the temporal construction of the reality of respective actors influences how they co-create organizations.

The flattening of organizational life takes place at the same time as interactive technologies become increasingly more prominent. One aspect is that of speed, but an equally important aspect is the temporal effects of coordination between actors with different historicities and ambitions at different locations and sometimes in different time zones. The connecting dynamics of organizational life and the formation of organizations need to be better understood, notably by better understanding how events—encounters between actors in the making—connect to each other and reproduce patterns or structures of events. For example, while the connecting power of social media has been demonstrated by recent political events, their importance in the definition of organizational life remains to be understood, especially because new forms of collaboration and exchange are emerging such as, for example, crowdsourcing, conceptualized as clouds or the foam of creative encounters. The very notion of crowds as arenas of organizational activity demands that novel analytical frameworks be developed.

At a more theoretical level the book may be seen as an appeal to an 'atomistic'[3] theory of organization, where ideas of organizational boundaries and structure are abandoned, and where the focus of analysis is on the connecting power of events, seen as encounters between heterogeneous organizational actors, rather than the connecting power of structures, systems, cultures, or the like. Consistently with process philosophy, order is seen as arising from flow and not vice versa, that is, there is not a unitary organizational actor that acts, but the making of organizational actors through acting. The flow of time gives rise to ordering attempts, which in turn give rise to organizations. This, I believe, is a feature of the world in which we find ourselves, where an idea in one part of the world, a piece of regulation in another, technology in the third, production in the fourth, and finance in the fifth may come together momentarily and set in motion an assembly of events and elements, which precariously yet vigorously reproduces itself from a growing past while continually changing for a different future. It is this sense of movement that traditional organization theory has withheld from organizational life. It is time to put it back where it belongs.

ACKNOWLEDGEMENTS

The Department of Organization at Copenhagen Business School (CBS) is a truly wonderful place for someone who wishes to pursue ideas in the crossroads between philosophy, sociology, and organization studies. I am deeply grateful for the many enlightening discussions I have had with my colleagues there. At the department, I have also had the fortunate opportunity of teaching and supervising in the department's Strategy, Organization and Leadership Programme (SOL), where I have had the privilege of working with inquisitive, demanding students whose comments and questions have prodded further reflection on the ideas in this book. I am also grateful to the students in various CBS PhD programmes for challenging me to explain and position my ideas. I am indebted to the BI Norwegian Business School, which offered multiple opportunities for academic enrichment from 2000 to 2008. An important source of institutional inspiration has been the international Process Organization Studies symposia held on various Greek islands that provided invaluable occasions to discuss ideas of process. I am also grateful to the organizations that I have had the pleasure to study, including the Ulstein Group and the LEGO Group. Finally, I greatly appreciate the insightful, thought-provoking discussions I have had with colleagues at Vestfold University College, Norway, over the last two years.

I owe special thanks to the following persons who took time to read parts of the manuscript while in draft form and provided indispensible advice on how to improve it: Tore Bakken, Robert Chia, Francois Cooren, Ann Cunliffe, Silvia Gherardi, Jenny Helin, Philippe Lorino, Saku Mantere, James G. March, Reijo Miettinen, Anne Roelsgaard, Ted Schatzki, Majken Schultz, and Steve Woolgar.

Conversations and delightful moments with friends and colleagues in various settings and from various institutions over the years have helped inspire and shape the ideas found in these pages. Thus I would like to thank: Elena Antonacopoulou, Tore Bakken, Marie Bengtsson, Are Branstad, Thomas Brekke, Kjell Caspersen, Robert Chia, Michael D. Cohen, Robert Cooper, Hervé Corvellec, Barbara Czarniawska, Ida Danneskiold-Samsøe, Ward Egan, Susanne Ekman, Henrika Franck, Christina Garsten, Elana Feldman, Martha S. Feldman, Susse Georg, Mike Geppert, Mary Ann Glynn, Mary Jo Hatch, Elisabet Hauge, Jenny Helin, Daniel Hjorth, Thomas Hoholm, Robin Holt, Eirik Irgens, Rasmus Johnsen, Peter Karnøe, Peter Kjær, Morten Knudsen, Martin Kornberger, Kristian Kreiner, Ann Langley, Anne Mette Langvad, Juha Laurila, Thomas Lennerfors, Jon Erland Lervik, Kajsa Lindberg, Philippe Lorino, Anders Koed Madsen, James G. March, Marie Mathiesen, Renate

Meyer, Anuk Nair, Richard Nielsen, David Obstfeld, Ansgar Ødegård, Anni Paalumäki, Rebecca Pinheiro-Croisel, Ursula Plesner, Mike Pratt, Kätlin Pulk, Lakshmi Ramarajan, Anne Roelsgaard, Gerhard E. Schjelderup, Kield Schmidt, Dennis Schoeneborn, Barbara Simpson, Peter Skærbæk, Matt Statler, Jonas Söderlund, Jesper Strandgaard, Silviya Svejenova, Are Thorkildsen, Kjell Tryggestad, Hari Tsoukas, Ib Tunby Gulbrandsen, Mike Tushman, Andrew van de Ven, Fredrik Weibull, Elke Weik, Ann Westenholz, Gail Whiteman, and Mike Zundel.

I am particularly indebted to Majken Schultz for numerous stimulating conversations about time and temporality in various forms of organizational life.

CONTENTS

1. Introduction   1

PART I   SOME PROBLEMS OF ORGANIZATION THEORY AND THE POTENTIAL OF PROCESS ORGANIZATION THEORY

2. Why Assumptions in Organization Theory Do Not Work for Explaining Organizing in a World on the Move   11

   2.1 Why it is Important to Assume a World on the Move   11
   2.2 Correspondence Assumptions and Some of their Problems   16
   2.3 Misplaced Concreteness Assumptions   19
   2.4 Homogeneity Assumptions   21
   2.5 Circumscription and Proximity Assumptions   26
   2.6 Stability Versus Change Assumptions   29
   2.7 Inert Temporalities Assumptions   31

3. Assumptions for Organizing in a World on the Move   39

   3.1 Becoming in a World on the Move   39
   3.2 Ongoing Temporality   44
   3.3 Endogeneity of Process   47
   3.4 Actions, Acts, We-ness, and Actors   53
   3.5 Organization as Connecting   59
   3.6 Potentiality, Actuality, and Contingencies   65
   3.7 Process and Structure   67

PART II   TOWARDS A PROCESS THEORY OF ORGANIZATION

4. Temporality and Process   75

   4.1 Temporal Structuring   75
   4.2 Organizational Presents and Living Presents   80
   4.3 Organizational Presents and the Becoming of Events   87
   4.4 Temporal Agency and Event Formations   92

5. Organization, Meaning Structures, and Time — 99

   5.1 Event-Objects and Delineation of Things — 99
   5.2 Organizational Meaning Structures — 104
   5.3 Organizing as Articulation of Organizational Meaning Structures — 115
   5.4 Articulation, Time, and Memory — 117

6. Articulatory Modes and Agency — 123

   6.1 Setting the Stage — 123
   6.2 Articulation and Modes — 124
   6.3 Events and Agency — 128
   6.4 Intersubjective Articulation — 130
   6.5 Practical Articulation — 134
   6.6 Material Articulation — 136
   6.7 Textual Articulation — 139
   6.8 Tacit Articulation — 144
   6.9 Events and Meaning Structures — 149

PART III PROCESS THEORY AND SELECTED ASPECTS OF ORGANIZATION AND MANAGEMENT

7. Process Theory, Organizational Continuity, and Change — 155

8. Managing and Leading in Time — 163

9. Organizational Culture, Identity, and Institutions — 171

   9.1 Organizational Culture as Memory — 171
   9.2 Organizational Identity as Spatio-Temporal Distinctions — 173
   9.3 Institutions as Stubborn Facts — 176

10. Some Thoughts on Studying Process — 179

11. A Plea for Mystery — 183

ANNEX: THE THEORETICAL FRAMEWORK IN BRIEF — 189
NOTES — 191
REFERENCES — 219
NAME INDEX — 235
SUBJECT INDEX — 239

1 Introduction

> But why would one be interested in adopting and promoting a process perspective? The simplest answer is that, as mentioned above, since time is an inescapable reality, process conceptualizations that take time into account offer an essential contribution to our understanding of the world that is unavailable from more traditional research-based conceptual models that tend to either ignore time completely, compress it into variables (describing decision making as fast or slow, or environments as dynamic or stable).
>
> (Langley and Tsoukas 2010: 10)

> In any attempts to bridge the domains of experience belonging to the spiritual and physical sides of our nature, time occupies the key position.
>
> (Eddington 1928: 91)

Process is more a disposition than a model or theory, as Chia has reminded me. As a disposition it can help to focus critically on things that otherwise are liable to be taken for granted in organization studies and which impede our understanding of organizing in a 'world on the move', a phrase meant to be consistent with Whitehead's 'the passage of nature'. 'A world on the move' invites the suspension of things as finite units and instead directs attention towards a world in a continuous state of flow. The flow we are talking about, however, is not the flow of money, people, or goods. It is about the flow of time. But time is not confined to the regular ticking of the clock or the appointments marked in an electronic calendar. Instead we find ourselves on the slippery slope of the relentless passage of time, time as eternally perishing, as Whitehead pointed out. The slope of time is slippery in the sense that keeping on one's feet depends on the ongoing drawing of appropriate temporal distinctions between present, past, and future. Nowhere is this more important than in organizational life, where heightened uncertainty combined with increased speed and accelerated rates of change sometimes provides decisions and choices with a heightened sense of acuteness.[1]

As human actors we find ourselves 'thrown' (Heidegger 1927) into the flow of time, as it were, and in the flow of time we carve out the temporal existence of things past, present, and future. In Heidegger's terms, we temporalize from time; and in Garfinkel's (1967: 166), we operate in the 'inner time' of recollection, remembrance, anticipation, expectancy'. Time, then, becomes the very resource from which temporality is created. Temporalization is proper to the entities in question as they project their past upon aspirations in an ongoing present. The past, while being re-enacted, is open to re-interpretation, and the future is an open canvas onto which selected interpretations of past experience are projected, while at the same time this canvas provides a basis for the evoking of past experience. The past–future articulation takes place in an ongoing present characterized by indeterminacy and improvisation. It is not before that present becomes past that it becomes possible to make sense of what the actions and gestures of the present that has passed pointed towards, even though the connecting of the various gestures and utterances were meaningful to the actors during the present. This is when the lived present becomes an 'event', an entity endowed with meaning in such a way that it blends into the spatial, yet fluid construct that is seen as the organization. Therefore the idea of the present plays a key role in the understanding of organization as process. The present—turned—event exhibits agency by reaching out towards other present-turned events, but it is a volatile sort of agency, perpetually in need of reproduction.

Thinking about process[2] is about coming to grips with the phenomenon of being in the flow of time. It is not about the flow of things, but about the things of flow. The things of flow include the actors who find themselves having to organize the world around them in the flow of time. They cannot simply step out of the flow, decide how to organize others, and then step back into the flow, because such an ideal scenario would presume that one could stop time, even reverse it, and start it again. The point is that even by freezing time, by going on leave, taking vacation, or, very unlikely, by *ordering* everyone to do nothing and turn off all machines, does not stop the flow of time. Attempting to substitute that which is with emptiness does not put an end to what is happening. Instead the actors have to organize while on the go, while in the flow of time, staying entangled with everything else that makes up the flow.

This may sound like the usual way to introduce process thinking and it may invite the usual sceptical reactions. If everything is changing all the time, then anything is possible, which runs counter to what we experience in real life, where some things are experienced as stable, thus providing a sense of how and when they change. People in organizations operate within structures, technologies, and legal systems that cannot be changed at will. They are burdened with histories, including heroic stories from the past that are not of their own making. Corporate strategies, visions, and goals are imposed on them, which, incidentally, may or may not work. And they have to follow temporal logics imposed by budget cycles and deadlines. Taking all these experiences into account is important, because they are experienced as real. A process view accepts this as the actuality of organizing, while simultaneously investigating how experience creates, enacts, and defines the phenomenon under study. As an actual state of affairs the organization is seen as a synthesized and coalesced set of ways in which things are perceived as functioning that is neither wrong nor misplaced. Process thinking also invites, however, a view of potentiality, which in turn prompts the question of how things become the way they are in view of the multiple possibilities of becoming. Process thinking invites reflection on the relationships between the given state of affairs and the multiple possibilities for things to turn out otherwise. The adage that there is always more than meets the eye is basic to process studies, which demands that phenomena are studied in their openness and indeterminacy, while accepting that they may provisionally appear closed and determinate.

Studying things as process is obviously not about comparing states of being in time or in space, but about how something persists and changes in view of becoming 'otherwise possible', to paraphrase Luhmann (1995: 133). More than anything, the task is to explain how things persist, and how some configurations achieve stabilization whereas others do not. Our task then becomes to investigate what produces these stabilizing and channelling effects that are typical of organizational life (Latour 1996). Ordering in such a world is not a result of inertia, but more like what Whitehead calls creative order. Chia (1999: 224) nicely states, 'Acts of organizing, much like the ceaseless building of sand-dykes to keep the sea at bay, reflect the on-going struggle to tame the intrinsically nomadic forces of reality.'

I believe that such thinking is far from alien to people who struggle to organize collective activity. If anything, it is more of an issue for people who theorize about organization than for those who actually do the organizing. If we assume that organizational actors are caught in the flow of time, maintaining a coherent past requires effort. For example, it requires no work to convince people in a quickly growing company that keeping things on track and retaining coherent practices over time entails hard work. Organizations are part human systems, and past memories need to be brought to life on an ongoing basis if they are to persist as a basis for a different future. Archives and artefacts, for example, need to be acted into existence: if not, their content perishes from sight as meaningful sources of coherent organized actions. What is more, efforts to keep things alive need to be organized for a coherent past to be maintained. Maintaining a sense of coherent identity, for instance, may require persistent reminders about where it all started and concern, for example, influential founders, their ideas, visions, commitment, and self-sacrifice. The use of narratives is but one of several ways of keeping the past coherent. Some organizations, for example, use corporate museums to keep the past alive. Naturally, keeping the past alive is not just about the past, but also about having a way to look forward. Caught in the flow of time, actors bring the past to bear on a desired future state, although they are aware that they will probably not attain this future state. Many leaders and practitioners are aware of this fact. They also know that if nothing is done to keep things on course, things could get off track, engendering consequences they might find difficult to tackle. So when we work hard to keep things on track, we work hard because we know that if we do not, things will turn out differently than we expected. Anyone who has tried to write a book, train for a championship, apply for a job, prepare a special meal, or pass an exam knows this. Maintaining continuity is hard because there will always be events that threaten to throw things off course.

Working to keep the past alive is not a purely retrospective exercise confined to the bringing forward of memories. As the theorists drawn upon in this book remind us, we are always inescapably in the present, which includes both the past and the future. To be sure, there are pasts that went before the present (present) just as there are futures that come after it. Still, the point is that the pasts and the futures are experienced in the present. What differentiates one present from another is how and how far back into the past and into the future the projection occurs. This is why this book works from the premise that actors operate in an ongoing present. Actors have the ability to evoke the past selectively and make choices about future aspirations informed by the selected past, aided by what Schultz and Hernes (2013), inspired by Mead, refer to as the materials of the present.[3] When the past is evoked in a social setting, we are talking about a living present (Deleuze 2004). The same applies to the future. Even if we consider the future as a goal to be achieved in ten years' time, it is an imagined state that is perceived within the confines of the present. We may say, along with Deleuze (2004), that the past and future are *dimensions* of the living present. But the present more than just includes the past and future, it *shapes* the past and future. An important implication therefore emerges from this, which is the need to examine the 'agency of the present', and in particular how it connects to other organizational presents, past and future, to maintain or alter organizational arrangements.

As process thinking begins to take hold in organization studies, there is a tendency to fall for the temptation of liquefying the notion of process to the extent that the view becomes of little use. Weick (1979) may have inadvertently planted some seeds to this effect when he pitted the verb 'organizing' against the noun 'organizations'. In the eagerness to make process the antithesis of the noun, a sort of Parmenidean world view where nothing moves, it becomes tempting to romanticize a view according to which everything flows, and to then embellish flow with notions such as change, disorder, freedom, innovation, multiplicity, chaos, and creativity.[4] However, to say that everything flows is first and foremost an ontological stance that actually challenges us to look for how flows are stabilized, bent, or deflected. It is precisely such a stance that invites study of how different forms of stabilization come about, including seemingly robust forms such as bureaucracies. The beauty of process thinking lies in leaving open what actually emerges from processes. For example, how institutions evolve depends on the processes, likewise the persistence of institutions depends on the processes that make and sustain them.

All these concerns are oriented towards the future along the arrow of time, while forcing attention towards what has been up until the present. Every organization involves routines, equipment, people, technologies, etc. that exist in the present, while stretching through events back into time. Like a tail of history, they all weigh in on how the organization sees itself in the mirror of its possibilities. It should be obvious that engaging in this process requires not just work, but even some degree of creativity.[5] Quite some time ago now, it was established that organizations should not be considered cultural dupes. A process view such as the one presented in this book challenges us to go much further than that and to consider them capable of assessing alternative courses of action even as they stick to their current course of action (Hernes and Irgens 2013). Assessing alternative courses of action requires imagination about how they might otherwise become even if they are not pursued. Therefore, purposely not changing things is not necessarily a sign of indifference, ignorance, or incompetence. On the contrary it may well be a sign of creativity, imagination, and persistence. For example, it may demand considerable imagination and persistence to organize collaboration with an outside firm in order to keep producing the same product, just as it may involve imagination to consider why it should not be changed. The reason why this requires creativity is that the world is assumed to be on the move, and the time in which to bring about a sense of ordering is evanescent. Things (markets, people, relations, products, beliefs, etc.) change as time moves on, and they sometimes change in surprising ways. Potentiality involves imagination about how things might become in the light of the possibilities that lie ahead, but also about how things of the past might be perceived differently. This is why potentiality is germane to a process view.

To come to grips with some salient features of process, I rely on a collection of thinkers in philosophy for whom temporality was central, notably Henri Bergson, Martin Heidegger, Alfred Schütz, George Herbert Mead, Gilles Deleuze and Alfred North Whitehead in particular. This seems like a broad choice of thinkers for one book and indeed it is. I could have undoubtedly written about organization and process by leaning on just one or two of them. Schooled philosophers might well criticize me for selectively drawing isolated ideas from thinkers who deserve a considerably more thorough understanding and treatment. It may be considered a work of bricolage, as it attempts to build a picture from diverse, although not irreconcilable, sources. There is, however, no standard in the social sciences for how deeply one should engage with a philosopher's thoughts and ideas in order for social theorizing to be seen as validly building upon the ideas of the philosopher. There is, I suppose, a point in social-science theorizing at which the philosophical validity is compromised, philosophical depth is left behind, and social-science criteria for theorizing begin to take over. This is a point at which the philosophical moorings are cut. Whether or not it is the right point will be known neither from an exclusively philosophical viewpoint, nor from an exclusively social-science standpoint. It matters what the aim of the writing is, and the aim of this book is to contribute a novel view of organizing and organizations rooted in process philosophy, to which temporality is essential.

Viewing the world as process, the thinkers from whom I draw ideas in this book developed insights into the temporality of process, notably on the notion of past, present, and future. A common assumption is the primacy of the present and the present as locus for the immediacy of past and future experience.[6] To be sure, there are significant differences between the thinkers concerning, for example, the role of the human and the social in temporal processes. Whitehead's event-based process philosophy is perhaps the one most devoid of actors, using what he called 'actual entities' as its most basic unit of analysis, where entities are constituted by events composed of tempo-spatial experiences rather than things of substance, such as material or human actors. Heidegger, while also working from a non-substance viewpoint, applied the notion of *Dasein*, which refers to the spatio-temporal entity that emerges from engaging with the world. Heidegger's *Dasein* differs from Whitehead's, whose metaphysical scheme aimed at reconciling natural process with that of experience. Still, from a process perspective, Whitehead and Heidegger held parallel views about the relationship between process and entities, whereby they viewed entities and their structured relationships as emerging from processes, and not vice versa.

With Bergson, who applied a human-centred, introspective view of duration and memory, individual human beings get to play a more concrete role in process thinking. For this reason, he could probably penetrate deeper into questions of the passing of time, memory, continuity, and change than many had done before him. Most notably his understanding of the indivisibility of change in time is of importance to process thinking and organization, and the difference between the understanding of time and space. His urge to try and think in terms of movement rather than a series of immobilities, and of duration as the continuous progression of the past, rather than a discrete series of 'nows', encourages a rethink of how time (and hence process) is viewed in organization studies.[7] Mead, a fourth example of a process thinker, drew upon the role of the social far more than the other three philosophers, as did Schütz. Although the different theorists operate with differing notions of the role of the human and the social in temporal processes, the main common ground between their ideas, which to my mind legitimizes the use of them in the same book, is their view of temporality, and particularly their view of the role of what this book refers to as an ongoing present.

The book is to be read as an attempt to develop a temporal process theory of organization, where actors find themselves continually 'thrown' into time.

The importance of time is that it cannot be stopped; it represents the relentless passage of nature, as Whitehead formulated it. Organizers are well aware of this. Whereas they appear to be organizing what is there today, they are in effect also organizing for what might not be there tomorrow. The first represents actuality, the second potentiality. The first is well documented in organizational research; the second remains to be developed further. When we better understand how the two work together, we are in a better position to unravel some of the mysteries of organization, such as what happens when a small idea, a passionate person, an available technology, and an accommodating institution connect to make something novel for the future while activating something that belongs to the past.

The book ends with a plea for mystery in organization studies. There are fascinating stories out there waiting to be told. Alas, many, if not most of them suffer from being sentenced to rejection because they are not set within legitimate theoretical frameworks. As per today there still seems to be a schism between, on the one hand, studies leaning towards natural science logics and, on the other, studies leaning towards constructivist logics. There is no reason, however, why organizations should be treated as either predictable objects anaesthetized by variance theorizing or as amorphous organisms doped by excessive *in situ* theorizing. Neither of them holds much promise of mystery. The one is devoid of life, and hence, force. The other suffers from a lack of form, and hence, a rationale for life and force. Form and life, however, are not antitheses of one another, but forces that play out in time. It is the passing of time that enables us to treat some things as open and indeterminate, as in-the-making so to speak, and others as provisionally closed. This is how we can be in a meeting and experience its outcomes as indeterminate, yet potentially consequential, while at the same time experience that which happens outside the meeting as provisionally stable and given. Closure, in this view, is not about leaving things behind unchanged, but about taking them with us and letting them be changed on a journey of new encounters. The whole point lies in being experimental in life about that which is provisionally given to us with form.

Part I

Some Problems of Organization Theory and the Potential of Process Organization Theory

■ **SUMMARY**

The overall aim of this part is to contrast the basis of traditional organization theory with the demands for a theory that explains organizing in a world on the move. Organization theory was developed to explain the functioning of large formal systems. Although multiple developments have been made in the field to make it more applicable to a contingent, fluid world, some of the basic assumptions of traditional organization theory remain in place. The part contains two main chapters. The first chapter explains why certain assumptions hamper the ability of traditional organization theory to explain organizing in a world on the move. The second chapter discusses elements from process theory that necessitate theorizing organization differently.

2 Why Assumptions in Organization Theory Do Not Work for Explaining Organizing in a World on the Move

■ SUMMARY

This chapter proposes six assumptions that underlie traditional organization theory that have been directed towards the view of organizations as stable, delineated entities circumscribed by boundaries that separate them from their external environments. However, a number of changes have been taking place over the past couple of decades that invite a view of organizations as emergent processes of interaction between heterogeneous entities of widely different sizes, operating from different times and from different places. This makes it necessary to study the extent to which dominant assumptions underlying traditional organization theory respond to the emergent economic and social realities. The chapter begins with arguments about why it is important to assume a world on the move and then examines each of the six assumptions in turn.

2.1 Why it is Important to Assume a World on the Move

> Organization studies and theories are based on time-free statements.
> (Gherardi and Strati 1988: 149)

> No concept of motion is possible without the category of time.
> (Sorokin and Merton 1937: 615)

Almost forty years have now passed since Weick (1974), in a relatively little-cited paper in the *Academy of Management Journal*, urged scholars to pay attention to five types of settings, which he called 'someplace else' than large, established organizations. The five 'someplace else' that he suggested were: (a) everyday events, (b) everyday places, (c) everyday questions, (d) micro-organizations, and (e) absurd organizations. His point was that by looking at places other than large, established organizations, we would become better at generating hypotheses about the larger, more established organizations. Given the present texture of organizational life, we can take his argument yet one step further and claim that events, micro-organizations, and absurd organizations[1] *constitute* contemporary organizations, together with the more formal structures: they are not mere illustrations of what goes on in more complex and formal organizations, they *are* those organizations.

Organization studies is still largely dominated by a view of organizations as bounded systems of social actors whose actions are regulated by various types of social, cognitive, or material mechanisms. The view has given organization theory a place and an important voice in areas such as management studies, economics, sociology, and political science. Its success at gaining a foothold in the social sciences, however, has come at the expense of analytically isolating the organization as an atemporal entity composed of social actors, mediated by technologies and surrounded by a neutral, external environment.[2] This conditional success is similar to that of institutional theory within organization studies, which, as Lawrence, Suddaby, and Leca (2011) pointed out, has been successful in generating intellectual excitement around macro-sociological understanding of organizational life. Both traditional organization theory and institutional theory have achieved success by assuming some sort of invisible equilibrating mechanisms at work. It is hard to find a more convincing footing for scientific legitimacy, although studying equilibrium without allowing for the possibility of being surprised by disequilibrium makes the very assumption of equilibrium a dodgy one.

The field of organization studies grew out of a concern to define formal organizations as social systems distinct from other social systems, such as groups, families, institutions, or markets.[3] Early contributors, such as March and Simon (1958), Thompson (1967), and Perrow (1986) carefully differentiated organizations as formal systems of coordination from other types of systems, and investigated them on those premises. Thus formal organizations have been seen as goal-oriented socio-technical systems, and the task of organization studies has been conceived as working out how such systems operate, evolve, change, and maintain themselves, as well as their effects on humans, the environment, or society. Concerns about phenomena such as rationality, power, emotions, gender, and many other matters have emerged over the years and are explained in the light of organizations as systems exhibiting particular characteristics, including the urge to be rational and coherent.

The preoccupation with the character of organizations as a species of systems has come at the expense of understanding the nature of organization as particular types of socio-material connecting processes. I find it necessary to insist on 'socio-material' in the sense that it is not a question of either socio or material, nor two concomitant but different connecting processes, but of hyphenated socio-material, where the social and the material act as an entangled unity. Such composite connecting processes may lead to the temporary formation of groups, companies, corporations, laboratories, think tanks, institutions, brands, etc., which spur connecting processes in turn. Beyond being socio-material, they have the virtue of connecting actors of various types and sizes while paying attention to their respective histories and ambitions.[4] In other words, not only are the connecting actors heterogeneous, but so are the means by which they are connected.

The idea is to search for generic processes that extend and stabilize socio-material configurations in time and space. In this view, organizations seen as connecting processes would form part of phenomena as diverse as social movements, families, religions, corporations, think tanks, and brands, and not be seen as a sociological phenomenon apart from them. Organization may be described as a particular formation of connecting processes, such as in a family, a group, or an institution, as much as it characterizes a formal organization. For example, rather than study how an organization impacts gender relations, or how gender is conceived, one might study how gendering takes part in shaping the particular connecting dynamics associated with, say, a company or institution.[5]

The contingencies of the organizational world are poorly captured by frameworks and variables commonly used in organization studies. To be sure, no framework can fully capture the actual complexity confronted by organizers. But a problem with common theories is that, rather than address the actual complexity faced by organizers, they confine complexity by locating it within organizational boundaries, as if managers were like Weberian officials trapped down in an administrative bunker, grappling more or less competently with neatly parcelled chunks of complexity. This 'confined complexity' gives ontological priority to the organization, such as by assuming the organization as a context for action and thinking, rather than assuming that actions are what make the organization. Conventional views in organization studies are susceptible to giving precedence to the environment over the organization, and precedence of the organization over actions. This reflects a penchant in the social sciences that goes a long way back.

Alternatively, the complexity facing organizers may be seen as spatio-temporal tangledness, which includes their immediate environment but transcends organizational boundaries to include happenings in faraway places and different times in history. Tangled processes may evolve and interact to form various entities, including individuals, groups, political parties, brands, services, institutions, or products. The temporal dimension is important, because what we perceive of them at the moment is the result of how they have developed over time. In a sense, they 'are' their historicities, which makes it difficult to gain access to the processes that shape organizations and institutions unless we better understand the temporal nature of their making.

Their historicities are tangled and do not evolve neatly apart from each other. Consequently they elude the models of understanding that are commonly applied to them, and also the models organizers apply to create, maintain, and change them.

To illustrate how entities 'are their tangled histories' the following passage from Wallack (1980: 276), in which she illustrates a Whiteheadian view of a stone by contrasting it to the view of a stone as an inert, self-contained, simply located object, illustrates the interconnectedness and contingent nature of the world:

> The Whiteheadian stone, however, is one stone occasion in a society of stone occasions, the antecedent members of which contribute to (by causing) the given stone occasion, the nature of which also causes subsequent occasions, whether stoney or otherwise. The given stone occasion is not fully describable, without considering its antecedents and its efficacy. For, the features of its own constitution, its structure, its mineral content, its layers, and streaks and crystals, its markings and fossils, its hardness, surface, and texture, are present effects of the past. They essentially refer to the stone's history, the route of occasions both of stone and of many other elements and compounds that have culminated as the present stone. And the stone is not fully describable without taking account of its real potentiality for effecting other occasions, not only other occasions of stone, but also occasions of perception, occasions of soil enrichment, occasions of certain uses to animals and plants, and so on. The present stone essentially refers to both antecedent and subsequent occasions, both stone and other sorts, which have acted upon it and upon which it acts and are consequently a part of its nature. A present stone that has no present and no future, no membership in a lengthy society of stone occasions that has been affected by water and air and living things is not understandable as a stone: we understand by a stone an instance of an apparently interminable enduring object, weather-beaten or earth-worn or animal-trodden or otherwise used. And a present stone that has not the real potentialities to be seen and felt—a stone without efficacy upon subsequent occasions of human perception—is not understandable as a stone. The stone's internal constitution and its real potentialities essentially refer not only to other occasions, past and future, of its more or less immediate environment, but to the remote environment as well. The entire stoney society may date back to the sedimentation of muds on the bottom of an early ocean and the antecedents of the mud go back to the origins of the planet, the historical route of which extends back to the birth of the universe. And the present stone occasion will have effects on occasion after occasion extending to the end of the cosmic epoch.

Organizing implies attempts at creating a meaningful and predictable order out of a tangled world. A meaningful world is not one that is known as such, but one that is believed to be as such based on one's own *experience* (Bakken 2014). It implies bringing together strands of a tangled whole within some selected and temporally evolving structures of meaning. Alas, the histories of entities are entangled and consequently do not evolve neatly, as illustrated by the above passage. Consequently, the world in which ordering (Law 2004) takes place eludes the models used to understand and order it. Although organizers may act as if they operate in a closed system, it is in every respect an open system; the unknown forms parts of the known, either as what Spencer-Brown (in Bakken 2014) called the 'unmarked state' or somewhat parallel to what Polanyi (1967: 302) called 'subsidiary awareness'.[6] Luckily, actors are aware, albeit tacitly, of operating in an open world while acting as if it was a closed one. A main challenge for those who study organizational life through the process lens is to try and understand how the assumption of a closed world and the reality of an open one interact with one another.

Privileging connections means assuming flatness, in the sense that actors are not given more agency because they appear larger, more central, more important, or more resourceful. On the contrary, flatness is a way to open for a broader view of practices and mechanisms that serve to stabilize organizational life, but their role in stabilization cannot only be verified by studying how they take part in stabilization. Flatness assumes that whatever takes place at 'other levels' is subsumed by acts and their connecting. Take, for example, the following quote from Friedman (2005), which illustrates the ongoing socio-material connecting in the making of a cartoon segment:

> This efficiency has allowed us to contract with fifty 'stars' for the twenty-six episodes. These interactive recording/writing/animation sessions allow us to record an artist for an entire show in less than half a day, including unlimited takes and rewrites. We record two actors per week. For example, last week we recorded Anne Heche and Smokey Robinson. Technically, we do this over the Internet. We have a VPN [virtual private network] configured on computers in our offices and on what we call writers' 'footballs,' or special laptop computers that can connect over any cat-5 Ethernet connection or wireless broadband connection in the 'field.' This VPN allows us to share the feed from the microphone, images from the session, the real-time script, and all the animation designs amongst all the locations with a simple log-in. Therefore, one way for you to observe is for us to ship you a football. You connect at home, the office, most hotel rooms, or go down to your local Starbucks [which has wireless broadband Internet access], log on, put on a pair of Bose noise-reduction headphones, and listen, watch, read, and comment. 'Sharon, can you sell that line a little more?' Then, over the eleven-week production schedule for the show, you can log in twenty-four hours a day and check the progress of the production as it follows the sun around the world. Technically, you need the 'football' only for the session. You can use your regular laptop to follow the 'dailies' and 'edits' over the production cycle.
>
> (Friedman 2005: 72)

This is an example of what a flat world may be like and it is closer to what many people around the world actually experience compared to what is assumed in mainstream organization theory. Although the example is from media and is naturally quite focused on technology, this is not what I intend to show. What the example shows is that there are multiple ways to connect actors between different settings, and because there are many different ways of connecting, the mode of connecting is open to choice. Two observations are needed to argue why this is of importance to organization studies. First, connecting makes the actors and not the other way around. This is basic to process theory: actors' identities emerge from processes and not vice versa. Second, connecting and hence the making of actors is not exclusively influenced by organizational boundaries. Actors are not assumed to act in a certain way because they belong to such and such an organization, but because they form parts of various settings, including their local organizational setting.

There is a need to explain organizational life while suspending the idea that it happens within organizational boundaries and while allowing it its true contingent nature, whereby actors other than human are given agency as organizers, and where time and temporality are given their due emphasis. Before moving on to develop a process-based framework that goes some way towards that aim, I will explore briefly how current organizational theory responds to such criteria.

2.2 Correspondence Assumptions and Some of their Problems

In a world that is studied from the safe distance of generalized abstraction, contingencies take the form of causality, necessity, and indispensability, where a stable state of affairs is assumed to exist in response to another state of affairs. Such assumptions are not only convenient, but they are also extremely powerful tools of analysis. Causality, necessity, and indispensability are persuasive modes by which arguments can be heard in the social sciences. When they connect to large populations of organizations, they may even be seen as reality itself, rather than ways of seeing reality. Somewhat paradoxically, the further removed the researchers are, the more weight their voices carry. Key to such thinking is the idea of correspondence.[7] Correspondence is a deadly serious idea, because it touches upon the very notion of truth, that is, the point from which our very understanding departs.[8] A central aspect of it is the assumption that truth lies in correspondence between what is experienced or enacted and something else. Correspondence does not necessarily imply similarity, but may imply being different from something else. There may, for example, be correspondence between an organizational state and what is perceived to be the external environment to the organization. Or there may be correspondence in time, such as between a present state of the organization and a previous state of the same organization.

Chia (1999: 215) makes the point succinctly in relation to organizational change:

> A 'correspondence theory of truth' is thus assumed, in which linguistic terms are taken to be accurately representing an external world of discrete and identifiable objects,

forces and generative mechanisms. This *representationalist epistemology* also implies that it is more important to focus on the *outcomes* of change rather than on the process of change itself. Change, according to this view, is merely that transitory phase which is necessary for bridging the various *stages* of any evolutionary process. Underlying this intellectual attitude is an unshakeable assumption that reality is essentially discrete, substantial and enduring. It is this fundamental ontological assumption which provides the inspiration for the scientific obsession with precision, accuracy and parsimony in representing and explaining social and material phenomena, since these are now regarded as relatively stable entities.

A problem with the correspondence assumption is that a more underlying idea of a one-to-one relationship between environment and organization develops, and it is an assumption that is questioned or even refuted by systems theorists such as Luhmann (1995) and organization theorists such as March and Olsen (1975).[9] Nevertheless, even in attempts at thinking processually about organizations and organizing, the idea of correspondence stands strong. For example, Pettigrew, Woodman, and Cameron (2001: 700) claim that, 'If the change process is the stream of analysis, the terrain around the stream that shapes the field of events, and is in turn shaped by them, is a necessary part of the investigation.'

Several schools within organization and management theory take context, that is, the idea of correspondence in space, as the determining factor with regard to processes. In recent decades such a view has been a predominant feature within central schools in organization theory, such as organizational ecology (Hannan and Freeman 1989), new institutionalism (DiMaggio and Powell 1983, 1991), resource dependence theory (Pfeffer and Salancik 1978), evolutionary organization theory (Aldrich 1999), and economic sociology and business systems (Morgan, Whitley, and Moen 2005). The main line of thought underlying these schools is that processes within organizational boundaries are as they are because they correspond to the state of the external environment of the organization. Organizations respond to the demands in their external environments by, for instance, adopting structures deemed legitimate and timely among actors in society at large. This is why new institutionalism, for example, regards forces such as imitation and coercion as a powerful influence when it comes to adopting management ideas. The sources of imitation and coercion are both located outside the organization. For others who are less interested in the symbolic aspect of adaptation and more in economic performance, external factors such as competition and regulation replace the influence of norms and needs for legitimacy. There is a vast literature on business performance that seeks to explain how competition works as a mechanism for performance-based selection. There are similar examples in other parts of management theory, whereby the adoption of certain management styles, for instance, is seen to correlate with certain types of problems.

The idea of correspondence is strongly embedded in much social science, partly because it is a relatively 'safe' way to truth. It lends the impression of safety because understanding can lean on the transposition of observable—and sometimes measurable—phenomena. For example, traits of an organizational culture may be seen to correspond to beliefs of a leader and compared to similar leaders elsewhere in the world. The power of correspondence legitimizes generalization of findings, which often facilitates the publication of research in peer-reviewed journals.

The most common way to criticize correspondence is to lump it together with positivism and sometimes rationalism. Thus a frequent argument is that the world is fragmented, ambiguous, and subjective, rather than coherent, unequivocal, and objective. But beyond the paradigm wars, their polemics and straw man projections there are logical problems with the idea of correspondence. Let me briefly suggest three principal problems associated with the assumption of correspondence.

One problem has to do with the multiple, or nested quality of organizational environments. For example, a representative and well-known line of argument is to assume that organizations embedded in more turbulent, ambiguous, and uncertain environments will tend towards management practices and organizational structures that are more dynamic and adaptive. The line of argumentation goes back at least as far as Emery and Trist's (1965) paper entitled, *The Causal Textures of Organizational Environments*, in which they argue for the virtues of organizational matrix structures in turbulent environments. Spatial correlation, however, is bound to be a conspicuously weak basis from which to derive conclusions. For a start, it relies on a monolithic view of the environment, whereby it is synthesized into a mass that can be described by simple parameters. However, environments may exhibit turbulence at one level precisely because they are strictly regulated through institutions at another level. Second, what is perceived as turbulent at one point in time may not be perceived as such at another point in time. Emery and Trist were right in pointing out that turbulent environments may become perceived as 'normal' if the turbulence persists over long periods of time. It is not really feasible, however, for researchers to pose as atemporal judges about whether something is more or less turbulent, unless the actors themselves consider it so. Only the actors themselves can judge the importance of their own histories.

A second problem has to do with organizational environments as possibility, or potentiality, as opposed to actuality. Correspondence is an assumption based on the idea of actuality in terms of a perceived state of affairs. It is this assumption that may lure researchers to assume a one-to-one relationship between what happens in the environment and the organizational response. Bakken, Hernes, and Wiik (2009) point out on the contrary:

This is not, as assumed in traditional organization theory, a situation where the environment imposes unilaterally its demands on the organization. On the contrary, the organization realizes itself by engaging with the possibilities offered by its environment. This means—and this is relevant to the question of innovation—that the *irritations potential* in the organization's environment increases. The concept of irritation is related to that of information, but not quite the same. Irritation may be seen as an undefined surprise that is *based on the environment,* yet remaining a product of the system itself. When the fire alarm goes off it is not the surroundings that are irritated but the fire brigade. The question poses itself thus: Where is the fire? And how extensive is it?

A third problem relates to temporality and correspondence. The idea that we may search for correspondence between different states at different times rests on the assumption that different states are objectively comparable. It assumes that a former state may be retrieved the way it was experienced then. However, this is an impossibility given the effects of the passing of time: the past cannot be lived again as it was. It would be impossible for something to be experienced as identical a second time because the second time would include the experience from the first time plus that of the second time. Process philosophers, such as Deleuze and Kierkegaard, while making repetition the essence of being, insist that repetition, seen as sameness, is impossible. This is also why Schütz (1967), influenced by Husserl, used the term 'retentional modification' for the act of evoking past experience. The expression 'retentional modification' signals how past experience is immanent in the present while at the same time being different from the 'original' experience. In other words, every act of retaining past experience in the present implies an element of modification.

2.3 Misplaced Concreteness Assumptions

When looking to describe organized entities one generally chooses to study what takes place within the boundaries of the organization. In other words, we search for some dominant, achieved state within those boundaries, which means that an imaginary line is drawn within which it is assumed that the entity exists in a fairly homogeneous, stable state believed to remain that way over a certain period of time. The stable state that prevails over some duration of time is liable to be described in terms of, for example, behaviour, actions, or discourse performed by the entity associated with that stable state.

Working from the assumption of organizations as circumscribed entities continues to be in good currency. The mindset is clearly evident from various handbooks on organizations or organization theory (e.g. Baum 2005; Clegg et al. 2006; Tsoukas and Knudsen 2005). Organizations are assumed to circumscribe sensemaking and actions in ways that allow the analyst to connect them internally as well as to other organizations or institutions. Thus, when we speak of the organization's operations they become described as relations between entities in space. We do not have adequate theoretical frameworks for how various connecting operations relate—and consequently shape—those entities while allowing for the making of entities outside organizational boundaries.

Much the same goes for distinctions between, say, the individual and the social, which are seen as delineated entities that may interact but are not seen as constitutive of one another. Although a social group is seen as an aggregate of individuals, it cannot really be seen as the sum of all the experiences of the individuals involved. Nor are individual experiences simply parts of the aggregate referred to as the group. The point is that we cannot really draw a line between the individual and the social level as though there is a social level that is separate from what goes on between individuals, or pretend that they are two levels that interact dialectically with one another.[10] Instead, the social is an ever-evolving product of social interaction, yet it cannot be seen as something separate from the interactive processes that produce it. The social, as much as the individual, is an abstraction that aids the sensemaking of what is going on.

The thing about abstractions is that they are useful, but also potentially deceitful for our understanding of the world. They are useful because they enable us to make progress in our understanding of our experiences, which are the primary source of knowing. However, abstractions may also become dangerous because we have a propensity for forgetting that they are abstractions from experience, and not the actual experience. The danger, Whitehead (1929a: 2) wrote, is that we then become victims of 'the fallacy of misplaced concreteness'. According to Whitehead, it is therefore essential to recognize that because objects are abstractions they are never present in a final state, but rather are perpetually in the process of becoming. Nothing can ever be as we perceive it, nor can it become as we want it to be. Everything is in the process of becoming, perpetually.

One example of this is institutions, the basic unit of analysis of institutionalism, where studies are inclined to work from a definition of institutions, which is then used to empirically locate the institution as an object of study. However, the assumption that phenomena, such as institutions, are perpetually in the making, would mean that the focus would have to encompass the various ways in which institutions evolve and co-evolve with other phenomena. An example of one such study is Verzelloni's (2009) institutional study of how judges in Italian courts operate as translators of written law with the help of fascicules:

> The fascicules are a centerpiece of the juridical institutions. These specific objects contribute to guarantee the dynamical stability of the contexts. In their materiality the trial papers crystallize a particular 'institutional asset' continuously confirmed in the different actors' practices. These 'containers' of knowledge are direct and clear expression of the 'order' that countersigns the organizational structure of every court of justice.
>
> (2009: 16)

Rather than assume that the institution 'infuses' actions, Verzelloni analyses the institution of law in the making and how it is being produced and reproduced by materially mediated practices, while analysing how those practices become 'infused' with the institution of law. One might well imagine how that would enable analysis of how the institution of law can evolve differently as novel contingencies arise in the practices related to it. Herein lies the strength of insisting on the becoming and the contingent nature of things; by not assuming that an institution ever exists in a steady state it is precisely the dynamics of the making of the institution, and possibly its unmaking, that becomes central to analysis.

By simply speaking of an organization we turn it into sets of abstractions, because making it an abstraction is necessary, not only in order to speak about it, but actually also to 'act' on it. This is a point where I diverge from writers such as Chia (1999), Tsoukas and Chia (2002), and in part Weick (1995) who, while rightfully lamenting the excessive noun-making in organization studies, argue in favour of organizational life as flux, translated into streams of consciousness. What is needed, while paying careful attention to the flux nature of organizational experience, is to explore how the flux arises from and turns into nouns and abstractions that make collective organizing possible; in other words, investigating how verbs produce nouns, while not treating them as antinomies.[11] It is worth quoting James here:

> Perceptual flux means nothing…(I)t is always a much-at-once, and contains innumerable aspects and characters which conception can pick out, isolate, and thereafter always intend.…(O)ut of this aboriginal sensible muchness attention carves out objects, which conception then names and identifies forever—in the sky 'constellations,' on the earth 'beach,' 'sea,' 'cliff,' 'bushes,' 'grass.' / (T)he intellectual life of man consists almost wholly in his substitution of a conceptual order for the perceptual order in which his experience originally comes.
>
> (James 1996: 49–51), italics in original, from Weick 2011: 10)

The making and unmaking of institutions, like organizations, describes a journey from the concrete, living experience, via abstractions, and back to concrete, living experience. Not only do social scientists engage in the making of abstractions, but so do organizers. The difference between social scientists and organizers, however, is that organizers have to live with the return of the abstractions to concrete, living reality, whereas social scientists can remain in the world of abstractions. Where studies have attempted to penetrate the concrete realities of people, abstractions have sometimes been expelled from the analysis, as if they were to be abhorred. An answer to avoiding misplaced concreteness (the concrete being the living experience) is not to avoid abstractions (because they are indispensible), but to be mindful of the journey back to living concreteness, that is, back to organizational life as it is lived.[12]

2.4 Homogeneity Assumptions

Since the 1950s, organization studies has veered towards viewing organizations as social systems conceived as collectivities of various sorts. Parson's (1951) sociological framework, which has influenced much mainstream organization theory, emphasizes the social collective as a building block of understanding social life. What makes collectivities attractive as a focus of analysis from a social-science point of view is that they can be granted agency in the shaping of organizations as well as societies. Agency is granted as and when collectivities are assumed to represent sharedness of meaning, which is widespread in mainstream organizational literature. However, the very notion of shared meaning may be misleading, especially when it is taken to signify agreement between people.[13] Questioning the assumption of sharedness of agreement as a requisite for social action hardly needs arguing. The pragmatist underpinnings of organization theory illustrated by the works of March and Weick clearly defy agreement as a basis for social action. Over the years, however, the idea of 'the social' has been treated various ways, each warranting criticism.

Social constructionist views are likely to see organizations as embodying social meaning construction 'in here' about a world 'out there'. When, for example, Smircich and Stubbart (1985: 727) define organization as 'a set of people who share many beliefs, values, and assumptions that encourage them to make mutually-reinforcing interpretations of their own acts and the acts of others', they boil organizations down to systems of shared meaning and assumptions among homogeneous actors. Although they may be different people with different dispositions, they are of the same kind. Homogeneity, however, is not necessarily inferred from what is actually going on, but forced upon actors by the analytical assumptions of the researchers. A pragmatist view, on the other hand, may take the world as meaning structures within which connections are attempted to be drawn and redrawn by actors. The world of the organization is not external to the meaning that actors make of it: it *is* that world. Actors inhabit that world, act upon it, and move with it. This is where organization theory has been conspicuously narrow-minded in its approach.

Lindahl (2005: 63), for example, observes how a machine, rather than forming a background for various social actions, works as an active connector:

> It is true that an engine does not 'draw' cables, pipes and other machines in the full sense of the word, but it 'draws' attention. Performing an installation with an engine as a point of reference means that some actions, or action sequences, become more likely than others. They also become more or less likely if the reference point had been defined as the generation of 30 MW or as the transaction of 600 MSEK.

The point is that it is difficult to see developments as driven exclusively by human actors within organizations deciding to do something 'out there'.[14] Human actors, as much as concepts and material objects, are 'made' by connecting processes, as are organizations. Connecting processes are composites of actions, which, although they may be planned, create contingencies that are both partly unforeseen, partly beyond identification, and partly beyond control, while also setting the stage for developments that are beyond the control of the actors who initiated them.

If both the assumptions of the exclusively social and the a priori identity of actors are abandoned, it means working with an open notion of the actors' identity, such as is the case in Actor-network Theory (ANT), in which elements may reveal themselves as persons, concepts, or material objects (Czarniawska 2004) as a result of processes of mutual translation rather than as pre-defined identities. It is striking how, in any organized system, social actors depend on materiality for their creating and maintaining their identities.[15] A litmus test of the inevitability of materiality in organized systems would be if the most secretive organizations, such as the Mafia, would be able to exist without material means. One would have thought that such organizations would ideally like to avoid any material traces of their activities in order to avoid that any 'material making' of their human members could be established by investigators. As it happens, even the Sicilian Mafia boss Bernardo Provenzano, who hid from Italian police for more than forty years, was not able to escape material tracing, however ingeniously he concealed his whereabouts. The following extract is from an interview with Giuseppe Gualtieri from the Palermo police force:

We had to be careful with our movements. Anything different from the ordinary was immediately noticed and reported back to him. That would have led him to change his hiding place, his habits, and for us to start all over again.

Afraid that police could intercept phone calls or computer messages, Provenzano issued orders through hundreds of little notes, known in Sicilian dialect as pizzini. Many of the messages were in a code that investigators are now trying to decipher. The key could be in a Bible found in Provenzano's hideout that police say contained numerous annotations.

A police investigator who has seen dozens of the notes agreed to show us how the Mafia boss carefully prepared his messages, making them easy to hide and making sure they moved as fast as possible to be hard to intercept. [...]

Investigators followed a suspect they thought was a Mafia messenger to a farmhouse outside Corleone and then set up a surveillance camera from a nearby hilltop. From a distance, police also were watching the house of Provenzano's wife a mile away in Corleone. From there, they noticed that bags of fresh laundry would travel through town, going from messenger to messenger. When they finally followed a bag all the way to the farmhouse that was now under surveillance, Provenzano made his biggest mistake. [...]

We saw a hand reaching out to pick up the bag. It was strange, because that part of the house was supposed to be empty. That's when we realized that the phantom of Corleone was no longer such, but actually a person in flesh and bones.

(<http://transcripts.cnn.com/TRANSCRIPTS/0604/21/ywt.01.html>
accessed 5 November 2013)

The transcript illustrates not just how human and material existence depend on each other, but also how difficult it is to empirically separate them from one another, even if they are analytically seen as separate. The little notes, for example, point towards the fugitive existence of the Mafia boss, and the laundry points towards his solitary existence, an existence that partly defined his identity as a leader during that period. In other words, the material artefacts articulated the meaning of his leadership, meaning which was created and re-created on an ongoing basis.

Another distinction commonly made is between the collective (such as the group, the team, the organization) and the individual. An abundance of studies has treated groups, organizational units, organizations, or communities as units of analysis. Once considered as units of analysis they have been given attributes (composition, norms, patterns of behaviour, etc.) to explain how they impact on individuals, or, much less frequently, to explain how the individual influences the collective. Once social units have been defined they have been seen as acting units, as if they were individuals acting upon their environment. A reduction of complexity is taking place whereby social units are frozen in time and space while also being homogenized into social wholes.[16]

Homogenization of the social is subject to being an obligatory exercise when abstracting from one to several. We may appreciate the various qualities of one object and retain that object's specificities for a later stage in time, but once we group several objects, homogenization imposes itself. Bergson's (1910) discussion about the possibility of accounting for experience in time makes this point. His example is the counting of sheep, which, if we count them one by one, is an exercise in multiplicity, where counting one sheep is not a recurrence of counting an earlier one. Accounting for a flock, however, inevitably becomes spatial as successive sheep become seen as additions to the ones that have been counted: 'In order that the number should go on increasing in proportion as we advance, we must retain the successive images and set them alongside each of the new units which we picture to ourselves: now, it is in space that such a juxtaposition takes place and not in pure duration' (Bergson 1910: 77).

Freezing in time–space and homogenization are extraordinarily crude approximations to reality, however. It is not for no reason that Strum and Latour (1987: 791) point out, with more than a hint of irony, that 'Modern scientific observers replace a complexity of shifting, often fuzzy and continuous behaviours, relationships and meanings with a complicated array of simple, symbolic, clear-cut items. It is an enormous task of simplification.' The vertical distinction cuts off social units from the processes that make them and pretends that, once formed, they can exist in a vacuum. It would be obvious to consider, as do ANT researchers, ways in which material means serve to uphold social units.

Weick (2001) nevertheless provides a socio-cognitive framework that accounts well for how social units are formed and re-formed. Working from social formation as a combination of interpretation and commitment he explains the ongoing processes that underlie social formation. Weick avoids the idea of social units, but tries instead to articulate the sensemaking process as it moves between individual and group levels. The first element ('the first' does not imply chronological order, as sensemaking processes never start and never end (Weick 1995)) of the process is that of actions (or acts), which, unless the process stops with the individual act, creates inter-acts, assuming that more people are involved and respond. Acts, in my understanding, may be verbal as well as non-verbal. Being faithful to the pragmatist tradition, Weick sees inter-acts as engendering social commitment to what is going on (several acts create implicit commitment to continue acting in accordance with inter-acts), for example by repeating a customary greeting or carrying on a discussion. Finally, 'committed interpretation' takes place as the justification of actions and their meaning. It is also a stage in the sensemaking process where larger structures, such as institutions, may be evoked to provide justification for inter-acts.[17] The advantage of Weick's treatment lies in the fact that he does not pin sensemaking down to individuals or groups, but instead follows the process of how actions and interpretations relate to create commitment, which may be seen as social glue, not of people, but of actions and interpretations.[18]

Nevertheless, the majority of studies consider the social as given, such as patterns of communication in a group, the identity of an organization, the identities of individual people, or the social structure of an organizational unit. Social entities are treated as givens, with definable boundaries around them, exhibiting particular characteristics. The problem, as Strum and Latour (1987) point out, is that we then get little or no knowledge of *how* a social entity becomes a social entity with the characteristics we ascribe to it.[19] We may, for example, describe an organization as hierarchical, which means that hierarchy then becomes the main descriptor we use for that organization. But hierarchy, although it may be understood in terms of overarching principles when ascribed to an organized system, is upheld by certain reproductive practices. If we wish to know more about the hierarchical characteristics of an organization we are better off investigating how the practices we associate with hierarchy come into being, maintain themselves, change, or dissipate.

Hierarchy is but one of many types of attributes, the point being that the social unit is defined first and then features are attributed to it. This is the case, for example, in Bechky's (2003) study of occupational communities, which identified three different communities within an organization, consisting of engineers, assemblers, and technicians, respectively. Studying misunderstandings between the three groups, Bechky revealed how they overcame misunderstandings, notably through what she calls the co-creation of a common ground of understanding. Such studies aid in understanding how people, understood as individuals, gain different knowledge through sharing, but these studies also make two assumptions. One assumption is that knowledge or understanding is located with individuals, meaning individual physical bodies (an assumption that Weick (2001) avoids, as pointed out earlier) organized into groups. Yet, the social groups are nowhere to be found in a pure form. To be sure, organized bodies are comprised of them and they are depicted in organizational charts and encoded in personnel registers. But, to locate knowledge with bodies is to confine complex processes to things, based on yet another assumption, that when action takes place, it is the body that acts, just as groups act and organizations act. Analytically, this implies that there are entities within which feelings, thoughts, ideas, and projections exist that provide a basis for outward action. This is how we can talk about the sharing of knowledge, but the problem is that knowledge sharing is seen to take place between bodies as entities. Consequently, bodies come to be seen as existing prior to actions. Similarly, when it is assumed that 'organizations act', the underlying idea is that organizations are bundles of social groups that form opinions and norms upon which decisions are based.[20]

In a world considered on the move, it should be assumed that any entity or actor is part of a heterogeneous assembly of entities or actors, including the historical processes that made them. Consequently, it is always possible that an entity may become defined by another assembly as a result of certain events or developments. For instance, a product may become a norm for other products; an in-house routine may become a procedure to be followed in other organizational settings; a personal style of leading may become a myth, a narrative, or a model to be held up to others. In this view it becomes problematic indeed to retain a distinction between the social and the material, just as it becomes problematic to retain a distinction between the conceptual and the material, or between the functional and the symbolic.

2.5 Circumscription and Proximity Assumptions

Locating 'the organization' has been—and will continue to be—central to the study of organizations. For example, organizations are located in various corners of society and the economy, helping us to gain overviews of where they are, how they act, and how they influence the ways in which we live. When we extend our study of organizations from industry, public administration, and services to sectors such as the media and sports, we are in a position to better understand the actions of actors such as CNN, *The Times*, the International Olympic Committee, Manchester United, and many others.

Studies locating the organization as a circumscribed entity also help classify the shape and size of the world in which we perceive organizations as existing. They tell us, for example, how organizations shrink and outsource activities to concentrate on their core competencies. Such observations enable us, again, to ask pertinent questions about employment policies, industrial democracy, home–work boundaries (Nippert-Eng 1996), and ethics (Garsten and Hernes 2008), to name but a few. Influential early studies, such as Chandler's (1962) study of the spread of the multi-divisional form, or M-form, not only located a form of organization within the strategies of international firms, but also prompted questions concerning the origin of the M-form. Chandler's study is based on the idea that the M-form follows naturally from the strategies particular to large, diversified multinational firms.[21]

When we classify organizations based on certain criteria we become aware when our criteria no longer apply, which encourages us to push the boundaries of our inquiry. For instance, when our image of the multinational corporation of a large unified entity no longer applies, as argued by Morgan, Kristensen, and Whitley (2001), we are forced to search for alternative frameworks of interpretation. Their book is interesting in that it shows how large multinational firms are fragmented but somehow simultaneously act in a unified way. In the book, Morgan, as well as Kristensen, Zeitlin, and others, conclude that studying internal dynamics over time and space will provide explanations for how tensions, paradoxes, and conflicts are acted out and resolved. In other words, considering organizations as achieved, identifiable states equips us with a platform to undertake correlational analysis work (Hernes 2004).

The assumption of organization as a bounded (Chia and King 1998) form is thus one that enables a number of important observations. This assumption, however, is also problematic, as drawing a line means making a distinction between what is and what is not, and, by implication, the assumption is made that that which is within the line represents a homogenous state. We establish categories that exist because they are seen as being internally homogeneous and mutually differentiable. This is done for analytical convenience more than out of empirical relevance or correctness. For example, du Gay (2006) makes the point that bureaucracies are susceptible to receiving labels such as red tape *tout court*, which neglects the variety of ways in which bureaucracy is practised in different spheres of organizational life.

Most importantly the assumption of circumscription freezes the 'in-here' versus 'out-there' assumption into a situation that effectively isolates the organization from the world in which it operates. The assumption leads to the following paradox. In order for the organization to continue to exist usefully in the world it is assumed that it has to change, such as when its culture is seen as being out of touch with what is going on in the outside world. Such an observation typically leads to a decision to try and change the culture to catch up with what are assumed to be the prevailing norms outside the organization. But the attempt includes blocking off the organization from the very world within which it operates, a world which is changing; hence, while change is being made it corresponds to a state of affairs that no longer prevails. Thus, even though the aim is to change with the world, the opposite actually occurs.

Instead of moving with the world, the organization is isolated from the world. Paradoxically, in an attempt to become more dynamic, the organization actually becomes more static.[22]

Therefore, we owe it to our analysis to investigate what happens if the analytical boundary were to be drawn differently. Notwithstanding the merits of studying organizations as bounded entities, once we draw boundaries for analytical purposes we are obliged to think about what to leave out of our analysis when we assume boundedness. Bittner's (1965) discussion of the concept of organization made precisely this point: in order to assert anything, we must leave some things unsaid. Such things, says Bittner, stand under the *ceteris paribus clause*. Bittner's position, however, is that the use of the *ceteris paribus clause* is restricted, and that its contents are always open to scrutiny (Bittner 1965: 244). Taking this particular issue further, Nayak and Chia (2011: 286) draw attention to the dangers of not exposing the bounded state to scrutiny by pointing out that the unquestioned assumption of the boundedness and simple location (an expression taken from Whitehead (1929a) of individuals as well as organizations leads to an 'overwhelming preoccupation with the formal organization, its environment, its infrastructural qualities, its people and technology, and its preoccupation with actor intentions, rational deliberations and calculative action'.

A related assumption to circumscription is that of proximity. By analytically drawing a boundary around the organization, an assumption is made that interactions between actors within that boundary are not just more significant than interactions with actors outside the boundary, but also largely independent of interactions with external actors. Analyses will consequently be predisposed to focus on those that take place within the boundary and be inclined to exclude those that extend beyond the boundary. In short, there is an implicit assumption of spatial distance determined by where the boundary is drawn. Within this boundary, relations and attention are presumed to be stronger than outside it; consequently, the causal power of singular events may be seen as weaker if they take place outside organizational boundaries rather than inside them.

The problem is that the boundary drawn for analytical purposes may reflect poorly the experience of being in organizations, where occasions of intensive experience may take place between actors in very distant locations. Several empirical studies show how seemingly weak or peripheral processes may be central to organizations. For example, Kreiner and Schultz's (1995) study of R&D professionals shows how they form networks in the margins of organizations and engage in a mutual bartering of services that may be central to the actions of formal organizations. Similarly, in their study of innovation processes at 3M Company, Van de Ven et al. (1999) show how events at a research unit in Australia were decisive for the development of the cochlear implant in the United States. Such studies typically focus on how novelty emerges in a world on the move, which may explain why they are more concerned with potentialities outside organizational borders than more conventional organizational analysis. However, such studies should not be categorized as mere innovation studies, as opposed to what is normally done. Instead they represent an aspect of organizing which is more common than is ordinarily assumed in organization studies based on assumptions of circumscription and proximity.

2.6 Stability Versus Change Assumptions

> We had a 100-year war! You don't get much more stable than that!
> (John Oliver, *The Daily Show*)

If we were to ask almost anyone in the process of carrying out a task whether the task being carried out reflected change or stability, the person is likely to respond that she does not know whether what she is doing represents change or stability, at least not before she has stopped doing what she is doing. She may respond that what she is doing is different from what she used to do previously, yet what she is doing now has some similarity to what she used to do. Assuming that she is right in the middle of doing something, she may have a hard time telling us whether or not her actions represent stability or change, precisely because she is in the middle of it, and the contours of the actual act are as yet indeterminable. She may, of course, intuitively sense that actions are *changing*, but the intuitive image is likely to be too complex to convey to an outsider. Assuming that our question takes her out of her ongoing stream of consciousness, she is likely to resort to a spatial image of time, whereby she considers particular sets of actions as pertaining to particular periods of time, such as by noting that what she was doing differs from the way she would have carried out the same task compared to, say, ten years ago. In this way she may be able to tell us whether or not what she is doing corresponds to what she did under similar circumstances during a certain period in the past. What she then is doing, is projecting an image of her actions upon a similar set of actions during a selected period of time, which will enable her to provide an answer to our question. In short, the account is likely to be highly subjective, selective, and, in fact, random. This brief, incomplete and hypothetical, yet realistic scenario suggests how elusive conceptions of change and stability really are. The only 'true' answer is likely to be the intuitive feeling that the person has of actions changing, but the problem is that that understanding is virtually impossible to impart to an outsider, and even less so to the person who eventually reads the outsider's account.

'Stability' is in itself a complex term. The very word evokes immobility, but immobility can be defined in various ways. Stability may mean immobility in the sense of an object staying firm and fixed. A factory where the people or machines do not move is stable because there is no movement. But this is not what organizational researchers mean when they refer to stability. What they mean is a stable state of recurring patterns of activity. In the context of the factory it implies that people move and machines turn, and that if we identify the cycles of movement, those cycles remain relatively identical over time. There is movement, but it is repeated, and the repetitions do not change significantly. The immobility then referred to is the similarity and regularity of repetitions. As a result, when change happens it is because the patterns of movement change.

However, the criticism levelled at the stability versus change assumption has relied on the idea of stability as immobility, and organizational evolution over time as a series of immobilities. Invoking Bergson's idea of movement, Tsoukas and Chia's (2002) paper is a notable critical contribution in this regard. Bergson (2007: 121) most forcefully rejects the series of immobilities view by making a case for viewing the world as 'indivisible movement'.[23] In so doing, he harkens to one of Zeno's paradoxes by invoking Zeno's ancient parable of the race between Achilles and the tortoise. They begin the race at the same time, with Achilles starting further behind the tortoise. The paradox is as follows: when Achilles has run to where the tortoise started, the tortoise has moved on a certain distance. The same happens when Achilles reaches the tortoise's second position. Every time Achilles reaches the tortoise's most recent position, the tortoise has moved on. Hence, Achilles can never overtake the tortoise. To Bergson, Zeno's paradox is no paradox at all, because movement is indivisible and cannot be divided into a series of immobilities, as is done by Zeno.

If organizational life were reduced to the type of inner duration that Bergson describes, we could accept his rejection of immobilities. However, organizational life, as it depends on social action, has to rely on the spatialization of reality, a point made by Bergson about human intellect, that is, that reflection relies on spatialization. Now, if the immobilities we speak of are in the form of stable states of activity rather than inner human experience, would that cancel out the series of immobilities argument? Returning to Zeno's parable again, but this time accompanied by Whitehead, the 'paradox' can be seen as a fallacy of temporal thinking. Whitehead (1929a: 68–9) points out the temporal fallacy of seeing durations as having begun anew every time Achilles reaches the tortoise's previous position, which implies that each duration has a before and an after. This, however, contradicts the very idea of becoming, and consequently a processual view of reality. Much organizational theorizing, however, especially when it comes to questions of change, falls prey to Zeno's paradox, where periods of time are assumed to have a beginning and an end. As Chia (1999) points out, the consequences of such organizational theorizing at the level of practice should not be underestimated, 'Indeed, it has instilled a set of instinctive "readinesses" (Vickers 1965: 67) among Western management academics to construe organizational change as a "problem" which needs to be "managed"' (Chia 1999: 214). Falling prey to Zeno's paradox, however, is unnecessary if the analysis incorporates the effects of the actors' spatialization of reality (e.g. calendars, plans, and strategies) as part of the process under study. It is in evoking past events, for example, that actors resort to spatial images to articulate what has taken place and its significance.

One way to deal with the stability versus change conundrum is to replace stability with continuity, and accept that there is continuity in change, which implies taking a temporal view of organizational life.[24] A temporal view implies coming to grips with how continuity and change become understood with the passing of time. Whereas a continuous change view assumes that actors operate in time only, a temporal view directs attention at how the past and future are brought into the present. Evoking the past, for example, constitutes both continuity and change. On the one hand, it represents continuity by 'containing' past events and experiences, thus representing a recognizable repertoire of experiences to organizational members. On the other hand, it also represents change because the present is inevitably a novel present (Chia 1999; Mead 1934; Schütz 1967), which takes part in defining the patterning of past and future events.

2.7 **Inert Temporalities Assumptions**

Time and temporality represent a long-standing conundrum, not just in organizational research, but in the social sciences as well.[25] Yet, the passing of time is primordial in the shaping of organizing processes, and temporal analysis becomes essential for understanding organizational life. Moreover, time is not merely a 'dead' factor (Lorino and Mourey 2013) of process, but the very life of it, and this is what temporal analysis needs to contend with. When the word 'process' is used in much organizational research, it tends to denote a progression of discrete events and acts in time and space (e.g. Langley et al. 2013). Many works are apt to describe a more or less orderly accumulation of events and acts, as reflected in the use of expressions such as 'knowledge creation processes', 'change processes', 'communication processes', 'research processes', 'sensemaking processes', 'strategy processes', 'inter-organizational processes', 'diffusion processes', 'decision processes', and 'M&A processes'.

But time matters, not only by being a vital force of becoming, but also by shaping the things (people, technologies, concepts, etc.) of organizational life.

On the one hand, it matters when and where events and acts take place. The paradox of a systematic lack of attention and the degree of importance to temporality was pointed put by Ranson et al. (1980) in suggesting that change has been considered timeless, yet understanding of change is incomplete without an understanding of the temporal dimension of change. They argued that we should, therefore, locate actors temporally. In this view, locating actors temporally basically means situating them along a temporal scale, thus allowing actions and events to be defined as taking place before or after other actions and events, alternatively allowing the duration of time between actions and events to be decisive for organizational developments.

However, even though this view pays attention to temporality, it seems content to locate events in terms of where in the order of events they appear. Attention, however, is not being paid to how what happens at one event creates and re-creates that which happens at other events, past and future.[26] This is what is meant by giving agency to time, and requires that we do away with the idea that past and future periods of time are merely discrete segments of duration. Temporality as an active force has yet to take on importance in organization studies. The 'mattering' caused by time, by which entities are given their form by the passing of time, remains as yet largely unexplored. To provide an overview of the treatment of temporality I shall discuss briefly the forms of temporality that have characterized the field and also supply a succinct presentation of the form of temporality dealt with in this book, which I term 'ongoing temporality'.

2.7.1 SOCIALLY CONSTRUCTED TEMPORAL LOGICS

It is possible, within certain limits, to choose between experienced time and linear time, and the choice of one or the other may have implications for how the process is experienced. Take the example of going for a long drive in the countryside. To a certain extent, you can choose between the experienced time and linear time. You may impose linear time upon yourself by keeping an eye on the clock. If you check the time every minute or so, the drive will feel about as long as the number of minutes and seconds it takes. If you drive for several hours, the time will seem almost interminable, especially if you are terribly looking forward to meeting someone special upon arrival at your destination. Imposing linear time means focusing on the device that measures time and not on the surrounding scenery. Failing to concentrate on the time-measuring device would allow the passing scenery to define your experience of time. For example, suddenly and unexpectedly discovering a herd of wild animals, then watching them run, might not seem to take very long because you pay rapt attention to their movements. The surrounding scenery may, in fact, offer a different experience of time. Now, imagine directing your attention on the scenery rather than the clock and leave the technical device that measures time in equal intervals behind. Observe the changes in scenery, the repetition of specific formations, and the scenery as it fades away behind the car, or note how a point on the horizon grows bigger as you drive towards it. Perhaps dwell on things you recognize from previous trips. Performing these acts of observation undisturbed by the chronological device serves to establish the feeling of travelling in one's 'experienced time' as opposed to in chronological time. The experienced time is a staging of the duration of one's experienced time experience, developed from the experience of the journey and belonging exclusively to the journey. Still, when looking back on or forward to the journey, the time will be expressed as a mixture of experienced and linear time.

A decisive break in the organizational literature since the 1980s provides a more differentiated view of time than conventional linear notions of time represented by the clock and the calendar, although socially constructed time as a phenomenon was recognized by the social sciences in prior decades. Sorokin and Merton (1937) contributed a seminal paper in which they distinguished the Newtonian notion of objective linear time from socially constructed, periodical time. Their paper points specifically towards the relationship between the complexity of social systems and their requirements for concerted action on the one hand, and the complexity of the temporal scheme on the other. Seeking to extricate the field from the assumption of the universality of clock time, some organization theory literature has considered the different ways in which time orders human activity and how this differs between different organizational settings. Whipp, Adam, and Sabelis (2002), for example, use the terms 'time control' and 'temporal reach' to describe the change in the ways that time influences human activity in organizations. Temporal effects relate, for example, to speed, punctuation, regularity, prolongation, acceleration, and time cycles. Various terms are used to categorize the different temporal logics at work, such as chronological codes (Clark 1990), temporal regimes (Hylland-Eriksen (2007), time-ordering systems (Whipp 1994), temporal structuring (Orlikowski and Yates 2002) and temporal realities (Bluedorn 2002).

Much of this literature (e.g. Clark 1985) has drawn inspiration from studies in social anthropology that show how cultural and ethnic groups may be differentiated by the different ways they relate to time.[27] Arguments have been made for the need to explore alternative temporal logics, such as what Clark (1990) calls heterogeneous chronological codes, which are codes that have different origins and are driven by different needs and by different social groups.[28] In an earlier and influential paper Clark (1985) demonstrated the need to broaden understanding of organizational time from the prevailing conceptions of time as unitary linear[29] clock time in the organizational literature. Working from the assumption of time ordering as subjectively and socially constructed, Clark showed how different industries drew upon different 'repertories' of rules, structures, and forms to meet the demands imposed by rhythms in their external environment.[30]

Inspired by Giddens' (1984) structuration theory, Orlikowski and Yates (2002) offer a distinct view that attempts to avoid the dualism between modernist and social views of time, notably by embedding the enactment of time in practices and by assuming a recursive relationship between practices and temporal structures. Temporal structures are understood as both shaping and being shaped by ongoing human action, and thus as neither independent of human action (because they are shaped in action) nor fully determined by human action (because they are shaping that action). They argue that temporal structures, viewed as the various temporal logics related to, for example, meeting schedules, project deadlines, and financial reporting periods, tend to specify parameters of acceptable conduct while in turn being modified by actions.[31] Interestingly, Orlikowski and Yates' study of a geographically and organizationally dispersed group of artificial intelligence language designers in the early 1980s shows that their communication shifted from an *open-ended* temporal structure enacted early in the project to a *closed*, deadline-bound structure by its end. They also illustrate how the project moved between linear and cyclical temporal structures, as well as how *universal* temporal structures were *particularized* in practice.

In later years instructive contributions taking into account broader institutional factors demonstrate how temporal logics influence business and project cycles. In a recent study, Bengtsson (2008), for example, shows how a logic of cyclical time applies in the clothing industry, which is entrained by the cycles of the fashion industry. Her study of the clothing chain H&M shows how it not only complies with the cycles of the fashion industry, but how it manages the interrelationship between product and fashion cycles when extending its network of shops. Huy (2001: 613), paying attention to rhythm and change, makes the point that each organization can find a dynamic internal change rhythm that permits it to alternate between differently paced changes. From a project management perspective, Dille and Söderlund (2011) argue how projects that take place between institutions come to adopt similar temporal logics, which the authors appropriately refer to as 'isochronism'. Finally, Garsten (2008) discusses how temporary work, or temping, gets shaped by the temporal demands imposed as temps lead a fluid existence, moving in and out of various jobs and meeting timelines in various job contexts, as well as how this challenges them to develop, for instance, a transferability of skills.

The emergence of electronic communication and the options for instantiating human contact across the globe spurred interest in the effects of time combined with space. Harvey (1990) discusses what he calls the 'time–space compression', which, with the emergence of communication technologies, has imposed novel demands on human activity. Harvey makes the point that the time–space compression imposes an acute sense of the present— 'the present is all there is'[32]—which is experienced as an overwhelming compression of space–time that is stressful, challenging, exciting, deeply troubling, and therefore capable of sparking what he describes as a schizophrenic experience of time–space.

Views of time as subjectively constructed, as opposed to being seen as an objective, universal, regular entity (as Orlikowski and Yates (2002) argue), are important because they show how different social groups or organizations construct time through their practices, which again provides a sense of belonging, meaning, and continuity to actors. As a functional example, an alarm that goes off in a fire station sets a particular fire-fighter drill in motion. As a symbolic example, text messaging expresses how people are always on the move, sending multiple messages to multiple people who are also on the move. However, making time subjective rather than objective still does not accord an active role to time. Orlikowski and Yates' (2002) conception of temporal structuring involves the temporal logics that are shared and enacted in everyday practices by organizational members and are what they in turn draw upon in the enactment of their organizations. Still, this conception lends the impression that temporal structuring, although it takes part in shaping practices, and hence the organizational life experienced by people, has connotations of what Shotter (2006: 591–2) refers to as mechanical assemblages. Rhythm and speed become socially defined labels that characterize organizational life, but they do not say much about its 'inner dynamic', which describes how the 'parts' of assemblages are 'on the way' to becoming more than they already are, due to what happens at certain events in time, and as events connect to other events. Borrowing from Shotter (2006), this is why temporal structures, even though they are labelled subjective, do not express the specific shape of the 'temporal movement' of the unfolding of organizational life.

2.7.2 PERIODIC TEMPORALITY AND DURATION

In their introduction to a 2013 special issue on process in the *Academy of Management Journal*, Langley et al. make two main points about temporality and process research. First, they point out that, given the critical importance and inescapability of time, it is ironic that time is likely to be excluded in management research. The second main point they make is that organizational activity needs to be considered *over time*, and they discuss how, viewed as succession, time enables the emergence, development, growth, change, and termination of organizational practices. Their first point is basically a criticism of what they refer to as variance theory, which is apt to take a spatial view of the interacting entities taking place independently of the passing of time. Their second point, however, describes the current state of temporal theorizing of organization more than what is actually presented by process philosophy. The idea of succession or sequentiality of time implies a linearized image of the passing of time in which time is seen as a succession of events. This is also the view that Whitehead associates with Zeno's paradox, illustrated by the idea that Achilles would not be able to overtake the tortoise. When Langley et al. present this as the process view of time they actually allude to a picture of the prevalent view of time represented by traditional longitudinal studies, rather than the active view of time held by process philosophers.[33]

Thinking about time as divided into periods facilitates a temporal *representation* of organizational life, which again serves as a temporal basis for concerted action. This is what may be called a 'periodic temporality' (Schultz and Hernes 2013), which means that the temporality is represented as periods of time where a state of affairs is assumed to remain relatively stable over that period of time.[34] In the case of organizations this means that they are assumed to exhibit certain stable characteristics, such as central claims, labels, associated meanings, shared understandings, or practices, until they are upset or challenged by external perceptions, concrete events, new strategic aspirations, or organizational changes, thus leading to a new period with a different set of characteristics (Schultz and Hernes 2013). When time is considered as a regular, linear stream of units of time, it also implies that the spatial entities (such as goals, technologies, rituals, behavioural patterns, etc.) are considered unchanged over the construed period. I use the expression 'construed period' because it is not a natural period in time per se. It is at best fictitious because the period does not correspond to an observed reality but is an averaged-out state of affairs based on an incomplete observation at one (or several) points in time.

When temporality has been considered, organization studies have traditionally adhered to a periodic view of temporality. The field of organizational identity exemplifies this tendency, although it applies to most temporally informed research on organizational phenomena (i.e. strategy, organization design, decision making,[35] and power, to name but a few). Informed by empirical studies, a line of debate about organizational identity has examined conditions under which identity changes or is upheld. Corley and Gioia (2004), for example, addressed the issue of consistency between past and future identity, arguing that it is reconstructed in the present driven by various discrepancies, such as between present identity and future desired images (Corley and Gioia 2004). From an organization-environment perspective, Ravasi and Schultz (2006) studied identity change in response to changes in the external environment to the organization. Dutton and Dukerich (1991), on the other hand, showed how a port authority would continue to develop its identity while working on its perceived image in the face of reactions from stakeholders. Contributions to the identity debate include frameworks and studies that tend to explain organizational identity as a stable state of affairs punctuated by discoveries and events. For example, Gioia et al. (2000), by suggesting identity should be treated as potentially adaptively unstable, suggested implicitly that identity is a relatively stable condition lying there to be upset and changed in the wake of environmental pressures. Although actors in organizations represent change as the difference between before and after a point in time, it is also important not to take this as the actual change taking place, but to study how such representations, when translated into narratives (Czarniawska 1997) or texts (Cooren 2004; Putnam and Cooren 2004), perform in shaping their sense of identity.

Periodic temporality, similar to McTaggart's B-series,[36] comes close to what may be called an 'inert' view of temporality, by which I mean that time is not seen to do active work, but represents a series of discrete moments or periods. Events are seen as a discrete series of what Bergson calls instantaneous 'nows'.[37] The word 'discrete' is worth paying attention to, because it signals that an instant, or 'now', is seen as separate and distinct, although not isolated from other instants. The relationship between instants is characterized by a before-after logic, as in McTaggart's B-series. For example, instants (or events) may enter into a pattern of instants or events, such as recurring annual events that comprise changing the clothing collection in a chain of clothing stores, as discussed by Bengtsson (2008). Importantly, discrete events are related, but not *constitutive of* one another. That is, they are what they are: experiences in time whose ordering matters, but not how they matter. Similarly, Heidegger (1927) referred to a series of 'nows' as the ordinary interpretation of time. His critique was that when time is represented as 'pure succession' (Heidegger 1927: 474) the *significance* of experience is lost. The point is that every act exhibits some potentiality for what may come, and even for what has been. For example, people may draw up contingency plans that enable a specific course of action to be pursued under certain conditions, should they arise in the future. Contingency plans are but one concrete example of potentiality in organizing processes which may lead to an actuality that is different than if they had not been prepared. In this view, temporality 'does active work' in the sense that the contingency plans are structured by the passing of time and based on previous experience. In such a view the actual process of evocation as well as projection becomes central to how the plan is developed as well as how it relates to what comes after.

An example in organization studies of an 'inert' view of temporality is Isabella's (1990) paper on evolving interpretations during the unfolding of organizational change. Focusing on how managers construe different types of organizational events, Isabella divides the sensemaking process into three phases: anticipation, confirmation, and culmination. Her view of temporality as discrete 'nows' is demonstrated by her suggestion that during confirmation, managers' frames of reference draw upon conventional explanations and comparisons to past events. This suggests that the present experience may be compared to previous experiences, as if they are distinct temporal units that can be held up against one another. Moreover, her framework assumes that there are so-called 'trigger events' that signal transition from one stage to another, that is, from one relatively stable state to another. Similarly, in Jarzabkowski and Seidl's (2008) analysis, events are seen as logical—but separate—outcomes of previous events. Events are linked, but they are not afforded 'temporal agency'[38] in the sense of being able to redefine the meanings of future as well as past events.[39] It is possible, for example, to view an organizational meeting as exhibiting temporal agency to the extent that it leads to reframing the meaning of past meetings while contributing to defining, say, the agenda for future meetings.[40] In a process temporal view, strategizing would be directed towards the past as well as towards the future, as the past would be strategically 'historicized' together with the future.[41]

Concluding this part of the book with the notion of temporality is fitting because the meaning given to time, and especially the passing of time, is something that clearly differentiates a process view from conventional organizational theorizing. Similar to Heidegger's conception of *Dasein* as being constituted by its temporal existence, organizations can be usefully understood as created in time. To do so, however, we need to assume that 'time does work' upon the entities we wish to study, even better, that they cannot exist outside of time. We need to get away from inert temporalities and move to active temporalities to appreciate the mattering created by time. In order to theorize a temporal phenomenon, however, a number of assumptions need to be discussed, which is what the next chapter sets out to do.

3 Assumptions for Organizing in a World on the Move

■ SUMMARY

This chapter discusses process theory assumptions rather than organization theory assumptions. It examines central assumptions in process thinking that are seen as necessary for conceptualizing organizing in a world on the move. The assumptions relate to temporality, the role of the social versus the material, modes of connecting, the roles of action, and the nature of process, notably the idea of actuality and potentiality. In a world on the move, focus is on connectedness rather than size, flow rather than stability, and temporality rather than spatiality. Process thinking may be used to understand how process constitutes organization as a provisional entity emerging from connecting entities in the flow of time.

3.1 Becoming in a World on the Move

In mainstream organization theory, organizations are commonly conceptualized as entities adapting to the environment, and analysis consequently becomes focused on the work of adapting to an environment that changes between successive stable states. Therefore, organizational change has commonly been seen as a stepwise adaptation to changes in the environment, and consequently analysis loses out on the possibility of understanding the dynamics by which organizational actors work to make a difference. From a process perspective, the focus is inversed: it is stabilization, and not change, that needs to be explained, because the world is continually changing and organizing consists of attempts at stabilization to create a predictable world amid multiple possibilities. But the work of stabilization is fraught with uncertainty and ambiguity. It demands that actors envisage what may become actuality while preparing for various future potentialities, rather than adapting to some externally given quasi-stable state of affairs.

A common way to distinguish process thinking from other approaches is to associate it with the becoming of things. The idea of using the word 'becoming' is to explicitly indicate that things are not to be considered as existing in a final state, and that whatever entity we are considering (a human being, a machine, a routine, a goal) is in a continuous state of becoming through the work of connecting it with other things. This is the very basis of relationality, as expressed by process sociologists such as Elias (1978) and Emirbayer (1997).

The meaning of becoming can only really be understood through the lens of temporality. This is a point that has not been explicated in the literature, which pits becoming against being, but without specifying the role of temporality. Chia (1996), for example, contrasts what he calls a 'becoming realism' with a 'being realism', but the terms remain somewhat vague, as is also the case with Rescher (1996), who has influenced the thinking of several organizational process scholars. Left at an abstract level it may suffice to use becoming versus being as a reminder that processes views should not assume the sort of entitative conception (Chia 1999) associated with a being-realism.[1] Still, several questions about the actual process of becoming are left unanswered.

The idea of becoming does not need to be left to abstract philosophizing. In fact, although it seems like a highly abstract way of considering a thing, such as an organization, when companies are assessed in the marketplace they are effectively assessed as processes of becoming rather than their actual state of being. At the time of writing, a topical issue among corporate analysts was the share value of Apple, which presents an interesting paradox, at least to those not initiated to stock-market analysis. Following the death of Steve Jobs in October 2011 Apple continued to grow, and in May 2013 was more affluent, dominant, and profitable than ever before. And, even though major status quo indicators seemed overwhelmingly positive, analysts spoke of a crisis. And to them it *was* a crisis, also in numerical terms, since the Apple share value had dropped in recent months from almost USD 700 to USD 400 per share. Such a drop would appear to be a mystery given that the real-time figures in terms of sales, market share, and product portfolio were overwhelmingly positive. Part of the answer lies in seeing the company as becoming as opposed to being. Apple's success has historically been associated with its ability to regularly take the world by surprise and present novel products that would take competitors, current and potential customers by surprise. Jobs' famously ritualistic 'one more thing' at the end of his appearance at Apple's public product launch meetings signalled a near permanent ability to surprise. In a temporal sense, every time he used this phrase he evoked multiple occasions in the past that heralded a future to come, while at the same time heralding the potential new future at that 'present present'. When analysts now speak of crisis, their worry is that the current situation is not a reflection of a past in which Apple would lead by regularly re-defining the reality to come. They seem to worry about Apple's becoming rather than its being, and its becoming is purely perceived in temporal terms.

The idea of becoming should not be seen as 'becoming something else', or the 'successive becoming of something different', as that could suggest a continuously changing entity, and the question would be whether or not it is changing and how much. A major implication is that becoming is an experience in time and that the only reality that matters is the experience of the entity in question. The entity is not to be taken as an individual person or social unit, but a relational whole, which may be taken as the organization.² An important contribution from process philosophers is the idea of explaining how processes make the subject rather than assuming that the subject exists prior to the processes, while granting primacy to time. What sometimes distinguishes process philosophers from process sociologists is that the notion of 'the process' is not confined to social processes, but is meant in a broader, sometimes metaphysical, sense.³ This is why the idea of the relational whole is important.

What we consider to be connected things or entities are transient appearances in the flow of time. For example, I may consider what I think of as 'me' to have been revealed in how I related to a friend, a problem, or a piece of equipment yesterday. If I wish to know more about 'myself' I enter into experience in which I sense myself as both acting and reacting to what exists in the world around me. This brings me to a second point about becoming, which is that things, such as organizations, rather than existing as a priori entities that can be cognitively comprehended as entities, reveal themselves to us through experience. Here lies not only the pragmatic, but also the phenomenological basis for process thinking, which is that understanding comes from acts of experiencing.

In this view, organization can be seen as attempting to make tentative connections that may develop into a stabilizing configuration. A stabilizing configuration is about connecting and re-connecting elements into a meaningful whole. How connections develop and how they feed into the surrounding world cannot be determined at the outset, nor can they be fully controlled by those involved. They can, at best, be inferred retroactively, but since we are talking about retroactive reconstruction in a later temporal present, they cannot be evoked as they took place, but are more like a *trompe l'oeil* of what took place, since it is in retrospect that connecting moments are given meaning in the light of their perceived consequences. In Bergson's (1922: 128) words we are witnessing a counterfeit of what has taken place; likewise, as Mead (1932: 30) made abundantly clear, elapsed presents are forever unattainable, and even continual reconstructions will not approach them with increasing exactness. March (1994: 11) provides much the same view of temporality in his discussion of how decision makers, caught in the flow of time, force impressions of the present upon past experiences:

Understandings adopted by decision makers tend to stabilize interpretations of the world. For the most part, the world is interpreted and understood today in the way it was interpreted and understood yesterday. Decision makers look for information, but they see what they expect to see and overlook unexpected things. Their memories are less recollections of history than constructions based on what they thought might happen and reconstructions based on what they now think must have happened, given their present beliefs.

Becoming is related to the iterative nature of organizing. From a process view there may be reiteration, as Whitehead (1925a: 133) formulated it, but not repetition in the sense of sameness. Whitehead's (1920: 34) notion of 'the passage of nature' was for Whitehead more fundamental than the abstraction 'time'. According to Whitehead, the underlying dynamics are reflected in the passing of events from which time and space are created in the form of abstractions.[4] We are immersed in the flow of events, past, current, and potential. On the one hand we are faced with current events, such as meetings, encounters, breakdowns, rituals, and many others, which we observe or are part of, and which, once they have taken place, fade into the past, and become, using Heidegger's (1927: 326) expression, 'having-been'.[5] On the other hand there are events that have yet to take place (Heidegger refers to them as 'not yet') and which can only be anticipated in the form of possibility. The ways in which possible events are anticipated to take place and the actions taken to enable them to happen or, on the contrary, to avoid them happening, are likely to affect the course of events. In other words, organizing is seen—also by Chia (2000) and Tsoukas and Chia (2002)—as *attempts* at stabilization in order to create a more predictable world. Predictability applies both to the future and the past. Although predictability is normally associated with the future, as in making it a likely occurrence, there is no reason why it cannot apply to the past, as in making it likely that, by acting in a certain way, a certain meaning gets to be attributed to past events. Herein lies the becoming of the present event.

Actors are continually in the process of pursuing possibilities while preserving a sense of continuity. The aim is to stabilize sets of actions and routines to render certain events possible.[6] It is the object of ongoing stabilization that may be said to constitute what is seen as the organization, which is constituted by actors doing the stabilizing work. The organization, cannot, however, be reducible to those actors. Because stabilization may be done in different ways, the particular forms of stabilization that are being pursued are unique to every organization. Some organizations rely more on discourse, others on written rules, others again on artefacts, such as design and technologies. Stability, insofar as it may be seen to be taking place, is the exception rather than the rule. Change is reflected in the fact that the possible event represents something different from what is associated with past events of a similar nature. For example, in internal political games, actors resort to various tricks to ensure that a certain decision or allocation is made, or that it is not made. In the case of external relations a company may file for bankruptcy to avoid being taken over by another company. Examples are rife in the organizational literature of actors working to enable the occurrence of events that are hypothetical at the time when acts are conceived to attain them.

In a temporal sense, what forces pursuit of possibilities is the precious nature of available time. In other words, time is a precious restraint that forces acts of organizing to make plausible the occurrence of certain events. Hypothetically, an abundance of time would save organizers from having to make all their hard decisions. But because time is in limited supply, it forces the pursuit of certain possible events and the appropriate choice of means to make them likely has to be made, because the same choices are unlikely to return. And in some situations not succeeding in making the right choices may threaten the entire system.

One difference between organizations may be the acuteness of making choices in terms of timing and importance. In some organizational settings the importance of the choice may be considerable, while its timing may seem of lesser importance, such as the decision to invest in a major infrastructure programme or choosing to engage in researching a new drug, which typically takes several years of development and testing before being brought to market. In other organizational settings timing may be of utmost importance, whereas the importance of choices for organizational survival may be of less significance. For example, every day thousands of aeroplanes take off and land at major airports. A mistake in timing may have fatal consequences for an aircraft and its passengers but does not jeopardize the airline's survival or that of the airport.

An example of an organizational setting where both timing and importance are crucial to the system in question is where social systems interact with nature. An illustration of the urgency of this is provided in Gell's (1992: 86) study of temporal patterning of activities in relation to the changing of the seasons. He describes, for example, the practices of the Muria Gond people in India as follows:

Paddy cultivation pits man against nature and the inexorable passage of the seasons in a way that sago production never does. Certain processes, notably sowing, weeding and harvesting, have to be performed within temporal parameters set by the biological requirements and growth pattern of the rice plant. The seed rice must fall onto waterlogged earth, weeding must be complete before the grain-bearing shoots mature, harvesting before the grains begin to be shed. These demands, emanating from the nature of the cultigen, and the fact that it is being grown in an artificial environment rather than where it would occur naturally, place exceptional demands on labour resources and management skills at 'life-crisis' stages in the life of the rice plant.

This example illustrates the temporal acuteness of activities and how social organization is carried out to enable temporal patterning in the face of the threat of systemic disintegration.

Gell's work illustrates not only the temporal patterning of activities, but also how social acts are performed to engage the members in meeting the demands of the temporal patterning, being mindful that rituals and procedures are a way to anticipate developments in a world where people and their relationships potentially face new challenges. Rituals represent continual attempts at the stabilization of temporal occurrences and their relationships.[7]

Becoming signifies the becoming of events and also the becoming of a certain converging pattern of past and future events formed by rituals. In order to appreciate this point it is useful to see events not as a sequence of happenings, but more like a formation of events that are spread out and yet connected in a pattern that exhibits some degree of coherence. Thinking in terms of multiple events invokes an atomistic view of organizational life, where events are both parts of a whole and signify the unity of the whole. Just as events are in a state of becoming, so is the whole of events.

3.2 Ongoing Temporality

> It takes time to change the past.
>
> (Elana Feldman)
>
> It's never too late to have a happy childhood.
>
> (Wayne Dyer)
>
> The novelty of every future demands a novel past.
>
> (Mead 1932: 31)

The introduction to this volume draws a distinction between two different conceptions of process. One sees process as identified processes, such as flows of tasks, goods, information, or people that can be studied, labelled, and categorized, as is the case, for example, in research on routines (Feldman 2000). Another view sees process as constitutive *of* the world. A similar distinction may be drawn between different views of temporality, where one view, commonly applied in cultural studies, seeks out the various temporal logics that order human activity. The other view, consistent with a view of process as constitutive of the world, assumes that the passing of time is an intrinsic quality of the world. This is a view characterized not by temporal logics, but by the ongoingness of time, and directs attention to the temporal construction of organizational life performed by organizational actors.

The first view of temporality, which does not confer agency upon the passing of time, may be called 'periodic temporality' (Schultz and Hernes 2013), which is represented in longitudinal perspectives on organization. A longitudinal perspective implies viewing things over a linear duration of time and plotting the relationships between events and actors over that duration, but without actually giving agency to the passing of time. Instead, what happens when a longitudinal perspective is taken is that time works as an external framework against which meaning is created. Time itself is not assumed to perform its work on the actors involved, but they perform work on each other during a defined span of time, hence periodic temporality does not confer agency upon time as such.[8] Chronological duration may be ascribed importance in the sense that phenomena may be seen as more or less important in view of the duration they are seen to occupy. For example, a set of practices that endures over decades may be seen as deeply rooted in a community. A periodic view consists of more or less arbitrarily dividing time into segments during which things are assumed stable, for the sake of facilitating analysis.

The second view is one that assumes the ongoingness of the experience of being in time, which Schultz and Hernes (2013) refer to as an ongoing view of temporality. An ongoing view implies that actors are seen as always being in the present. Past and future are not temporal elements distinct from the present, but *dimensions* of the present experience (Deleuze 2004). From a temporal perspective one could say that we are constantly in the middle of doing something while attending to things we no longer are in the middle of doing, and preparing for things that we might be in the middle of doing at a later time. The passing of time throws us continually into situations in which we recreate past and future, either by continuing through habit or by changing the meaning of the past through conscious reflection and staking out a different future. It changes things around us because we inescapably form part of a moving world, and as we observe the changes around us, we respond to them and anticipate others, and our reactions and anticipations become part of our experiential past. When we are in the midst of carrying out an act, we pay attention to the immediate precedents and the immediate consequences of performing the act, whereas the passing of time converts our acts into past experience and our temporal span of observation becomes longer.

A world on the move signifies temporal evanescence, or perishing of time, as Whitehead formulated it, of the world that surrounds us at present. Instead of assuming that things stay the way they are, they are constantly threatened with disappearance, at least in their present form. What influences the work of practitioners, and consequently those who analyse their actions, is the acuteness associated with the perishability. For example, most dairy companies have a long history of applying science and technology, the application of which stems from the early days when problems involving the extraction, tapping, storing, and transport of milk had to be dealt with to meet demands for volume and timing. Milk is a most perishable commodity, which means that during the Second Industrial Revolution, when delivery distances increased, imposing greater demands on transportation, farmers were forced to pool their resources to form dairy cooperatives to overcome shared logistical problems (DuPuis 2002). Similarly, Bakken, Holt, and Zundel (2013) point out how organizational time grew out of the perishability of goods, in particular agrarian produce, requiring a temporally standardized, regularized, and transparent organization of mechanized production across wider physical spaces.

From a temporal view, 'passage', or perishability, refers to the perishing of the present, which marks the ontology of becoming. Whitehead (1929a: 126, 196) describes time as 'perpetually perishing', by which he meant that the experience of particular duration is forever perishing. It comes into being and then vanishes; it never really is, except in the imagination. Continuity, therefore, is an imagined state of affairs over duration. Whereas passage may be seen as the ontology of becoming, its epistemological 'remedy' consists of imagining continuity, and with it, change. This is why rituals hold such enormous importance in organizational life (March and Olsen 1989), and why they become more important the more volatile life appears. The photographer Robert Capa shows a glimpse of this in a wonderful photograph from a London air-raid shelter during the Second World War, where a man wearing a helmet and a woman sit in front of an improvised table with a white tea towel and tea cups on it. Although in the relative safety of an air-raid shelter, that safety could be shattered at any moment. The photo bears witness to a situation of passage, of perishability, in which continuity is actively constructed, as time is held onto through the ritual of drinking tea.

A central point is that as much as the future is open, so is also the past. For example, forming a project team consisting of people from various backgrounds is initially an encounter between people with different pasts (Erdem and Eilertsen 2013). As they begin to work together their individual pasts form the beginning of evolving joint pasts that blend in with the individual pasts. Whereas Levitt and March (1988) and March (1999b)[9] make the point that the past may be experienced as potentially ambiguous and uncertain, an ongoing view of temporality invites the possibility of the past being open to re-interpretation, and therefore consequential for the anticipation of future acts. Mead (1932: 21), for one, is explicit on this point:

The pasts which they spread back of us are as hypothetical as the future which they assist us in prevising. They become valid in interpreting nature in so far as they present a history of becomings in nature leading up to that which is becoming today, in so far as they bring out what fits into the pattern that is emerging from the roaring loom of time, not in so far as they erect metaphysical entities which are the tenuous obverse of mathematical apparatus.

However, as will be discussed later, the present should not be seen as a point in time that divides between absolute past and absolute future. The past, while taking part in shaping the future, changes some of its meaning as it takes part in shaping a different future. For example, for many years, the organization Norwegian Red Sire (now called Geno) kept samples of DNA of cattle, mainly to record the evolution of the most common breed of cattle in Norway. In recent years, however, ox sperm has become a commercial export success, the reason being the superior health of some Norwegian cattle over breeds used in a host of other countries. DNA cannot be sold unless it is well documented, which is precisely what had been done by the organization. In the light of today's commercial utility the past activity is cast in a new light. As the activity is partly used for future export purposes, the past activity of collecting records takes on a different meaning in the light of its future usefulness.

Recording, analysing, reporting, marketing, selling, distributing, etc are ongoing activities. When they take place at specific points in time, meaning when they are associated with certain actors, such as researchers and technologies, they are events rather than just activities. As events they provide historicity to the overall process as the formation of events that organizational actors experience contains both past and future events. Actors experience past, current, and future events as a formation in which past (lived) and future (possible) events form a living whole in which they continuously create and re-create each other.

3.3 Endogeneity of Process

To better understand organizing in a world on the move, it is necessary to understand everything as being in process, including organizations. This implies that it is not tenable to assume any stable contexts as framing processes, since connecting is seen as the essence of organizing. In a world on the move the ability to conceptualize the emergence of novelty as part of process is important. Novelty cannot, however, be outside process: it must be an integral part of process, just like reoccurrence of the known. Novelty implies connecting to untried possibilities, which may be distant from actors, both in time and in space.

This is not, however, the way that process has been traditionally considered in organization studies. Traditional process views, such as presented by Pettigrew[10], seem to assume that processes are framed by relatively stable organizational contexts, which is what Hernes and Weik (2007) refer to as an exogenous view of process. According to an exogenous view, flows such as actions, communication, behaviour, and so on are assumed to be influenced by the external context of the process, which may consist of entities such as rules, institutions, customers, and competitors. At an analytical level the view corresponds to seeing organizations as consisting of processes within structures, and seeing context as something within which interaction takes place. March and Olsen (1975: 152) argue against such a view, stating:

Sometimes we observe a considerable impact on the process of the temporal flow of autonomous actions. We need a theory that considers the timing of different individual actions, and the changing context of each act. Most theories imply the importance of the context of an act. Typically, however, they have assumed that this context has stable properties that allow unconditional predictions. We observe a much more interactive, branching, and contextual set of connections among the participants, problems, and solutions in an organization.

The context assumption also represents the sort of thinking that Giddens (1984), among others, takes issue with, that is, seeing context as a spatially defined framework within which interactions are correlated. Inspired by Giddens, Boden (1994) points out that we need to abandon the idea that rationality is 'big' (and stable) and action 'small' (and ephemeral). Instead, action should be seen as reflexive, in the sense that it instantiates the very framework that it both constitutes and emerges from. In this way, following Boden, all that takes place as macro can be seen through micro-level interactions.[11] It follows, then, that whatever we see as macro level, consists of interactions at micro level. Boden suggests further that through their interactions, actors create a 'matter-of-factness' of the world, which they in retrospect treat as real and constraining.

To state an endogenous view of process implies simply saying that all is in the process. 'It's all in the game', as gangster Omar Little says in the television series *The Wire*. According to an endogenous view, processes are analysed without assuming the direct influence of an external context. This implies, of course, not a rejection of the importance of context, but it considers context to be important only as it is responded to, and hence converted into experience, through the organization's response to environmental factors. In this view the organization responds in turn, not to the context as such, but to the way it itself experiences external context. Such a view is in line with, for example, Mead's thinking, where he emphasizes the meaning of external objects (other individuals, gestures, physical objects) as the response to the 'calling out' of an actor and thereby arousing in the actor the actor's own response.[12] At a systemic level this means that whatever context there is, is constituted by the actions of the acting system, rather than by those of the system's context. Where conventional views would treat context spatially, assuming that organizational actors respond to external influences, a temporal view would see external influences as a past experience and a future opportunity to be explored and pursued.[13] A financial crisis, for example, is a future opportunity to change organizational strategies based on selected past experience. As steps are taken in exploring opportunities, those steps successively become additions (and consequently changes) to the organizational experience, enabling the emergence of different possible futures.

A basic tenet of a temporal process view is that the passing of time forces actors to carve out their own temporal existence. When feeling stifled by bureaucratic routines, company employees may evoke the early days when feelings of optimism, entrepreneurship, and risk-taking reigned. In another company, the arrival of a new leader may herald a completely new future at the expense of forgetting the good old days. In each case, a sense of 'having been' together characterizes the past. Such evocation is a collective effort consisting of individual contributions, but not reducible to those individual contributions. Each individual keeps traces of his or her experiences within a collective system, but those experiences that matter for organization as process are the collective manifestations of experience. An endogenous view of process assumes that process establishes its own time and that there is no spatial context beyond the process. Naturally, this is an analytical distinction and there is no clear distinction between our own experience and others' experience. Some past events may have a certain 'ownness' about them, in the sense that they both feel unique to the organization in question and they are interpreted as being significant for its patterning through time.

A litmus test of temporal structuring is whether organizations can be observed as operating 'in their own time', meaning that they establish their own distinct historicities that weigh in on their acts in the present. An interesting example is Pickering's (1984, 1995a) detailed studies of developments in particle physics, which show how two different organizational settings with similar points of departure operating in similar contexts develop different temporal trajectories of acts. It is worth paying attention to his observations because in a field such as physics choices can be traced back in time, just as future effects of choices can be traced. This is much harder in organization studies, partly because records on decision making are lacking, partly because decisions do not have to be documented and justified with reference to the past, and partly because justifications are sometimes purposely left vague. Still, if we assume, as I suggest we do for a process-based organization theory, that the present embodies the past, then findings from communities other than organization studies, but with more stringent demands for referring choices to past choices and their respective outcomes, can indicate something about what to look for when we conceptualize the temporality of organizational life. And particle physics research, the way Pickering describes it, does in fact exhibit characteristics that are recognizable in organization studies. What I have in mind is his description of particle physics as being both theoretical and phenomenological, a description that physicists apply themselves when discussing doing theory versus doing phenomenology (Pickering 1984: 91). The phenomenology of particle physics contains conceptual modelling which is open ended in the sense that it points towards novel possibilities while containing actualized facts in scientific practice. The mangle between, on the one hand models, which are conceptual, and experiments and theories on the other, which are scientifically more tangible, resembles organizing, which constantly vacillates between measurement, prediction, and sensemaking, where the former two are based on precision and the latter based on plausibility (Weick 1995).

The experimental nature of science, Pickering argues, subjects it to contingencies, which means that experiences or facts may intervene in the process and spur new and unforeseen developments. Experimenters orient their actions towards desired future outcomes while being prepared for outcomes that differ from what they tentatively expect. For physicists, for example, the choice of one model over another may well influence what they obtain in the way of results, which may yet again trigger other courses of action. Between theories and experiments, however, lie models, and this is where Pickering offers a phenomenological addition to the world of theories and testing. Models are phenomenological because they are open, pointing towards possible explanations while expressing the culture within which the scientists operate. 'Culture', as Pickering uses the term, consists of various kinds of elements ('things of science'), such as skills, social relations, machines and instruments, scientific facts, and theories. Models, then, are integral to the culture of the scientists as they enable the making of possible connections and the production of associations and alignments between disparate cultural elements (Pickering 1995a: 139).

Pickering's treatment of process and temporality comes in principle close to the treatment in this book. One point of resemblance is the use of history, or historicity, where he emphasizes the retroactive nature of making sense.[14] Another point of resemblance is the idea of conceiving experience as taking place in time, rather than over time. Pickering, for example, employs the term 'temporal emergence', by which he means that contingencies emerge in time during scientific practice, which may alter the vector of experimenting and theorizing. A third point of resemblance is to allow for the co-existence of process and structure. The use of meaning structures in this book may be compared to Pickering's use of culture, and the articulation of meaning structures has parallels to Pickering's use of models.

Pickering (1984, 1995a) describes in some detail the development of two projects in two different geographical locations (Genoa and Stanford) in particle physics, both of which had similar starting points and aims, but took different paths and resulted in diametrically opposed conclusions. The starting point of the process consisted of common knowledge and assumptions within particle physics about the nature of non-observed particles (quarks) thought to make up elementary particles called hadrons, of which protons and neutrons are examples. As the field evolves through what Pickering calls the symbiotic interaction between experiments and theorizing, with experiments being prospective and theorizing being retrospective, the organization of the scientific activity gets caught up in its own evolving logic of events. At both locations, even though the basis of the scientific activity rested at that point in time on what had been developed in the search for the nature of quarks, the exploration of quarks pursued different paths, used different equipment, and leaned towards different models. In Genoa, for example, the researchers worked from the idea that isolated quarks could be observed empirically (Pickering 1995a: 98), and experiments and models seemed to be built on this conceptual idea. At Stanford, on the other hand, the researchers proceeded in a significantly different manner. The point is that the two processes started from a similar point of departure, the so-called Millikan oil-drop experiment in the 1960s, and with similar aims, but worked with different types of equipment. While engaging in a similar quest—the search for empirically supported theories explaining quarks—they arrived at diametrically opposed conclusions, quarks for the Stanford researchers, no quarks for the Genoa researchers (Pickering 1995a: 210). According to Pickering, the reason for the Genoese researchers' no-quarks conclusion was that they searched for isolated quarks using bench-top experiments. The Stanford researchers, on the other hand, operated with the idea that quarks could only be composite, which enabled them to conclude the existence of quarks.

Pickering is explicit about ascribing the different outcomes of the two research teams to the different ways in which the two processes unfolded. By experiencing different emergent temporalities in which concepts, equipment, and theories supported each other in staking out different courses, the teams came to experience the stabilization of different cultures around the facts they produced. The analysis points towards the central role played by contingencies in processes and is primarily explained from the view of organizations operating in their own time. With time, different historicities evolved supporting the respective trajectories of the research groups. Pickering shows with considerable clarity the making of an organization's own time, that is, its own unique path of unfolding supported by its own specific contingencies, the production of its unique past, and its own unique choices for future aspirations, all derived from its own particular culture.

Pursuing the assumption of the endogeneity of process implies that organizational experience attains agency when it enters the organizational memory. In this regard, I follow Levitt and March's (1988: 327) point that it is not experience as such that enters memory, but *inferences* drawn from experience. Inferences may be interpreted in social interaction. They depend on the inferences of individuals, but they are not reducible to them. Individual experiences, in turn, derive partly from collectively articulated inferences. However, differently from Weick, who focuses on the making of sense from singular occasions, it is important to consider how experiences actually become part of memory, which is a *structured form* of experiences, and not the experiences in themselves. An organized system includes an almost infinite number of experiences every day and no experience can be retained as a self-contained experience. Such may be the case with individuals, such as when we remember a distinct sensorial experience, but it does not hold when we consider organizational life, which remains a phenomenon dependent on socially and materially mediated action.

The assumption of endogeneity becomes yet more reasonable with the notion of ongoing present (Schultz and Hernes 2013) introduced above, by which the past–future articulation takes place in an ongoing present that is a present characterized by indeterminacy and openness. Taking this point into the discussion about organizational context, it means that, although events are encountered, felt, and experienced, they have yet to be given form through evocation, reflection, and social processing before actors can begin to have a sense of their emerging implications.

The point is that every contextual experience is made endogenous to the organization and is not to be considered in the way of structure or the banks of a river. Once context (be it in the form of technology, money, people, politics, or institutions) is experienced, it works itself into the immediate organizational memory and adds to the existing organizational memory.[15] In other words, every experience is immediately historicized, as every new experience fades immediately into the past. Memory is not to be confined to long-term memory. It may refer to instants in a meeting or it may refer to decades. In a meeting, for example, a statement about a sudden event in the organizational context, once uttered, becomes past to the persons who respond to it. As and when several persons converge towards a sense of apparent agreement about what has happened, the contextual event enters the organizational past, even if it is only a question of a few instants.

The following conversation between two scientists from Latour and Woolgar's (1979: 165–166) study of micro-level interaction in a laboratory illustrates how, in the present, actors perceive events from the context of their work. In particular, as the conversation progresses, it shows how their perceptions of context become history in their ensuing conversation:

> A: We have an interesting thing for you... we gave a single dose of B; killed the animals by microwave... of course we have some controls without any injection
> B: Hum, hum...
> A: and we assay them for Beta and Alpha.
> B: The whole brain?
> A: Yes, and our big surprise was that two and a half hours later...
> B: [writing carefully] Two and a half hours...
> A: it was still 40% the value of Beta... the values are here [pointing out a scribbled sheet of paper]...
> B: Now this is unbelievable!
> A: Of course, the Beta assay is not perfect but we can trust...
> B: I think in this case the misreading of Beta cannot be important...
> A: No, no, I think
> B: [looking at the sheet] Is this point statistically different?
> A: Oh yes, I have done it... anyway it is different from the control...
> B: What is the control?
> A: The control is a brain extracted in the same way... but we may say something, in the control there is 25 times more Beta than Alpha.
> B: That much is already getting interesting.
> A: The value is...
> B: It's too late to send an abstract to the Federations?!

Latour and Woolgar point out how perceptions make their way into the interaction as it progresses. For example, they point out that, 'Expressions such as "this is unbelievable" and "big surprise" stemmed from the expectation that the peptide Beta would degrade quickly and from the contrary indication of the data. B's use of the word "interesting" towards the end of the extract can be understood against a background of controversy over whether either of Beta or Alpha are artefacts' (1979: 166). They point out that the ability to answer or anticipate the various questions that arose depended upon the local setting, but that the two scientists were constantly at work to eliminate alternative explanations in an effort to arrive at a statement in one particular direction. They are couching their propositions so that they point towards a synthesis of future aspirations. Their conversation, in other words, even though it brings forward the past, points continually towards future possible syntheses.

Considering process as endogenous means that we reject the idea that there are any stable sources of truth or knowledge outside the process. To be sure, most sources of experience lie outside the process, but they only attain meaning as they enter the process of experience and become part of memory, whether in the space of a few seconds, such as in the intimacy of the social interaction described above, or in the space of several years, such as represented by organizational archives, artefacts, and stories. This locking-in of processual impetus demands a great deal from analysis. It forces, for example, consideration of the connecting between events and asking what connects events and what makes an event an event. Such thinking rejects the assumption whereby anything residual can exist in terms of qualities, people, technologies, organizations, or institutions that enables the connecting of events. The events instead connect by their own accord, by the temporal agency they exhibit.

3.4 Actions, Acts, We-ness, and Actors

> There is no 'being' behind doing, effecting, becoming; the 'doer' is merely a fiction added to the deed—the deed is everything.
> (Nietzsche, cited in Carlisle 2005: 138)

> When I cut logs for next winter, there is no fire yet, but I (along with others) am imagining the fire in the hearth: this anticipation in the action in progress (cutting logs) and this projection into the future is required for the situation—in this example, my efforts to cut logs—to make meaning. The piece of wood is made to mean 'log' well before it is actually used as a log, by a specific meaning-making perspective (winter will require fire, fire requires logs...).
> (Lorino 2014, discussing Charles Sanders Peirce)

Process thinking is closely related to pragmatism in philosophy,[16] which in many ways is the study of actions and meaning. Whereas James (1904) made the connection between the term pragmatism and the Greek word *pragma*, Mead (1934) made numerous references to the relationship between action and meaning in social contexts. Meaning, however, is not to be seen as a teleological purpose or aim in the narrow sense of the word:[17]

> A pragmatist turns his back resolutely and once for all upon a lot of inveterate habits dear to professional philosophers. He turns away from abstraction and insufficiency, from verbal solutions, from bad *a priori* reasons, from fixed principles, closed systems, and pretended absolutes and origins. He turns towards concreteness and adequacy, towards facts, towards action and towards power. That means the empiricist temper regnant and the rationalist temper sincerely given up. It means the open air and possibilities of nature, as against dogma, artificiality, and the pretence of finality in truth.
>
> (James 1904)

Following James, meaning resides in the *possibilities* of nature rather than in the dogma of what nature is about, and possibilities are realized through actions rather than through fixed principles. Organizations are about possibilities rather than constraints, and as possibilities they reveal themselves through actions. This is an important implication of taking an endogenous view of process by assuming that organizations are processes, rather than seeing them as contexts for processes.

'Actions' has been used in many different ways to explain the making of organizations. Early works, from Taylor (1911) through the human relations movement (Roethlisberger and Dickson 1939), sought to understand human action in the light of the motivation of individuals, and actions were typically seen as productive activity. A more cognitive framework focusing on the informational basis for decisions was applied in the field of decision theory beginning in the mid-twentieth century (Cohen, March, and Olsen 1972; Cyert and March 1963; March and Simon 1958). In this framework, decisions were substituted for actions as the basic unit of organizational analysis. Later, organizational culture researchers (Schein 1985; Martin et al. 1998; Martin 2002) interested in the symbolic implications of actions related them to organizational norms and values. In the organizational culture literature, however, little agency has been given to actions, as they tend to be held up against relatively immutable organizational norms. In the wake of a 'practice turn' in the 1990s (Schatzki et al. 2001), researchers have given more agency to what people do in organizations, such as by considering organizations as bundles of practices and material arrangements (Schatzki 2006).

The centrality given to actions and practices, however, does not seem to have occasioned the emergence of a theory of organization around actions, with the exception of ideas such as Czarniawska's (2004) notion of action nets.[18] Attempts have also been made in the strategy-as-practice literature to link actions and practices to organizational levels (Jarzabkowski and Spee 2009), thus implying a level of meaning separate and distinct from the actions of actors. The idea of levels of organization, however, remains dubious from the point of view of organization as process. For example, to consider strategy as a higher level implies that there is a level of rationality that hovers above organizational actions that synthesizes them into an overriding teleological intention. No doubt strategy has its rightful position as an element within the organizational system, but it should be seen neither as an element that infuses every other aspect of organization, nor as an element that enjoys a privileged position above other elements of the system, which would presuppose the existence of a purposeful individual actor who can rise above the entanglement of organizational events, experiences, actors, and actions (Chia and Holt 2009).[19] Taking a process view of strategy, Chia and Holt (2009) suggest, instead, that we should look at the making of strategy as a process of wayfinding (rather than goal finding). In their view, strategy is not to be seen as developed by human actors who instigate actions to arrive at strategies. Instead, they advocate a softer view of human agency as constituted by practices.[20]

A point of departure for Weber's (1968) interpretive sociology was that actions are rooted in actors' subjective meaning. In his definition of sociology and social action he wrote, 'We shall speak of "action" insofar as the acting individual attaches a subjective meaning to his behaviour—be it overt or covert, omission or acquiescence.' The subjective meaning of the action could, as Weber saw it, be deciphered from the motive that the individual actor attached to the action. As to meaning as an object of study, it could be observed, either from the point of view of 'subjective adequacy' or 'causal adequacy'. Weber also distinguished between two main (ideal) types of intentionality. One is typically rational in nature and the other is emotional. The rational aims can be understood and deciphered by anyone besides the actor, whereas the emotional (irrational) cannot. Hence Weber's statement, that 'one need not have been Caesar in order to understand Caesar' (1968: 5).

Schütz (1967), influenced by Husserl's phenomenology and consequently Husserl's emphasis on temporality and consciousness, criticized Weber for a lack of attention to the temporal nature of actions and meaning. Leaning on Bergson's conception of time and particularly his notion of *durée*, Schütz drew the distinction between action and act. An act, in Schütz' framework, is a completed set of actions. For example, going to a friend's house (a 'phantasied future' in Schütz' framework) provides meaning to the actions, and as actions constitute the act, actions produce the meaning of the act ('the meaning of any action is its corresponding projected act' (Schütz 1967: 61)). Importantly, the action is not directed towards meaning, but produces or activates that particular meaning. When going to visit a friend, the visit to her house is made meaningful by my bodily movements towards her house. If, for example, I look at a photograph of her house without moving towards it, the visit does not hold the same meaning (which does not make it meaningless). In other words, this differs from Weber's assumption that meaning is provided by the object of the action. Instead, the action reveals the meaning (the act), which again provides the action with meaning.

One main implication from a temporal perspective, based on Schütz' conceptualization of actions and acts, is namely that because the act is anticipated, it cannot be seen as a purely future state. On the contrary, the anticipated future state accompanies the actions towards its accomplishment. In a counter-intuitive sense, the anticipated future actually forms a 'past' to the actions. This is why Schütz was loath to consider what he called foresight and hindsight as being located squarely on two different sides of the present event (Schütz 1959).[21] I will return to this point in the discussion of event formations as manifolds and the idea of futurity and pastness.

In the spirit of the performative view taken in this book it seems important to point out that the imagining going to my friend's is not purely a predicted state of affairs. On the one hand a prediction is a representation of a future state of affairs. On the other the prediction is an act that has agency in itself. If I had dreamt that I would be going to my friend's house, the act could be seen to be based on introspection alone. The desire to go there has no evident external motivation. If I call other friends to tell them of my intentions, however, the situation would be different, as I would perform an act of signalling commitment to the act. If, in addition, we coordinated our electronic calendars in order to meet in connection with my trip, the act of imagining would in itself perform agency and the act would not be a pure representation of what is to take place. An interpretation of the above would be that in the flow of time we act in certain ways because it is meaningful, whereas the *impact* of meaning is arrived at through reflection, as and when we turn back on time, to use Schütz' expression.[22] It would seem that acts, as opposed to actions, are accomplishments that may be given a thing-like character. The act is an image of a state of affairs involving entities having interacted in a certain way. Seeing a friend is an accomplished act that acquires meaning as it connects to a number of things related to that friend, such as other acts carried out together in the past, other common friends, the school you went to, etc.

Importantly, a temporal view of action and meaning allows a clarification of current conceptions of action and meaning in organization studies, notably Weick's sensemaking. Weick, Sutcliffe and Obstfeld (2005: 410), for example, make a point of separating the language of sensemaking, which, they suggest, captures the realities of agency, flow, equivocality, transience, re-accomplishment, unfolding, and emergence, from the language of variables, nouns, quantities, and structures. A temporal view, however, rather than separating out a 'language' of flows from a language of states, assumes that actors experience flow in action, but reflect on those actions in the form of patterned entities once the experience wanes into the past and becomes available for recollection. What happens during the interaction is that words, actors, signs, and the like appear as distinguishable entities, but their movements and interactions may carry multiple meanings in the making.

To see entities as emerging through actions, as opposed to actions emerging from entities, differs from the thinking of, for example, Weick (1979: 44), who suggests that 'connections among nouns are the stuff of process', where he does not mention the work of relating *as* the making of the nouns. The nouns, or entities, are better seen as the things that are extended from actions, articulated by actions. The nouns provide meaning to actions, or rather actions provide meaning to themselves by their designation of nouns 'in the making'. When I reach for a marker in order to write on a whiteboard, the marker, the whiteboard, and the words that I write are nouns in the making, while in my consciousness I experience a process of tentative connecting. While in the process of reaching out and writing the meaning, the nouns (the marker, the whiteboard, the words) are real, but virtual, in the sense that they are open possibilities, in spite of their thing-like qualities. Once I have finished the operation, it is provisionally closed and I can attach meaning to the event and objects involved.

The action–act concept pair enables understanding of how actions connect into acts. It is difficult, though, to conceive of an adequate theory of organization that does not include considerations of actors as well. People who work in the accounting department rely on a notion of the accounting department as an entity, external stakeholders rely on a notion of the company as an entity, staff rely on a notion of their trade union as an entity, etc. This is not to say, of course, that they are entities in an objective sense, but that they are seen as entities from a distance in time and space. When looking back on what they have accomplished, however, they may perceive themselves as a unit. When the accounting department is under threat of restructuring, transformation, or elimination, it is experienced as an entity by its staff, by top management, and the trade union (if there is one). It 'is' not that entity, because no-one can really see it (apart from being depicted as a box on an organization chart), but it is talked and acted into existence as an imaginary-yet-felt-as-real entity. Here we come to an important insight by Czarniawska, that actions, connected by translation, produce actors, or, one should say, images of actors. The main point is that actors do not exist independently of what is done to invoke them. In a similar argument to Czarniawska's, but directed explicitly at interaction at micro level, Schütz (1967) points out the making of the 'we' arising from the vivid co-presence of humans. The passage where he imagines two persons watching a bird in flight is particularly illustrative:

Suppose that you and I are watching a bird in flight. The thought 'bird-in-flight' is in each of our minds and is the means by which each of us interprets his own observations. Neither of us, however, could say whether our lived experiences on that occasion were identical. In fact, neither of us would even try to answer that question, since one's own subjective meaning can never be laid side by side with another's and compared.

Nevertheless, during the flight of the bird you and I have 'grown older together'; our experiences have been simultaneous. Perhaps while I was following the bird's flight I noticed out of the corner of my eye that your head was moving in the same direction as mine. I could then say that the two of us, that *we,* had watched the bird's flight. What I have done in this case is to coordinate temporally a series of my own experiences with a series of yours.... It is enough for me to know that you are a fellow human being who was watching the same thing that I was.

(Schütz 1967: 165)

In the example the 'we', however, is not perceived in isolation of the acts that have produced it. The 'we saw it together' is an accomplished act that produces a temporally informed meaning of 'we'. The passage illustrates the making of 'we-ness' through temporal connecting of experiences. The connecting takes place in the co-presence between human actors and is a collective experience that cannot be the same for those present, but is collective nonetheless. As Helin (2011) points out, the meaning-making process is shaped by the interaction as a joint effort. Consequently the we-ness lies in the action, and not the result of the action.

The we-ness is necessarily volatile and momentary, as it is created amid a stream of fleeting gestures. Importantly, though, we-ness is taken to represent community, or the noun of a 'collective person' (Muzzetto 2006: 21). Taking collective action necessitates actions oriented towards the future but with reference to a collective past (whether the reference is explicit or not). Moreover, it necessitates some form of explicit recognition of the basis for the action. It is not assumed that collective action is based on agreement, or shared beliefs, but merely that it is made with some degree of collective recognition of a *raison d'être*. Nor is it assumed that it is based on face-to-face interaction, but that it involves, by its implications, actors dispersed in time and space.[23]

Collective recognition of past and future cannot be based on fleeting gestures alone, but requires temporal reference to recognizable events that concern the collective in some way or another. Schütz and Luckmann (1973: 87) point out that once we have lived through a we-relation, or a they-relation, which consists of multiple and related experiences, we can make sense of those experiences, not as multiple and related ones, but as grouped experiences, thus allowing for some related experiences to be distinguished from others. For such a monothetic (as opposed to polythetic)[24] evocation to take place, it is fair to assume that experiences may be grouped, either by virtue of similarity or by temporal proximity to one another. This implies that when evoking experiences, although they have taken place in time and are experienced as such, once they are to be evoked and expressed as a totality, the successive experiences get to be seen as events.[25] In Schütz' (1967) words, experiences that were once intentional (i.e. temporal) become, when evoked, mere passive content that can be drawn upon in the present as they become grouped through monothetic evocation in the reservoir of experience. The various actors and acts associated with the event constitute the content of the event. Note, however, that although the content may be passive owing to the fact that it lies in the past, that does not prevent it from being re-activated or even changed back into the active mode, as it were. For example, the content of the event may change if the meaning of the presence of an actor or his gestures is modified at a later event.

Returning to Schütz' idea that actions add up to acts, and that actions are carried out with the intention of completing acts, we may infer that when making sense of the past in order to mobilize collectively for the future, the evocation of acts serves to 'make' collective actors. A monothetic view may be seen to group actions around acts, which may be ascribed actors. For example, soccer team players mobilize a feeling of who they are as a team by retrospectively relating actions (the way they played) to acts (their victories and defeats). Doctors may mobilize a feeling of who they are by relating previous acts, such as operations, each consisting of numerous actions. Likewise, when observed by others, acts may constitute a collective. One act alone, however, may not be sufficient for enabling a sense of actor-hood.

3.5 **Organization as Connecting**

Organization theory has traditionally been based on the view of organizations as providing contexts for actions, and management theory has traditionally worked from the idea that managers create contexts in which intended results are achieved (Hernes 2004). In these contexts people have been assumed to be 'connected' by a variety of mechanisms, such as rules, norms, contracts etc. Parson's (1951) powerful theoretical framework, for example, which has heavily influenced mainstream organization theory, posed as an assumption that communication—a means of inter-human connecting—is guided by a shared perception of the norms of the system. In response to mainstream theory, studies have uncovered the lack of success of connections. One example is the focus on the emergence of informal organization, where people are connected differently from how they are connected by mechanisms in the formal organization. The achievement of the Hawthorne studies was to demonstrate that mechanisms such as group loyalty could be more influential upon group performance than formal organizational mechanisms, such as incentives or supervision.

In a world on the move it becomes important to explain how heterogeneous sets of actors connect and reconnect. In such a world standards sometimes replace organizations, human judgement is sometimes replaced by audit systems, artefacts sometimes constitute memory, concepts sometimes perform institutional work, and brands perform the work of identification. The list is long. Acknowledging a heterogeneous world implies accepting that while human actors perform work upon concepts and artefacts, they are also performed upon by artefacts and concepts. What becomes interesting for analysis—and relevant to the world of practitioners—is to study the connecting work performed by humans, materials, and concepts. This calls for a view of organization which considers dispersed actors in a world in which they act upon—and are being acted upon by—other actors. It calls for a view of organization as the actually performed work of connecting and reconnecting within and into meaningful wholes.

Important questions are 'What status do we ascribe that which gets connected?', and 'To what do we attribute the power of connecting?'. In mainstream organization theory, people are seen as being connected by other people using social, cognitive, or material means. In other words, people, normally managers, employ mechanisms to connect others, normally their staff, in such a way that the actions and behaviour of the staff correspond to some set of stated organizational aims. Early organization theory attributed passive roles to people and assumed that mechanisms would more or less mould their actions and behaviour to fit the organization's aims. Later, organization theory has allowed more agency to the subjective experience of organizational members.

But what do we make of a process-based theory that aims to explain the connecting of heterogeneous actors? To start with, the word 'actor' needs to be treated with considerable caution. Actors are commonly understood as those elements that are ascribed agency, that is, the ability to act upon other elements. Elements can be human, material, or abstract entities, such as concepts or institutions, but their identities are shaped by the ways in which they come to be perceived of as actors.[26] There are examples of how human actors may ascribe agency to abstract entities. When growing up as a child on the coast of northern Norway, I remember fishermen referring to the weather as 'he'. Closer to the world of organizations, a friend of mine serves on the board of a major European financial institution, where the market is sometimes also referred to as 'he'. These are oral constructions of actors performed in intersubjective situations, which Mead (1934: 184) explains as part of the ongoing making and remaking of one's 'self'. By addressing 'the other', which may be a physical object as well as another human being, or a larger social system (in which case we are talking about the 'generalized other'), we imagine their response, which is the response to the 'me'. We may, for example, according to Mead, address clouds, the sea, or trees, and as they are imputed reactions they are abstracted into entities with their own rationalities.[27] This process of action–reaction is temporal. For example, when a person makes a gesture or an utterance, what the person is expressing is not known to that person until after the act, and that is when the person experiences a sense of 'me'. The 'me' is never the same, yet the 'me' that is experienced sets the stage for the next 'me' during the course of interaction. Thus 'me', in Mead's theoretical framework, becomes an ever-changing 'historical figure' (Mead 1934: 174): 'It is what you were a second ago that is the "I" of the "me." It is another "me" that has to take that role. You cannot get the immediate response of the "I" in the process'. The 'I', on the other hand, is an acting, experimenting entity.

As much as agency may be attributed to individual actors, it is not individual actors that produce effects, but their interactions in certain settings, which provide pulses, or energy, for interactions in other settings. Following Whitehead's thinking, the experiencing subjects are the meetings of entities of different kinds, what in this book is referred to as 'organizational presents'. It is the collective socio-material experience, or rather, enactment during organizational presents, that exhibit agency. Those experiences, or enactments, include contributions by individuals, but they cannot be reducible to the contributions of those individuals.

During temporal presents, experience is in the making, but as yet indeterminate, because the relationship with other presents is assessed after closure, at which time the present becomes an event to be related to other events. With the passing of time the present becomes a historical entity in the form of an event, consisting of the heterogeneous sets of entities and acts that are associated with it. From being temporal, the event becomes spatio-temporal, but where the temporality is not one of flow, but more like fixing in terms of when it occurred and which place it occupies in the overall order of events. Space is to be read here as relational space, and not as absolute space (Schatzki 2010: 26). Relational space is the space created in the relationships between entities that takes place when an event gets to be seen as entities interacting in a certain setting (a park, a meeting room, a Skype conversation, or an email exchange). Central to an event-based interpretation of organizational life is the idea that space resides in events, rather than events existing in space, just as time is in the events, rather than events being in time. Events embody time in the way that they relate to one another. In this way events provide historicity to organizational life, as entities and their articulated relationships becomes associated with time and place. The agency conferred upon the event is temporal, in the sense that what takes place in the event gives meaning to past events while making future events possible.

A little detour is called for here, because the idea of organizing as the ongoing connecting of actors is expressed in ANT, which is in many ways an application of a process view to areas of technology, economics, and organization. Some ANT literature considers, as is the case in process thinking, the emergent character of entities, whose character is thought to emerge as a result of connecting work. A guiding principle of ANT studies, ever since the earliest studies (e.g. Latour and Woolgar 1979), continuing via Callon (1986a) and restated in Latour (2005), has been to follow the work of actors assembling seemingly disparate and heterogeneous entities into intelligible assemblies (Latour 2005). There is, of course, no omnipotent connector, such as a manager (a creature dear to management studies), but actors connecting themselves into actor-networks. 'Managers', to the extent that they are seen to exist as actors, emerge through multiple connecting operations; they are temporarily given their qualities through the connecting work they are performing. Note, though, that the term 'temporary' is a mere optical illusion. Temporariness is not a state as such, even in human experience, which is ongoing, although it may be imposed through reflection.

A process view as discussed here takes into consideration the virtuality of things and 'moments of suspension', while ANT, even though it considers entities as emergent and connecting as ongoing processes, tends to consider connecting as temporarily accomplished facts.[28] Actors forming actor-networks are seen as either connecting or not connecting, and their interests are seen as either translated or not translated along the interests of the network. Although ANT is an attempt (and a very good one at that) at capturing the ongoing nature of socio-economic or socio-material life, in its application it is likely to end up considering connecting as a step-by-step process (or, rather, steps that have happened), and overlook the temporality of connecting. Human actors produce choices based on their experienced past and their future aspirations. Moreover these choices are tentative choices in the making, rather than happening in a step-by-step fashion, although there are times when choices appear more decisive than others in retrospect.[29] What sets human actors aside from artefacts is their ability to make sense of possibilities by creating abstractions (Whitehead 1929a) from an equivocal world (Weick 1995). Assessing the potentiality represented by an element while gradually turning it into an actuality of the network is a capacity that is reserved for human actors, although the process may not be done without the help of material actors.

'Connectedness is', as Whitehead (1938: 9) wrote, 'of the essence of all things of all types'. Without connectedness there is no process. Connectedness is indispensible for connecting, which implies bringing together things to form a basis from which action can take place and meaning be created.[30] Connecting, however, cannot be but tentative. Tsoukas and Chia (2002: 570) define organization as 'an attempt to order the intrinsic flux of human action, to channel it toward certain ends, to give it a particular shape, through generalizing and institutionalizing particular meanings and rules'. By defining it this way, they bring out the volatile yet purposeful nature of organization. The word 'attempt', however, is a bit vague for a workable definition. Although their definition provides a sound basis from which to work, what remains to be specified is the very nature of such 'attempts'. Attempts must inevitably form part of an overall activity, and hence take the form of work, in the sense of sets of activity carried out with a purpose. An important question that Tsoukas and Chia's definition settles is that organizing *is* the attempts at ordering, hence there is no dualism between the actual attempts and the resulting organization. There is no work 'in here' that can be compared to a world 'out there', or work that is considered complete versus work yet to come. Substituting work for attempts, organization becomes the work of ordering the flux of activity (I purposefully omit the term 'human action' used by Tsoukas and Chia) of various types of actors. Still, the process that characterizes 'attempts' deserves more precise description.

But what can be said about the relationship between attempts at connecting and that which connecting attempts are aimed at if temporality is allowed to play a role? Let's take a hike. In the French Alps you sometimes come across large herds of sheep. The herds or, rather, the herding, is an impressive act of organizing. As thousands of sheep flow through the landscape, a few dogs, under the watchful eye of the shepherd, work incessantly to keep the sheep together and on course. It is truly a fascinating view because *ordering* (to use Law's (1994) term) goes on all the time. Although it is never determinate (except maybe at night when the herd stays together in the same spot, the dogs and the sheep rest), sheep, dogs, and shepherd are always on the move. The moving formation cannot just be ascribed to the movements of the dogs. Although I am no expert on the social psychology of sheep, it seems that the sheep have a notion of where they are heading, presumably towards more grass and water. In Norway, where I come from, sheep by and large manage on their own for months without shepherds or dogs to guide them, which suggests that there is a meaningful purpose in their movements. In Norway you might encounter a few sheep together in scattered groups, but in the Alps the herds run into several thousand sheep, which means that there are emergent formations of groups that deviate temporarily from the rest, either because they have different agendas (heading towards different patches of grass, for example, or because the terrain makes it impossible for such a large herd to keep together). When a few sheep diverge from the rest for a sustained amount of time and spread out in space, the divergent stream may accumulate and pose a threat to the overall task of the sheepdogs. Hence, clever dogs, which Border Collies are, stem outbreaks before they accumulate. This is how they display a constant awareness of the potentiality of the herd to take a different form and direction. Thus, to the observer it is hard to figure out why the dogs make such and such a movement and bark in a particular way. It may be understood at times, such as when you see them chasing sheep back towards the herd, but at other times their acts of herding are mere warnings to stem what might otherwise happen. This means that the 'organization' is never in any final state because it is constantly on its way to becoming something potentially different. The connecting is done in anticipation of potentialities; in other words, those emergent changes that might lead to a change in the formation.

Where is the organization in all this? The formation of the sheep could be interpreted in different ways. It could, for example, be frozen into a still picture and the position of every sheep could be plotted graphically, which would be seen as a representation of the organization of the herd. Then another frozen image could be retrieved, and yet another, and positions could be weighted to provide an assessment of the average formation over time. Such an approach would reflect a classic view of 'the organization' as a given arrangement, depicted as a succession of immobilities in time and space. A more technical approach to understanding the organizing by the dogs and relating it to the organization of the sheep would be to plot the positions and the barking of the sheepdogs at corresponding points in time and then relate them to the positions of the sheep. Such an approach would be an exercise in schematization but would be close to meaningless as a description of the process of organizing and organization. It would assume that the organization of the sheep and the organizing (herding) of the dogs are different processes that may or may not happen to coincide. It would ignore the inherently relational aspect of organizing and organization.

A different approach would be to focus on the ongoing movements of organizing aimed at maintaining some kind of coherence. Three words stand out in this sentence. I will take them in reverse order. 'Coherence' means that the overall movements of organizing respond to some 'framework' common to dogs and sheep and which represents continuity of meaning over time. If we work from the rudimentary assumption that it is mostly about grass and water, and some geo-physiological factors (sheep are not good climbers, for example), the organizing of the dogs and the movements of the sheep all enact these factors and thus provide sense to what is going on. 'Maintaining' means that movements beyond being isolated acts are intentional, aimed at what might happen. When a dog, for example, takes up a certain position, it is in anticipation of what might happen. Therefore, mapping the position does not in itself tell us anything about what eventuality the dog has in mind. Maybe that eventuality would not have happened after all, but the positioning of the dog is still part of organizing movements. 'Ongoing' means that movements take place in the present, draw upon a past, and are projected upon future aspirations. In the present, memories from previous presents may trigger reactions both with dogs and sheep in order to achieve something (like grass or water) or avoid something (like a steep slope). 'Ongoing' also means that actions of organizing reside with multiple actors, not just the dogs in this example, but also with the sheep.

Organizing and organization may thus be seen as the situated movements of sheep and dogs within a quasi-stable, permanently evolving framework enacted by movements. A group of sheep setting off towards a water hole or a patch of green grass enacts the framework. So do dogs when they chase those sheep back to the main herd again because the larger herd is headed towards a river where they can all drink. Hence there is never an organization in terms of positions, but ongoing movements related to different factors (grass, water, slopes). There is no 'negotiated order' in terms of one conclusive representative immobility because there is never a single order that can meaningfully reflect what is going on. Yet there is ordering, myopic, but directed nevertheless.[31]

In traditional organization studies, organizations are analytically reduced to a few orders, each corresponding to the mechanism that is assumed to connect the actors. In other words, actors are assumed already connected to some order. The connecting is seen as a fact (real or imaginary) and not a possibility for connecting otherwise, except in degree of intensity or strength of connections. From a process viewpoint, however, there is never really an accomplished order, but many possible orders of connecting in the making. Whereas organization theory has viewed order as given by the organization, process-based views shift attention to the work that is actually performed in trying to establish order. Drawing upon Law's (1994) terminology a move to a process view represents a move from order(s) to ordering. Law argues against the idea of social order, as well as the idea that there is one, and not multiple, orders. In seeking to denounce extant assumptions in social science related to ideas such as monotheism and purity, however, Law overlooks the virtual character of connecting. Connect*ing* depicts a process of acting towards some future aspirations, which is a double-sided process of moving from the manifest (or actual) to the latent (virtual), as well as the other way round. This double-sided process of connecting is what Cooper (2005a: 1693) calls relationality:

'Relationality relates the domain of the pre-objective and suspended with the objective world of realizable goals and purposeful action through the translation of the latent into the manifest. And, just as significantly, it re-lates the manifest world of objects and their objectives with the latent space and time of the pre-objective and suspended. In this sense, human agency is the expression of relationality, the continuous construction of the manifest out of the latent *and* the continuous inspiring of the manifest by the latent.'

Importantly, though, whereas the manifest may be perceived as a connected order, the latent is not an aggregate of things. Latency, as Cooper points out, is an open field of *possibilities*, always exceeding our attempts to fix and objectify it. This is what Whitehead calls 'relata', which belong to the discernible, but not the discerned, entities. Whitehead sees the discerned as comprised of elements discriminated by their own individual peculiarities, in other words those directly discerned. The discernible, on the other hand, is known as relata to discerned entities. Discernible entities are not known as entities as such, but as 'elements of the general fact which is going on' (Whitehead 1920: 49). In other words, they serve to fulfil functions of relata in pointing towards a broader picture.

3.6 Potentiality, Actuality, and Contingencies

One aspect that sets process views apart from prevailing views in organization studies is the notion of potentiality coupled with actuality. Potentiality is important because it signifies alertness as to the possibility of things becoming otherwise, and alertness to how things could be otherwise is what provides the experience of what the thing 'is'.[32] The passing of time brings with it concern, not just as to what may be created in the future, but also about the making of the past. In organizational language it may imply an ongoing concern about what the organization may possibly become, given what it has been, but also what it has been, given what it is in the process of becoming. As these concerns are expressed in the present it is through the projected possibilities that the organization acquires understanding about itself. In a sense it 'is' what it may potentially become, just as it is through its possibilities that it reveals itself to itself. As an athlete I understand myself in terms of the types of races that I may take part in. As a manager I understand myself in terms of the various projects that I can motivate my colleagues to undertake. As a company we understand ourselves in terms of the markets where we may excel; as an institution we understand ourselves in terms of the types and numbers of members we may recruit.

A process view, and especially one that emphasizes temporality, would argue that all the things we 'know' about being in the organization describe the actuality of being in the organization. As actuality, the organization is seen as a synthesized and coalesced set of ways in which things are perceived as working, and neither wrong nor misplaced. What a process view also argues, however, is that the world exhibits not just actuality but also *potentiality*. Potentiality represents that which provides forward and backward projection of process in time while offering realization of opportunities. Whereas potentiality is a notion that dates back to Aristotle, Whitehead (1938: 99–100) is explicit about potentiality as that which is particular to process thinking:

> The notion of potentiality is fundamental for the understanding of existence, as soon as the notion of process is admitted. If the universe be interpreted in terms of static actuality, then potentiality vanishes. Everything is just what it is. Succession is mere appearance, rising from the limitation of perception. But if we start with process as fundamental, then the actualities of the present are deriving their characters from the process, and are bestowing their characters upon the future. Immediacy is the realization of the potentialities of the past, and is the storehouse of the potentialities of the future. Hope and fear, joy and disillusion, obtain their meaning from the potentialities essential in the nature of things. We are following a trail in hope, or are fleeing from the pursuit in fear. The potentialities in immediate fact constitute the driving force of process.

Process thinking is a way to think about that which is otherwise possible, and in so doing capture the ongoing emergent nature of organizational life. It is a philosophy of possibility and creativity, without ignoring the restraints of the existing. It is about appreciating how processes contain potentiality for becoming otherwise without rejecting the idea that things are perceived in their actuality.

This is why, in its latency, a city, a school, or a small start-up company can be seen as a kaleidoscope of multiple possibilities; although in its manifestation it may be conceptualized as an order, or multiplicity of orders. Any attempt at arresting it as a fixed form only provides a partial glimpse of an order whose latency exceeds all representation (Cooper 2005a). For example, Pinheiro-Croisel's (2013) study of innovative urban development in France exemplifies the power of focusing on the processes of connecting rather than the things in themselves. Taking an organization process view inspired by Mead's pragmatism, Pinheiro-Croisel describes how innovative urban development projects depart from an open idea of the city space, which progressively engages actors (including city planners, citizens, politicians, engineers, and architects) to take collective responsibility for the end product and produce urban areas that exhibit uniqueness in terms of aesthetics, social life, and environmental friendliness. Her analysis derives from her focus on connecting processes by which actors and their collective role as designer emerges and is continually re-produced without staying the same, rather than assume that they are quasi-stable actors with pre-defined qualities or roles. Thus the city design in Pinheiro-Croisel's analysis is not a ready-made object to be designed and planned, but more like an open opportunity to fulfil certain functional and aesthetic needs in a given urban space. Connecting takes place around the 'virtuality' of the object rather than the object in itself.[33]

Things may be seen as vague possibilities that take form to become gradually more distinct. They may move from being possibilities to becoming more real through a process of actualization. Virtual realities come into being through *actualization*. As notes Heidegger (1927: 262):

Expecting is not just an occasional looking-away from the possible to its possible actualization, but is essentially a *waiting for that actualization*. Even in expecting, one leaps away from the possible and gets a foothold in the actual. It is for this actuality that what is expected is expected. By the very nature of expecting, the possible is drawn into the actual, arising out of the actual and returning to it.

3.7 Process and Structure

This book combines process with structure, because it is the process–structure relationship that enables the temporal qualities of organizational life to be understood. In this view, structure is not seen as separate from process; on the contrary, it belongs to process, much as process belongs to structure. An appreciation of temporality is created as structure provides a sense of both continuity and change to actors, and as events provide the structure with a sense of historicity. Similar to how airport signs provide a structure for destinations and ports of origin of aircraft, the departure and arrival times and blinking boarding/gate closing messages provide a sense of historicity and movement to the information on the signs.

Structure is intertwined with temporality because it provides a notion of continuity and change to actors who experience encounters in the flow of time. Continuity is produced as part of the process of experiencing the organization, and the organization 'is' its historicity as experienced in the present and projected upon future aspirations. The evocation/projection, however, is momentary and fades away as the present is left behind in the flow of time. A sense of continuity is provided as structure gives a sense of extension of present experience in time: it enables present experience to transcend the temporal diameter (Mead 1932) of the present and to live on as meaningful experience.

It may seem counterintuitive to combine structure with process. In its pure form process represents evanescence and the impossibility of repetition. Once an event has taken place it is gone, never to return. (I met a very good colleague today, as I do most days, and every encounter is unique and fades into the past as soon as it has taken place.) If we did not need to contemplate acting upon the world we live in we might as well live in a world of pure process. But in order to act upon the world we treat events as if they can be repeated, what Deleuze (2004: 8) calls pseudo-repetition. For example, I treat meeting my good colleague as a repetition, although I am aware that no encounter with him is really a repetition. In order to make it (seem like) a repetition I construct a map of the daily encounter that provides it with meaning, which means that I anticipate the encounter as I enter the office building, maybe even prepare for it, such as by thinking briefly about what to tell my colleague about what has happened since we last saw each other. In making my preparations I select what is meaningful to convey to him and that selection is a temporary structure of meaning for the encounter. I may, for example, relate something about the slow process of producing publications because of a temporary overload of teaching. In so doing I evoke in the present a segment of the institution that stretches into the past[34] and into the future. The statements I make may evoke previous encounters and create a possibility for what we may talk about at future encounters. Every encounter is, in a pure sense, unique and can never be repeated, but to enact a reality (meeting my colleague) we 'counterfeit' (Bergson) what has taken place) by conferring upon it a thing-like appearance:

Evolution in general would fain go on in a straight line; each special evolution is a kind of circle. Like eddies of dust raised by the wind as it passes, the living return upon themselves, born by the great blast of life. They are therefore relatively stable, and counterfeit immobility so well that we treat them as a *thing* rather than as a *progress*, forgetting that the very permanence of their form is only the outline of a movement.

(Bergson 1922: 128)

It is by treating Bergson's eddies of dust as things that they become elements of a structure of lived experiences. We treat them as things, even though our experience of them is in the form of events of encounters with them. Whereas evanescence is a fact of life, structure provides the means for evanescence gives way to continuity. It is not without reason that writers such as Heidegger and Deleuze made reference to structure, although their view of reality was clearly to treat it as an evanescent phenomenon.[35]

It has been—and continues to be—common in the social sciences to pit the fluidity of process against the immutability of structure. This is one of the unfortunate dualities that has arisen and been sustained by non-temporal views of phenomena such as groups, organizations, and societies. One major fallacy that such a view commits is that it assumes that structure and process are made from different materials, for example by assuming that process is about actions, practice, or routines, and that structure is about division of work reflected in an organizational chart. Even if a dialectical relationship is assumed between the two, it does not prevent structure and process from being seen as separate phenomena.

An example is Ranson et al.'s (1980) paper on the 'structuring of organizational structures', in which they apply Giddens' structuration theory to the study of organizations. Their paper is based on a discussion about the relationships between, on the one hand, interpretive frameworks, intimately related to Schütz' (1967) term 'provinces of meaning', and organizational structure on the other. Their definition of organizational structure is the social structures of relationships that reside in organizations. Actors' interpretive schemes, the authors argue, enable them to ensure a certain degree of continuity and predictability in their interactions, providing them with a *sense* of social structure. The interpretive schemes of actors constitute 'deep structures' that actors share and which facilitate their interactions, thus helping them resolve ambiguity in the meeting between interpretive schemes and structural frameworks. The gist of their paper resides in the distinction between the realm of meaning (represented by the interpretive frameworks) and structural frameworks (consisting of roles, rules, and authority relations), which are kept analytically separate. In other words, the world of structure is conceptualized as structural 'scaffolding' within which operate the worlds of meaning. It is between these two worlds that struggles for power take place, they argue, as different groups with different interpretive frameworks have different access to material and structural resources (p. 7). In short, their paper reflects prevailing assumptions in organization theory whereby a distinction is drawn between the world of meaning and the world of organizing.

In a comment to the paper by Ranson et al., Willmott (1981) points to the following basic problem in their paper, that is, that the separation between structure and interaction does not enable the kind of duality between action and structure that Giddens aims at. Willmott's point is that the aim from a structuration perspective would be to explain how structuring is actually accomplished, which is not possible as long as interactions are kept separate from the social structures they are seen to constitute. Willmott's point refers to Giddens' (1979) position on the duality of structure, where structure serves as both medium and output for actions, and hence embodies the essential recursiveness of social life.[36] Logically speaking, if structure serves as both medium and outcome for actions, structure and actions should be seen as 'cut from the same cloth', which is implied in Giddens' (1979: 62) definition of structure as that which 'tends to include two elements, not clearly distinguished from one another: the *patterning of interaction*, as implying relations between actors or groups, and the *continuity of interaction* in time'.

Assuming that structure and process are made from the same fabric, the difference between structure and process should lie more in their temporal properties than in substantive differences. A basic example is that of language, which provides a structure of words that enables words to acquire different meanings. Without the structure of language, words would be irreversible micro events that would not have any meaning beyond their microscopic duration. But the point is also that language, while being structure, also consists of words and does not consist of a different fabric than words. What changes is the passing of time in which words uttered in a certain context become labels that characterize that context; and as labels they confer meaning upon the utterances in the situation.

Language provides meaning to the flow of an event as it unfolds, such as the ongoing flow of gestures and utterances (Helin 2011: 63). While words and sentences are being uttered, they acquire provisional meaning in relation to one another, but remain in an indeterminate state until closure is reached as to their broader implications. Once they reach closure, their meaning may be altered as they are related to other words or sentences. If we pay careful attention to our ongoing experience of talking and thinking, we become quickly aware that while in the process of talking we are searching for words that correspond with our thought processes, but neither thoughts nor words are really complete or arranged before the next takes over. Still, we use them during the formulation of the sentence as if they are finite entities. Words could be seen as forming part of the structuring reality that we resort to while talking, but we reach out for the words without really knowing which words we are going to use and the consequences of using those words. We feel our way while we are uttering words. But words only make sense in linguistic structure. Therefore, as we feel our way we are guided by the structure of our language, which interacts with what we are in the process of expressing. As we search for an appropriate word, language is presented to us as multiple units (words), each of which represents a possibility. Once a word has been uttered, however, it has created a contingency[37] for what could come next. As we speak, we are literally speaking in time, where the word just uttered represents an immediate past, which is projected upon immediate future aspirations. As we speak we reach out towards the structure of language as a source of inspiration and structuring, while that structure frames what we try and express. This ongoing process is open and indeterminate. Also, the structure of language provides both scaffolding for what we are in the process of expressing and the means to understanding what we have expressed (when I see what I have said I will know what I meant).

'Pure' process is basically irreversible, which is why it needs structure for continuity. It is irreversible because it consists of events only, and once an event has taken place, it becomes a fact as having taken place and its occurrence cannot be done away with. I may carry out an action that I regret, such as having rebuked a colleague. But even if I apologize that does not change the fact that it took place. My apology may alter the meaning of the rebuke, but not the fact that it took place. It will add to the event of the rebuke while modifying the meaning of that event. Mantere, Schildt, and Sillince (2012) provide a good illustration of this point in their study of attempts at changing the sensemaking history in the case of a failed merger attempt in a company, where they found that the attempts at reframing the meaning of past acts would be remembered in subsequent change attempts. This is what Mead alludes to when he writes that the past is both irrevocable and revocable. On the one hand, what has taken place has taken place; it is what it was (Mead 1932: 36), while on the other hand, once it has slipped into the past and with the passing of time, its meaning will inescapably change as new presents emerge to change the past of which it forms part. Yet, in order to make it possible to even try and change the meaning of what took place, meaning needs to endure for that meaning to change. If not, the rebuke would sink without a trace and all that would be left was a rebuke that merely was what it was. Without the possibility of endurance of meaning there would be no way to experience a change in meaning of the rebuke.

The temporal difference between process and structure lies in the fact that structure enables evocation and projection. It provides events with the possibility of endurance in such a way that they acquire meaning in the light of the structure. Once they acquire meaning, that meaning may become subject to change with the passing of time. For example, the meaning of the rebuke may change with time as other events become related to it via a common structure of meaning. This presupposes, however, that the rebuke gets to be seen as an act between actors that remain identifiable as such over time. This is how structure provides for continuity, and why, by the same token, structure is essential to process. Continuity, however, is not given, but it has to be produced. It is not a property of a process but an experience *of* process. The production of continuity provides a sense of being, of experiencing the organization. The role of structure in the production of continuity is to provide the possibility of experiencing a durable whole.

Structure is the way that the organization understands itself and is articulated as a projection of the structure upon possibilities. Pharmaceutical companies, for example, launch new medical products that articulate their structure by conforming to certain ethical, technological, and aesthetic criteria that exist from the past as quasi-stable elements. As those products are targeted at a specific country or region in the world they articulate the structure in the direction of possibilities in those countries or regions, while evoking the conditions of past launches. Structure provides a sense of continuity, as it enables experience to acquire extension by becoming events associated with identifiable entities. This is how structure enables events to acquire apparent reversibility, because they may be 're-visited' and given new meaning as the repertoire of events grows. Still, structure and events are cut from the same cloth, as they are made up of congruous elements.

Part II
Towards a Process Theory of Organization

■ **SUMMARY**

In this main part of the book a theoretical framework is developed in response to the elements discussed in chapter 3. The main terms are temporality (including the role of presents and events), meaning structures, and articulation. The focus on temporality takes the reader into the implications of considering the idea of actors embedded in an ongoing present, by discussing the actual nature of presents, and how they form a basis for events. The temporality of presents and events lays the basis for understanding the structural aspect of organizing, as it provides structure with a sense of historicity and movement. Structure, on the other hand, provides a sense of continuity, which is basic to a process view. The connection between presents (and events) and structure is provided by the notion of articulation, which describes the process of enacting structures in time.

4 Temporality and Process

■ **SUMMARY**

This chapter develops the notion of living present, which is a temporary situation characterized by fluidity and movement and which involves human intersubjectivity. Living presents are characterised by temporal float, which signifies reversibility of experiences during the encounter. The passing of time forces closure upon presents, which turns them into events. Consistently with the atomistic view of events taken in the book, events exhibit temporal agency, which is defined as their ability to prehend ('reach out to') other events. The prehending of other events takes place in the living present, during which interactions mirror themselves in other events. Upon closure, temporal float is no longer possible and the living present becomes a spatio-temporal event associated with actors and outcomes. It enters what is referred to as 'event formation', which may be seen as a structuring of events in time.

4.1 Temporal Structuring

> ...*proximity* brings you closer to what happened, is responsible for the facts we glean, the artefacts we possess, the verbatim quotations of what people said; but *distance* is what makes possible the story of what happened, is precisely what gives someone the freedom to organize and shape those bits into a pleasing and coherent whole...
>
> (Mendelsohn 2008: 417)

> The ways in which people understand their own relationship to the past, future, and present *make a difference* to their actions; changing conceptions of agentic possibility in relation to structural contexts profoundly influence how actors in different periods and places see their worlds as more or less responsive to human imagination, purpose and effort.
>
> (Emirbayer and Mische 1998: 973)

Winston Churchill has been credited with saying, 'The more distant we look into the past, the farther we can see into the future', which is also a point March (1999a) makes and that Schultz and Hernes (2013) illustrate empirically. Looking back many years makes it possible to look forward a correspondingly long period of time. It is not obvious, for example, how one can look forward several years on the basis of looking back a few hours in time unless, of course, one has just witnessed a dramatic event, such as the news of a spectacular achievement or a disaster which, in its clarity and instantaneity, spells out a different future for years or decades to come. How far into the past and how far into the future one looks is partly a matter of choice. The choice, however, influences what is seen. Obviously, if the temporal span is a matter of seconds or minutes, the choice of what is seen is narrower than if the span extends to months or years. What is seen is also different in terms of detail in that a temporal span that lasts seconds or minutes may allow for a higher degree of vividness than one that lasts months or years.[1]

Temporal structuring implies taking into consideration the effects that the passing of time—including the shaping of past and future—have on the perceptions of spatial entities. Ultimately, perceptions of what an organization 'is' are spatial, in the sense that they are perceived as things—human, material, or conceptual—that are abstracted out and separated from one another so as to be reconnected into meaningful patterns. To take a temporal view does not mean to reject the idea of organizations as spatial phenomena. The point is that they are made spatial *in time*, meaning that spatiality is shaped by the passing of time. The organization chart, for example, is dependent on the temporal experience during which it is observed, not because it is expected to change from one point in time to the next, but because the point at which it is observed contains a past and a future, which are uniquely linked to the observation of the chart at that moment. Its past and future are both related to other spatial phenomena, such as concrete people who occupied—and may occupy—roles depicted in the chart. In this case our observation of the chart is dependent on the people we visualize as having filled certain roles that are depicted in it. Our present observation is also directed towards future possibilities for role occupations in the chart. For example, it involves the selection of who occupied which roles, and when, as well as the choice of other elements that related to the roles and the incumbents during that period of time. In this way time becomes decisive for how the chart is observed, not just because the actual time of observation matters (since the time of observation determines what the chart registers as past and future), but also because the observation takes place *in time* and each observation has its own past and future. The past reflects the conditions under which the chart was studied previously and the future reflects the actual intended use of the chart.

As the present of studying the chart reaches closure, it becomes an event, and as an event it remains open to definition and redefinition. As a temporal experience it evolves from an indeterminate experience in time to gradually becoming a condensed spatio-temporal event (composed of the observer and the chart) with the passing of time. It is as an event that its meaning may be redefined with the passing of time. The Storming of the Bastille in Paris in July

1789, a precursor to what came to be known as the French Revolution, is an example of the meaning of events changing with the passing of time, as it had a different significance on the day it took place than it came to have in subsequent decades and centuries. In fact, it was not seen as a revolution at the time, but more like an indeterminate unfolding of events. In July 1789 the attack on the Bastille related to events in the temporal immediacy of the storming. For instance, King Louis XVI's dismissal of Jacques Necker, his minister of finance, on 11 July 1789 (three days before the Storming of the Bastille) was an event that influenced the people to violent revolt. Necker was perceived as the person who had recently saved France from financial ruin while introducing a stronger element of financial accountability. The king's banishment of Necker was seen as a further manifestation of royal negligence of the economic and financial realities of the country and its citizens, and people took to arms to march on the Bastille. Though of limited military significance, the taking of the Bastille had enormous symbolic value (Sewell 1996). Its symbolic value enabled important articulation for political reform in the National Assembly. Political discourse for reform was strongly bolstered by the events in the streets and eventually led to extensive political reform. As a matter of fact, politicians in the National Assembly were against some of the events until they realized that those same events could lead to the type of reforms consistent with their own political agendas. Sewell (1996) points out that the density of events in the days leading up to the reforms played a significant role in justifying the actions that ultimately led to reform, although the great wave of reforms that came to be known as the French Revolution was unforeseen at that stage. The Storming of the Bastille represents a string of events that occurred in the attempt to solve imminent crises, while the French Revolution may, at best, have been an abstract idea at the time, similar to what Cooper (1976) refers to as an 'open field'. Sewell (1996: 845) points out that in such situations actors are rife with worry about how to get on with life, because they take part in what he calls the dislocation of structure. This disruption raises the emotional intensity of life as the longer time perspectives become uncertain. The events that occurred over a few days in July 1789 were in close temporal proximity to one another, and closer scrutiny would probably reveal how some events overlapped, helping to explain why they were so charged emotionally. As events took place to solve problems of a more immediate nature, events and actors were connected into patterns that held special meaning. For example, members of the National Assembly condemned the beheading of two officials by the crowd as barbarian acts, but also recognized that those very acts were, in the longer term, symbolic acts in the process of politically restructuring France.

With the passing of time, the cooling of emotions, and a changing understanding of the political and social consequences of the uprising, the temporal structuring of events and actors took on different meanings. With the revolution an established fact, events became clustered and linked to each other in time in ways that would not occur among those who were in the heat of the action. In retrospect, events are interlinked to make sense of how they led progressively to a revolution. With time the French Revolution has become more than a fact. It has become an institution, for which Whitehead's term a 'stubborn' fact applies, which makes and remakes ingression into processes of becoming in social and political life. Interestingly, once the actions in Paris in July 1789 became associated with revolution, the actors, material artefacts (such as the Bastille), and political ideas became related to one another differently than was the case in the days the events took place. It is open to speculation if some of the events seen as a nuisance as events unfolded, became viewed as paving the way for democracy with the passing of time. The change that has occurred does not so much involve the things (people, ideas, artefacts) that went into the revolution, but their *articulation* with one another.

Ongoing temporality entails a view of time as relentlessly passing, what Whitehead (1920) called 'the passage of nature', where time is irrevocably running away as a perpetually perishing commodity. In this view organizing is about making temporal entities from the past that can be projected as future aspirations in the flow of time. This involves giving temporal identity to entities in an effort to stabilize them into some form of configuration that appears desirable and/or plausible in the present. Actors are surrounded by other actors, who are also shaped by the passing of time. In such an optic, choices, problems, and solutions appear instantly in the flow as pressing necessities (Boden 1994: 22), offering possibilities of connection (Cohen, March, and Olsen 1972). Connecting, however, can only be done with a view of the temporal dynamics of other actors or entities.

Connecting is about tentative mutual stabilization among heterogeneous actors in time. The urge created by the passage of time to connect to actors influences the meaning that those actors take on, because connecting to them is a way to deviate from what they might otherwise become. The idiom 'strike while the iron is hot' applies here, as the passing of time inevitably leads to a cooling of the iron, and the possibilities of shaping it diminish correspondingly. In so doing they define the temporal features of that world, which is the past–future relationship of the actors involved. Farmers know that if they do not plant seeds they will miss an entire crop and suffer a loss of income. Under most circumstances, missing an entire season is unthinkable to them. They are caught in the flow of time and the corresponding ebb and flow of the seasons. But they also need to carve out their own temporality by sowing such that they can anticipate harvesting at an appropriate time, maybe by drawing upon the wisdom passed on to them by their ancestors. An example from organizational life is when a company hires a specialist (which means her past from other companies and possible future with the hiring company) in the nick of time, because this person was en route elsewhere and seen as a scarce resource. The hiring makes this individual precious, at least for a while. The work of connecting to actors on the move also serves to build up a past of connecting to them. The hiring of the specialist, for example, in itself constitutes the beginning of a differently evolving past of the hiring company, where a key moment is seen as the act of employment. The urgency of hiring the specialist and the desperate last-minute negotiations that went into the appointment form part of the emerging history of that actor in the organization and the view held of this person.

An example of temporal structuring is provided by Schultz and Hernes (2013), in which we analyse the evoking of organizational memory by managers in the Danish LEGO Group. LEGO was founded by an enterprising carpenter by the name of Ole Kirk Kristiansen in the small Danish town of Billund in the early 1930s. Kristiansen originally made wooden toys before inventing the LEGO bricks in the 1940s, which were originally made from wood. Early on, Kristiansen articulated the kind of a company he aimed to create through his motto, 'Only the best is good enough',[2] which he had engraved on a wooden sign in his office.

The sign, however, is associated with an experience he had with his son. In the 1930s when he manufactured wooden toys, Kristiansen once gave his son the task of painting wooden ducks that were to be sold to Sweden. He insisted that all toys receive three layers of paint. His son, having been delegated the task, delivered the finished ducks to the train station, proudly announcing to his father upon return that he had saved the company money by only painting the ducks twice. His father, not at all impressed, ordered him to take his bike to the train station, pick up the big box of ducks, and add the third layer of paint before going to bed. The son ended up working all night and never forgot his father's insistence on creating 'the best', whatever the situation. Engraving the sign was an attempt to project this experience into the future in order to manufacture top-quality LEGO products, and represents an effort to stabilize actors (people, machines, products) around the idea that quality can never be too good, in other words, that LEGO should always strive towards perfection in its products.

At another decisive moment in the company's history, between 2005 and 2007, when the company founds itself in a crisis, its new CEO chose to rely on traditional LEGO bricks as part of a strategy to focus on 'systematic creativity' (Schultz and Hernes 2013:12) rather than pursue a strategy of brand extension, which had been tried earlier. As part of this turnaround, LEGO focused its attention on its founder and his focus on superior quality more than seventy years earlier. In fact, the new CEO put the engraved wooden sign in his office—as had the founder—to symbolize the renewed focus on quality and simplicity. The bricks, the sign, and many other entities were in a sense given a temporal identity as they were infused with stories and artefacts from a distant past and directed towards future aspirations. It is not, of course, a story of copying the past, but of bringing the past into the present in an attempt to stabilize future entities and their relations.

The LEGO story suggests how a present (ordering the son to redo the painting) is evoked as an event at organizational presents decades later, and how the event is given new meaning in the context of of corporate renewal. In other words, not only do events change their meaning with the passing of time, but the ways they make their entry into the present remain open to interpretation. Key factors in the analysis are the nature of the present and its degree of 'livingness'.

4.2 **Organizational Presents and Living Presents**

> In thought...relations between entities...are expressible by definite propositions...Sense-perception knows none of these things, except by courtesy. Accuracy essentially collapses at some stage of inquiry.
>
> Whitehead (1929b:134)

The nature of the present has been subjected to considerable attention as well as controversy within philosophy. Mead, who wrote a volume dedicated to the present, saw the 'real' present as the ongoing projection of past experience onto future aspirations, whereas, following Whitehead, he called the 'specious present' that which is not a 'real' present, but that which is *conceptualized* as a present.[3] Kelly (1882: 167–8), believed to have coined the expression 'specious present', states:

The relation of experience to time has not been profoundly studied. Its objects are given as being of the present, but the part of time referred to by the datum is a very different thing from the conterminous of the past and future which philosophy denotes by the name Present. The present to which the datum refers is really a part of the past—a recent past—delusively given as being a time that intervenes between the past and the future. Let it be named the specious present, and let the past, that is given as being the past, be known as the obvious past. All the notes of a bar of a song seem to the listener to be contained in the present. All the changes of place of a meteor seem to the beholder to be contained in the present. At the instant of the termination of such series, no part of the time measured by them seems to be a past. Time, then, considered relatively to human apprehension, consists of four parts, viz., the obvious past, the specious present, the real present, and the future. Omitting the specious present, it consists of three...nonentities—the past, which does not exist, the future, which does not exist, and their conterminous, the present; the faculty from which it proceeds lies to us in the fiction of the specious present.

Somewhat paradoxically, we end up seeing the present as a reality while at the same time rejecting the reality of the present.[4] But then this is how we can view process philosophy as an invitation to conceptualize what we mean by 'the present' in organization studies: the present as a virtual reality. It invites elaboration and definition of how an 'organizational present' may be understood. Curiously, although several sociological and organizational writers acknowledge the importance of the present, very little has been done to elaborate a theory of the organizational present.

Organizations are special because they consist of numerous presents that are characterized by social co-presence, where gestures serve to mediate understanding in a flow of interaction. I have referred elsewhere in the book, quoting Schütz, to the becoming of 'we-ness' through gestures between two persons who become aware of a bird in flight. As pointed out earlier in the book, human co-presence in organizations has been dealt with by various writers, such as Boden (1994).[5] Mindful of the temporality of human interaction, I prefer to work from a definition of the present that considers more specifically human interaction in relation to the passing of time. I believe that this is relevant to organizational life, which, critically, is about doing things in the flow of time punctuated by temporal provisional closures, as I will discuss below.

A process theory of organization with focus on temporality calls for definitions of 'organizational presents', which would serve to lay the basis for a definition of events. While there are important insights in philosophy as to the different natures of the present, it is also important to develop notions of the present for use in organizational analysis. It is not important to define the duration of the present, but what sets it apart from what we would not call a present. A present is an experience in time and space that forms part of an organizational event pattern. A point of departure is to define the present as 'being there, then'.[6] 'Being there, then' signifies simultaneity, or co-presence, which may take place with or without human actors. A present, however, needs to signify some form of closure, however provisional that closure may be. Although actors are seen to operate in an ongoing present, a provisional closure of a present is necessary for that present to become an event. A purely material co-presence may, for example, be the encounter in a nanosecond between a computer and software, whereas a wholly social present is any encounter of two persons or more. A more composite situation arises when there is a simultaneous presence between humans and artefacts. This is described by Knorr-Cetina and Bruegger (2002: 923) in their analysis of traders, in which they distinguish between face-to-screen situations and face-to-face situations:

A key concept here is that of the face-to-screen situation, as opposed to the face-to-face situation. Traders work from trading floors located in banks in what are ostensibly face-to-face situations in which they are seated close together to be able to observe one another and feel the mood of other traders. Nonetheless, traders are not in a traditional face-to-face situation. Traders do not face one another but face their screens, an arrangement that transforms the face-to-face situation into, literally, a back-to-back situation. This arrangement implements a split in orientation in the interaction order, forcing, on the one hand, an orientation toward the screen that links the physically present person with a global sphere and, on the other hand, a secondary orientation to the local setting and the physically present others participating in it.

A 'human–substance present', is also found in Latour's (1994, 1999) description of Louis Pasteur's 'discovery' in 1857 that lactic yeast causes fermentation. Latour's discussion shows vividly how Pasteur interacted with the substances involved in his experiments, sometimes experimenting from hypotheses of what might happen, while at other times the experiments would 'speak back at him', forcing him to alter his course of experimentation. Together they formed processes that separated them, then blended them, then changed their respective identities. Actor-network Theory, however, which proceeds from assumptions of entities connecting, does not pay much attention to the actual 'connecting moments' of processes. The pasts of an entity reveal themselves during moments of connecting and it is during moments of connecting that agency is exercised. Human agency becomes crucial during such moments, because it is with the help of human agency that pasts may be selected differently and thus enable a different direction of events to be staked out.

Following Whitehead's event-based philosophy, presents constitute organizational life, which means effectively that there is nothing beyond the presents. On the other hand, if some presents, such as the ones formed between Pasteur and the lactic yeast, are highly influential upon further development, including a different meaning of the past, it becomes important to explain how some events, or some patterns of events, become particularly powerful in defining other past and future events.[7] This entails studying the temporal agency of presents, by which I mean the capacity to initiate change or reproduce the meaning of previous as well as future events.[8]

Living presents may be seen as a species of presents that involve human subjectivity. As much as organizations are about systems, material artefacts, and technologies, they are also about living moments where reality gets to be lived, defined, changed, or continued. This is what confers particular agency upon living presents that involve intersubjective presence of human actors. At a general level, organizational life is made up of multiple moments, or presents, regardless of whether or not they include human actors. Systems, for example, interact as they are connected by structured flows of data, and each connecting moment may be seen as a present that projects past encounters onto a possible future. However, the present, if it is to have agency, presupposes the co-presence of human actors whose interactions make it a 'living present', like what Whitehead calls a 'living occasion'. Similar to Whitehead's point that living occasions do not imply pure social presence, co-presence of human actors does not imply an exclusively social presence, as exemplified by

Knorr-Cetina and Bruegger's (2002) observations about face-to-screen situations. Still, only human co-presence can bring about change in the sense of exploiting the potentiality of a situation, because it has the ability to recall a different past as well as project a different future, which is what confers agency upon the present. Assuming that the present consists of co-present humans, an important question to ask is what characterizes their interaction that makes it an organizational present.

Living presents take place in what Bergson called *durée*, the 'pure' passing of time without perception of delineated entities, or what is also referred to as 'real time' (Schatzki 2006). Real time, he points out, is to experience something as it unfolds, and not later. As Schatzki (2006: 1865) points out, most events are not instantaneous, which means that their occurrence takes time; they form a passage from commencement to cessation, which is a movement in the sense of 'real time'. Unlike uncommitted talk, such as over a dinner table, however, organizations need to produce decisions in the flow of time. Decisions involve social commitment, and therefore living presents are normally conducted with a view to closure, whether or not that preclosure is planned.

How do we perceive actions, that is, what we do in a living present, as meaningful? Here Schütz (1967), drawing upon Bergson's work, provides an additional dimension of meaning, which relates on the one hand to the idea of pure duration and streams of consciousness, and on the other to the idea of reflection. He saw pure duration as the temporal passing of 'nows', a constant flux, a stream of conscious state (p. 45), which is a conception of living experience that draws upon Bergson. Importantly, however, the stream of consciousness is on-going and indiscriminate in relation to experience: 'The stream of consciousness is, by its very nature not yet caught up in the net of reflection' (p. 45).[9] The ongoing intersubjective process during an encounter provides a tentative, but not yet fully formed, understanding of what the encounter is in the way of constituting a collective actor capable of agency, that is, making a difference to what has been and to what is to come. As pointed out by Schütz (1967: 170), the pure 'we-relationship' of an intersubjective encounter is not grasped reflectively, but is *lived through*, enabled by the 'inter-locking of glances, this thousand-faceted mirroring of each other'; moreover, 'The many different mirror images of Self within Self are not therefore caught sight of one by one but are experienced as a *continuum* within a single experience' (emphasis added).

In living presents several minds are at work in converting experiences into expectations for the imminent future, moving continuously between the particular and the general while in face-to-face contact. I see the living present in such a context as the temporal horizon of interaction that allows contemplative activity (Deleuze 2004) to carry the process from moment to moment through a fusion of instants without closures that force reflection and action, which would automatically introduce past and future as distinct from the present.

A definition of the living present would capture the flow of social interaction in which minds work to fuse past, present, and future within the temporal horizon of the encounter. Within the temporal horizon of a living present it is possible to recall selected segments (utterances, ideas) from the totality of the present at an instant, such as by reminding others of what was said by someone at a previous instant without interrupting the interactive flow. What was said at that previous instant is then made available for contemplation as a candidate for the imminent future in the flow of interaction. Once the temporal horizon of the living present is transcended, the present ceases to be a present and turns into an event to become an object of historicizing.

Mindful that Deleuze does not discuss the social dimension of the present, his notion of the temporal unfolding of the present, and more precisely his idea of passive synthesis, in which past and future are not instants distinct from the present, seems useful for defining a living present. Deleuze (2004) describes the living present as the present where time is deployed, where it works as a synthesis contracting successive independent instants into one another. Both immediate past and immediate future belong in the living present. The past figures in the present insofar as the preceding instants are retained in the contraction; and the future is contained in the present insofar as its expectation is contained in the same contraction. Importantly, the past and future do not designate instants distinct from the present, but form dimensions of the present. Deleuze (1994: 9) calls this 'passive synthesis'; it is not carried out by the mind, but occurs in the mind.

The idea of immediate past and immediate future being contained in the present applies to principles of process thinking in general, but Deleuze's notion of passive synthesis applies to the living present in particular. Deleuze emphasizes the element of contemplation in passive synthesis. Passive synthesis may be associated with habit, which could be seen as the mere repetition of actions over time. This is not what is meant, however. Deleuze accentuates instead the role of the 'contemplating mind' (p. 95) in performing the fusion of instants into the present. The fusion performed by contemplation serves to carry on 'the project' of what is taking place. Therefore, when Deleuze uses the term 'passive synthesis' it is not meant to signify that nothing occurs: it means that that which occurs takes place in the mind that contemplates and not in the object that is contemplated. It may be externally passive, but internally active.

If we consider living presents in organizational life from this viewpoint, the contemplative activity that carries the process from moment to moment through a fusion of instants is what makes them 'living'. It is asymmetrical in the sense that it goes from the past to the future in the present, from the particular to the general, thus imparting direction to the arrow of time (Deleuze 1994: 91). The particular is that which is lived and experienced by the subject(s). The general, on the other hand, harbours the expectations for the imminent future generated by those particular experiences.[10] Again, it seems clear that although the term is passive synthesis, it also describes intense emotional and cognitive activity, which on a continuous basis converts particular experience to generalized expectations.[11] Not only does it constitute intense activity, but also inherently creative efforts to convert from the particular to the general in the flow of time.

The process of a living present is characterized by openness as to what it will produce. This is illustrated by Sheets-Johnstone's (2008: 485) description of dance improvisation, which brings to light the combined volatility and agency of the present:

> A dance improvisation is the incarnation of creativity as process. Its future is thus open. Where it will go at any moment, what will happen next, no one knows; until the precise moment at which it ends, its integrity as an artwork is uncharted. It is in view of its perpetually open future, its being in the process of being created, that a dance improvisation is unrehearsed and spontaneous. Because no set artistic product exists in advance or in arrear, the dancers have nothing in particular to practice or perfect in advance, nothing in particular to remember in order to keep. Their improvisation is process through and through, a form which lives and breathes in the moving flow of its creation, a flow experienced as an on-going present.

Yet, the meaning of an act is settled (although provisionally) when provisional closure is introduced (such as the end of a dance or the scheduled end of a meeting). This is when it takes the form of an event.[12] Hence, what distinguishes a living present from an event is that, whereas a living present is defined by the process that takes place, an event is a temporal experience marked by closure, then to become a spatio-temporal entity. A meeting is a living present, or a series of living presents, while it is taking place. Once it is over it becomes an event that can be talked about and related to other events.

Meaning is conferred upon actions through reflection, in other words after it has taken place while new meaning construction is taking place. This is when we are able to give a spatio-temporal ordering to actions, by relating them to the acts in a continual process of interaction. Acts are given meaning through reflection by turning a living present into an event, which takes place once the 'temporal diameter' (Mead 1932) has been left behind by the flow of time. Meaning is constructed as we 'turn back' on the flow of time and impose reflection upon it:

> At one moment an experience waxes, then it wanes. Meanwhile something new grows out of what was something old and then gives place to something still newer. I cannot distinguish between the Now and the Earlier, between the later Now and the Now that has just been, except that I know that what has just been is different from what now is. For I experience my duration as a uni-directional, irreversible stream and find that between a moment ago and just now *I have grown older*. But I cannot become aware of this while still immersed in the stream. As long as my whole consciousness remains temporally uni-directional and irreversible, I am unaware either of my own growing older or of any difference between present and past. The very awareness of the stream

presupposes a turning-back against the stream, a special kind of attitude toward the stream, a 'reflection,' as we will call it. (Schütz 1967: 47)

I infer from this passage that the experience of change is undifferentiated in the present. What may be differentiated are things and their movements, which provide tentative meaning to actions in the present. For example, when I offer a supportive comment to colleagues during a meeting, their reaction to my comment provides meaning to that comment. While talking and gesturing, the situation is essentially indeterminate, in other words open as to what the interaction will accomplish as regards the object of interaction. For example, when I am talking to another person, I am wholly in the process of constructing intersubjective meaning by the use of words and gestures, although I may be talking about entities that appear delineated. Even when I am in the middle of a sentence I do not really know how the sentence is going to end or how the other person will react to the sentence. As Mead (1934: 177–178) writes, '[W]e are aware of ourselves, and what the situation is, but exactly how we will act never gets into experience until after the action has taken place.' While I am speaking, for example, I appear as an open entity to the others present. Will I, for example, become a dissenter, an adversary, a bearer of bad news, or a saviour of the situation? While I am speaking and performing gestures, what matters for becoming an entity in the eyes of others is the punctuation of my utterances, which provide structure and hence meaning to what I am saying. Before the punctuation is provided (or attributed) my expression is indeterminate, and others are involved in the flow of my presentation. Once the punctuation is made, it becomes possible to make sense of what has been said and attribute that sense to 'me' as a temporary entity in relation to the social setting. Without punctuation, participants are held hostage to the contents of what actually is being communicated, but also held hostage by the indeterminacy of the situation, because the communication, if extended by another word, sentence, or gesture, may provide clues for a meaning other than what is experienced while in the flow.[13]

Interactions are given meaning in the light of the particular context of the meeting and its approaching closure. If a meeting is held to deal with interpersonal conflict, interactions are influenced by the need to make some progress towards solving the conflict by a certain time. Meetings, however, are but one form of encounter. Naturally, many encounters have no specific predefined agenda.

Before an encounter is brought to closure the broader meaning of the interactions going on within it remains to be determined. A reason for this is that the interactions within the encounter exhibit what we might call 'temporal float', by which I mean that utterances, gestures, and imageries may be brought forward, re-used, repeated, and re-defined in the flow of exchange.[14] Temporal float signifies not only that what goes on during the present may change, but also that it has not yet been brought to closure, i.e. its outcome is still indeterminate. The temporal experience of a living present is well articulated by James (1890: 611) in the following passage:

> The practically cognized present [i.e. the specious present] is no knife-edge, but a saddle-back, with a certain breadth of its own on which we sit perched, and from which we look in two directions of time. The unit of composition of our perception of time is a duration, with a bow and a stern, as it were—a rearward—and a forward-looking end. It is only as parts of this duration-block that the relation of succession of one end to the other is perceived. We do not first feel one end and then feel the other after it, and from the perception of the succession infer an interval of time between, but we seem to feel the interval of time as a whole, with its two ends embedded in it. The experience is from the outset a synthetic datum, not a simple one; and to sensible perception its elements are inseparable, although attention looking back may easily decompose the experience, and distinguish its beginning from its end.

Temporal float implies that intersubjective processes at living presents are temporally reversible. For example, I may refer to a certain gesture at the beginning of an encounter and most people present may know what I mean, as well as how that gesture makes a difference to—or bears out—what is being said at that very moment. The bow and stern mentioned by James are experienced as boundaries for temporal float during a living present. When that living present reaches closure, the bow and stern become seen as part of the framing of the event that grew out of the living present.

4.3 Organizational Presents and the Becoming of Events

> We may wish to mark off a period; but have we the right to establish symmetrical breaks at two points in time in order to give an appearance of continuity and unity to the system we place between them?
>
> (Foucault 1994: 50)

The transition from flow-like to thing-like experience is represented by the transition from presents to events. Transforming from a living present to an event implies transforming from a logic of intuition to a logic of analysis. Typical of a living present is the ability to apply intuition to the ongoing process, similar to Bergson's idea of intuition, which he calls 'intellectual sympathy', by which he means the ability to 'place oneself within an object in order to coincide with what is unique' in it, which according to Bergson is inexpressible (Bergson 1999: 7). In a living present, objects would refer to objects of talk, of thought, and reasoning, including the actors present. It is relevant to mention Mead again here, who reminds us that we impute expression not just to other human actors but also to supposedly 'non-living' objects (my expression), such as nature. From a temporal perspective, perhaps the most important feature of the living present is its openness and indeterminacy, which leaves open the possibility for innovation in the sense of imputing different meanings to past and future events. Concomitantly with openness and indeterminacy, however, there is what Bergson calls 'analysis' (parallel to Schütz's idea reflection mentioned above), which he suggests reduces objects to elements already known. This is when objects become representatives of categories, that is, when an object is reduced to 'elements common to it and other objects' (Bergson 1999: 7). Analysing involves the expression 'of a thing as a function of something other than itself' (p. 7).

Organizational life may be seen as pulsations of living presents within an unfolding pattern of collective action driven by reflection and analysis. Bergson (whom Schütz drew upon for a temporal understanding of action and meaning) sees reflection as that which enables concerted action. Although actors are seen to operate in an ongoing present, within that present they conceive past and future events as representing periods of identifiable states. Breaking up the flow of time into states, Bergson (2007) argues, enables acting upon things, and therefore we should be more interested in the states rather than the flow itself.

In order to appreciate the entangled flow-thing-like nature of organizational life it may be useful to consider micro movements in social interaction, such as winking, which consists of closing and re-opening one eyelid in a split second. During the split second that the eyelid moves, the experience of the other person or persons is of a flow-like character in that it is undifferentiated. During the movement of the eyelid the other person does not know what its implications will be. A number of potential lines of distinction exist, but they cannot be drawn until the wink is over and reflection becomes possible as to its possible meanings. Is it flirtatious, confirmative, consolatory, conspiratorial, or malicious? During that split second possible lines of distinction exist, but they cannot be drawn definitely. It is a moment during which possible meanings are multiple, a moment of indeterminacy.[15] In other words, the moving entities are experienced as indeterminate flow. Once the wink is accomplished it becomes a micro event whose meaning is provisionally settled as it becomes connected to other events, such as sentences, gestures, emails, etc. The moving of the eyelid, just like a string of words from a mouth or a computer screen, is experienced as flow, but once it is over, it becomes an accomplished event where the movement of parts took place. The wink has moved from a flow-like to a thing-like experience, carried by the flow of time.[16] What matters is how experiences are connected with one another so that singular experiences inscribe their place into a larger pattern of events. We may choose, for example, to relate the wink to the utterance that preceded it and the one that followed it, or we may relate it to the preparations and the aftermath of the meeting, in which case the temporal span is very different. If associated with other events, prior to or after the wink, it may take on quite different proportions, as it gets connected differently into a wider event formation.

Spatialization—or entification (Hernes 2008)—of experience amid temporal experience arises from the need to act. The ongoing spatializations may be compared to what Bergson calls 'halts'. Bergson makes the point that faced with the necessity of action we make sense of experience by spatializing that which in inner experience is strictly temporal.[17] Bergson (2007: 122) points out, however, that breaking up the flow in states should be seen as a means to act and not reflect a true picture of the flow itself:

> I repeat, there is nothing more natural: the breaking up of change into states enables us to act upon things, and it is useful in a practical sense to be interested in the states rather than in the change itself. But what is favourable to action in this case is fatal to speculation. If you imagine a change as being really composed of states, you at once cause insoluble metaphysical problems to arise. They deal only with appearances. You have closed your eyes to true reality.

A crucial question becomes, how can the relationship between presents (in particularly living presents) and events be theorized? Curiously few attempts seem to have been made in the organizational literature to explicitly make the notion of event an analytical element of theory building. There is a considerable literature on meetings in organizations,[18] but little that systematically relates meetings to processual issues, such as routines, practices, or strategy formulation. Jarzabkowski and Seidl (2008), for example, note a lack of studies that provide understanding of how meetings, despite their pervasiveness, contribute to strategy formulation in organizations. Although they confine their statement to strategy, their observation suggests that there is a general lack of studies of how organizational meetings connect temporally. Hendry and Seidl (2003) offer some interesting ideas here. Basing their paper on Luhmann's autopoietic theory, they employ the notion of episodes to understand how the bracketing off of formal and informal social encounters enables their temporal structuring. In their analysis they consider the temporal structuring as the effects the anticipated ending of an episode have on the structuring of the episode, as well as on how the episode connects in time to the broader discursive structure of the organization. In Luhmann's theory, episodes serve as events at which autopoietic reproduction is continued, while opening up the possibility that meaning may be changed during the episode. During episodes, consciousness may be disturbed and lead to re-interpretation of meaning structures (Luhmann 1995: 268). Meaning, because it is temporally produced and re-produced, is brought forward from the past, which is why Luhmann also points out that episodes contain *sediments* of earlier communication (Luhmann 1995: 407). In other words, the episode performs agency by re-establishing what has been before, while possibly changing it. Taken together this suggests the importance of conceptualizing how organizational presents, while forming part of the temporal stream of organizing, also constitute previous episodes and provide a basis for episodes to come.

Whereas philosophers express the present as an ongoing existence of undifferentiated flows, organizational life also demands concerted action, which necessitates invocation of spatial entities, even though actors operate in a living present. This is why it is insufficient for organizational analysis to insist, as Nayak and Chia (2011) seem to do, on invoking the 'pure present'. Their inspiration comes from Bergson, although similar points could be made on the basis of Deleuze. Where I depart from the exclusive focus on purity of the present derived from process philosophy is that when acting upon things it is natural to resort to spatial thinking, as Bergson (2007: 15) himself pointed out.

Once a present consisting of numerous flow-like experiences is broken up, its temporal float is broken and the gestures and reactions that took place in the meeting cannot be recalled under the same intersubjective conditions as continuous experience. If a gesture in the meeting is recalled after the meeting, it is more likely to be described as 'she reacted with that gesture in response to his remark that...'; in other words, the gesture is recalled in spatial terms (who did what) and as taking part in a succession (it happened after, or before something else.) Thus temporal closure in organizational life implies the making of entities, although provisionally, because the event—the act—produced will derive its meaning from the entities it is associated with. A main point is that the present shapes the meaning of past and future events by recreating them by the use of spatial terms.

Since past and future are in the present, observe Whitehead (1929b) and Mead (1932), there is agency in the present to redefine past and future. Hiring an expert sets the stage for changing the history leading up to meetings with this person, where participation—her living presents with others—serves to evoke and modify that history. In other words, a living present, such as in the form of a meeting, serves two purposes. First, it (re)defines the meaning of the history up and till that meeting by (re)arranging the entities associated with that history. Second, it takes part in shaping the passage of history for subsequent meetings.[19] In this trajectory of experiential events the expert is continuously being 'made' and remade' by projections backward and forward in time made in the living presents that the individual partakes in.[20]

The idea that the past may be changed, or rather that the meaning of the past may be changed in the present, requires some elaboration. Staying faithful to the view of an ongoing present, what is changed is not the past, or the meaning of it, per se, but the past is experienced by the way that the present mirrors itself in past events. When watching a documentary about Mohammed Ali's legendary boxing fight versus George Foreman in Kinshasa, Zaire, in 1974 the very setting of the match is experienced as important and is mirrored in other settings in which boxing matches have taken place. Two Afro-American boxing champions, one of whom (Mohammed Ali) was a symbol of youth defiance and an emerging African-American identity, meet in an African country no longer a colony, away from the prejudice and oppression in the United States. The boxing match becomes more than a boxing match, as it becomes related to the era, which is also an outcome of previously accumulated, interrelated eras characterized by struggle, for example slavery, the American Civil War, racial laws, and McCarthyism. When we speak of boxing, the Kinshasa match, being an emblematic match in the history of boxing, is part of what boxing 'is'. In other words, boxing, similar to an organization as we experience it, stretches back into time, made up of events with enduring associations. Although few boxing matches ever come close to achieving the symbolic value of the 'Foreman v. Ali Rumble in the Jungle' match, as it came to be called, even some insignificant boxing matches may be seen to take place against the background of that fight. By association, their taking place may be seen to stretch back to that match, and by so doing they may evoke the context of the match, even if it is not seen as relevant to the present-day context. When I use the word 'context' here it is not meant to signify context in the way of a stable body that lies outside the process, but other events mirrored by the event in question. The Rumble in the Jungle may be associated with, for instance, various television appearances by Muhammad Ali during which he declared black supremacy, poked fun at his opponents, or chastised the US government for its involvement in the Vietnam War. So when Mead (1929: 237) writes that, 'The assurances which we give to a remembered occurrence come from the structures with which they accord', I take 'structure' to mean the structured relationships between the remembered occurrences.

Adding Whitehead's notion of causality, which suggests that causality takes place not in virtue of the activity of the cause but through the activity of the effect, the present cannot but change the effects past events have on the present, the effects of which are created in the present. This idea is consistent with Kline's (1986: 221) discussion of presents (what he calls present existents), where he suggests that presents (or present existents) 'may, and regularly do, modify themselves by causally objectifying past existents in different ways'. This, according to Kline, is how the meaning of the past may be changed in the present. Importantly, however, the present also shapes itself in the light of the events it evokes. It is clear that the mirroring performed in the present—upon the present—of other events is a process involving several events as pattern, or structure, rather than individual events. No event can be seen in isolation from other presents-turned-events; on the contrary, it is seen as taking part in the formation of multiple, related events that, in turn, define individual events. Hence a present can never be a replica of other events because it cannot mirror itself exactly in individual events (maybe with the exception of particularly carefully scripted rituals). On the contrary, it is bound to differ, which means that once it has become an event it modifies the meaning of other events.

Of particular relevance in Whitehead's thinking (Whitehead is probably the philosopher who has gone farthest in developing an event-based theory) is that an event does not passively copy the past; rather, in the act of self-creation it refreshes the design of the past, thereby inventing its novel present and preparing for future aspirations.[21] This means that events (or presents) exhibit mutual agency by (re)defining each other.[22] Revising the design of the past, that is, bend the trajectory of its events pattern, requires work, as mentioned above. In organizations it involves activity, technologies, attention, reflecting, and time.

4.4 Temporal Agency and Event Formations

> That clocks are instruments constructed and used by people for quite specific purposes connected with the demands of their communal lives is understood readily enough. But that time too has an instrumental character is obviously more difficult to grasp. Do we not feel it passing ineluctably over our heads? Linguistic usage also clouds the issue: it makes it appear as if time were a mysterious something, the measure of which is determined by man-made instruments—clocks.
>
> (Elias 1992: 5)

> The research question then becomes, how does it happen that loosely coupled events which remain loosely coupled are institutionally held together in one organization which retains few controls over central activities? Stated differently, how does it happen that someone can take a series of loosely coupled events, assemble them into an organization of loosely coupled systems, and the events remain both loosely coupled but the organization itself survives? It is common to observe that large organizations have loosely connected sectors. The questions are, what makes this possible, how does it happen?
>
> (Weick 1976: 14)

Both of the above quotes are concerned with the workings of time. Still, the quotes convey complementary yet different views of time. Elias addresses the fact that the passing of time itself performs work upon social life and that social life emerges from temporal structuring. Temporal structuring takes place through work, in time, which gives it an instrumental character. Weick's quote places events in time but, consistently with his sensemaking framework, he sees events as making up causal patterns that are formed retrospectively by acts of sensemaking. The work, however, is done by organizational and institutional systems, which appear stable over time. Therefore, sensemaking is seen as activity that connects events that are already connected by organizational and institutional systems.[23] The actual events of sensemaking are not seen to perform the making of other events, but are merely strung together by institutionalized systems. Although Weick's insistence on 'making' in sensemaking suggests that sensemaking events do exhibit some agency in the flow of time, it is useful to develop further thinking about how actual events 'make' other events, both past and future.[24]

In a temporal process theory of organization, events need to be ascribed some form of agency, according to the following line of reasoning. First, some form of agency needs to be ascribed if process is seen as endogenous in the sense that only experience generated within the process matters. Second, if experience takes place in an ongoing present, it means that any action is confined to that present. In Schütz' (1953: 15) words, 'All projects of my forthcoming acts are based upon my knowledge *at the time* of projecting' (italics added). Taken together, these two assumptions signify that process takes place as the activity of projecting from one event to the next (both backward and forward in time). For example, I send an email to a colleague and the response to the message in the email is related to the wording of the email, which was composed in one event with the anticipation of the event of my colleague reading the email.[25]

The idea of temporal agency as it is conceptualized here is simple, in the sense that what happens at one time and place matters to what happens at another time and place, whether this other time and place precedes, succeeds, or takes place concurrently with the time and place in question. Some readers may object, 'But where are the agents?', 'How can there be agency without agents?', and 'What is the role of the individual and groups?' During an encounter, for example, people exert agency. The answer is that 'yes, they do', but only through their actions, word, and gestures, which become entangled with the actions, words, and gestures of others. An encounter is constituted by the activities of those present, including technologies and artefacts, but encounter cannot be *reducible to* those activities. Hence what produces agency is the outcome of the encounter as it reaches closure and becomes an event, thereby giving meaning to other events, while defining the encounter as well.

The agency of events lies in their ability to redefine the meaning of the past and define the contents of future events. The following is an excerpt from Whitehead's (Whitehead 1925b: 10) description of a somewhat special meeting at the Royal Society in London in 1919, at which they received the news that Einstein's general theory of relativity was scientifically confirmed:

It was my good fortune to be present at the meeting of the Royal Society in London when the Astronomer Royal for England announced that the photographic plates of the famous eclipse, as measured by his colleagues in Greenwich Observatory, had verified the prediction of Einstein that rays of light are bent as they pass in the neighbourhood of the sun. The whole atmosphere of tense interest was exactly that of a Greek drama: we were the chorus commenting on the decree of destiny as disclosed in the development of a supreme incident. There was a dramatic quality in the very staging:—the traditional ceremonial, and in the background the picture of Newton to remind us that the greatest of scientific generalisations was now, after more than two centuries, to receive its first modification.

Quite understandably, the meeting was one of several occasions at which the meaning of the Newtonian order up and till then was altered, while giving new meaning to future scientific work in the field of physics. The intensity of the present at the Royal Society did not by itself change the course of events, but it would probably be fair to say that it played its part in an overall formation of events (hereafter called event formation). It presumably gave a slight 'jolt' to the organizing structure of theoretical physics, including human actors, resources, technologies, concepts, and institutions in the field as the certainty dawned upon those present that a new era was definitely about to be begin. That jolt, however, can only become a jolt due to the way it is related to how other events mirror themselves in—and are mirrored by—the event produced by the living present at the Royal Society in 1919. In order for that to happen, the event needs to acquire 'eventness', a term used by Bakhtin (Cunliffe, Helin, and Luhman 2014). The eventness cannot be known as such, although it may perhaps be sensed intuitively. Taking part in an event may provide a prescient sense of the event being potentially eventful in the sense that it may influence both events to come and events that have taken place. For example, in a recent article, *New York Times* columnist Charles M. Blow (2013) writes about the current political events surrounding the right to same-sex marriage in the United States and that he senses history as taking place in 'real time' as statements and political votes are converging towards the eventual adoption of the right to same-sex marriage.[26] What Blow expresses, however, is not a definite eventness, but a prescient feeling of being there, then, when important changes are taking place.

The temporal dimension of agency is generally not given much attention in organization studies. Scholars tend to be better trained to deal with space than with time, which is convenient, because space lends itself to the mapping of stable locations and attribution of size, whereas the passing of time does not offer that sort of ontological safety.[27] Still temporal effects of events have been dealt with in several interesting studies. An example of temporal agency in organization studies is Gephart's (1984) study of how the meaning attached to an oil spill off the coast of California developed as more information and knowledge became available and integrated into the political processes of negotiation over the years subsequent to the disaster. Another example is Sutton's (1987) study, which demonstrates the effects of a future death of the organizations 'coming towards' their members, and how members engage in activities of disbanding and re-connecting as the ending of their organizations' lives are approaching. In both of these examples agency is given to the passing of time, but in very different ways. In Gephart's story it is the passing of time that enables activity, which again changes the meaning of a past event. In other words, time frees activity, which enriches experience, which in turn enables learning from the past that is different than if the information gathering had been concluded once and for all shortly after the disaster. In Sutton's case time works differently, and actions are triggered by the premonition of an ending as an event, such as Heidegger's (1927: 385) emphasis on the finitude of death as a means to understanding one's own temporality, including one's past, hence representing a possibility for being. The premonition of an ending imposes in itself a form of temporal agency as it is felt here and now, as coming towards the actors involved.

A point of departure for thinking about temporal agency would be by defining the work performed by organizational presents in shaping the meaning of past and future presents. In order to 'bend' the past-present-future event pattern's trajectory, a present needs to include not only past presents, but also to reframe those past presents in what Emirbayer and Mische call the contingencies of the (present) present. This presupposes, however, that presents 'co-create' each other in an evolving process. It implies being consistent with Whitehead's (1929a) urge that we not treat events as simple locations, but try and understand not just how they connect but how they reach out to one another, and in reaching out, recreate those events in the present event, what Whitehead refers to as prehension.[28] The co-creating of events through prehension takes part in the making of event formations, which are the provisional relational outcomes of connecting between events.

It is important not to assume temporality as a succession of pasts, presents, and futures, but to join in Whitehead's (1920) atomistic view of events, whereby events have precedents, contemporaries, and antecedents.[29] Consistent with his atomistic view of processes, Whitehead (1929a: 86) sees events as related in the form of a manifold, rather than as a succession in line. What characterizes a manifold beyond having different forms or elements is that elements are woven together in a continuum that has no endpoints, rather like planes that intersect and self-intersect. In mechanics a manifold appears as tubes spreading like a fan out from a central point, allowing liquid or gas to reach several spatially dispersed points simultaneously. The image of a mechanical manifold is already very different from the imagery of a line. When points are seen temporally, that is, as events rather than spatially, that is, as points in space, it means that multiple events both in the past and the future are affected by what takes place in the present event.

When Whitehead refers to a manifold, however, he means it in a mathematical sense, where it is seen as an n-dimensional figure where each point has its neighbourhood, like in a Euclidian space (one in which points are represented by linear coordinates), but which put together can take on multi-dimensional proportions, including a tangled curvilinear form of intersecting and self-intersecting sets of coordinates. Whitehead suggests seeing events in a four-dimensional manifold consisting of three spatial dimensions and time as the fourth dimension. The time dimension relates to the extent of distance in time between events (not as measured time, but as experienced time) and duration of events (again, not as linear or measured duration, but as experienced duration). Consistently with the mathematical conception of manifolds, events are seen to have their 'neighbourhoods', and a neighbourhood may be described in terms of continuity, connectedness, and convergence. These three descriptors suggest conditions under which actors, in a present, enact the connecting of events (including the one they are making in the present). Connecting events is about experienced relatedness of events and the feeling of creating continuity. Importantly, though, the relatedness is an evolving multidimensional pattern of events in time and space, which reproduces its form while remaining open to new connections, and consequently, new forms.

What the manifold imagery does is eliminate the idea of the present representing a temporal 'watershed', whereby some connecting processes apply to past, and others, to future events. Instead, intersection and self-intersection impose circularity of creation between past and future events. For example, I look back on letting an employee go to decide whether or not another person should be fired (future event); likewise I may fire someone to justify that someone else was fired in the past (which is how event formations self-intersect). Since both past and future events figure in the present, they are better seen as events that exhibit varying degrees of pastness and futurity than seen as belonging absolutely in the past (as having beens) or in the future (yet to come). A childhood memory, for example, exhibits pastness, but if I intend to repeat it, that event will in the present exhibit both pastness and futurity, as 'already seen' and 'yet to be seen'.

This may be exemplified by an experience I had in a recent research project at the Ulstein Shipyard on the western coast of Norway, a shipyard that had made a rather spectacular turnaround by building highly complex ships for the offshore industry. Their specialization is novel, innovative ship design, an area where they currently excel globally. The turnaround followed after decades of growth and internationalization that had begun around 1970, but which took a dramatic turn when the Ulstein Group, including its subsidiaries as well as the entire design department and some of the engineering functions, were sold to the Vickers corporation, then to Rolls Royce in 1999. In 1999 the Ulstein family faced the choice of either shutting down or re-entering the shipbuilding business with new, innovative designs. The owners—siblings Tore and Gunvor Ulstein and their father, Idar Ulstein—chose the latter option. One result of getting back into the business and reconfiguring their in-house capabilities was the so-called Ulstein X-BOW, an inverted ship's bow, which saw the light of day in 2006. The idea of the novel bow design was suggested by one of the shipyard's new designers, who had come from a competitor, where pursuing the idea had not received managerial support. Designers at Ulstein played around with the idea and featured a sketch of it on the front of their internal newsletter.[30] During a visit, the CEO of a ship-owner company caught a glimpse of the sketch, enquired about it, and was told about the possible virtues of the bow by the Ulstein designers. Ships have been constructed with an ordinary bow throughout the history of ship design. Thus, by traditional standards, the X-BOW has a counterintuitive design that ship designers, engineers, owners, and captains do not find pleasing to the eye (the design even features on <http://www.uglyships.com>). Still, intrigued by the X-BOW design, the CEO told the Ulstein designers, 'I want you to build that for me'. Once he had expressed concrete interest and the designer received backing from colleagues and the Ulstein management to pursue the idea, the opportunity was further articulated materially through calculations, models, and tests.

Of interest is how the various events leading up to the construction of the ship and the subsequent expansion of a fleet of ships connected to one another forward and backward in time. Noticeably, interviewees referred to when the customer ordered the design, the subsequent formal testing of the X-BOW's efficacy, and previous developments in the company. These events were not only experienced as significant moments illustrating the ability of the company to innovate and build accordingly, but they also 'co-created each other'. Their co-creation took place in relative temporal proximity (or neighbourhood) to one another, and consequently in relative continuity, such as the building of the mock-up, the model testing, and the design of the first ship with an X-BOW. As the process unfolded, the events surrounding the X-BOW became related to more distant events in the company's history that marked their ability to innovate. When they received confirmation that the bow design could successfully withstand wave tests, the events of the tests somehow confirmed the rightness of their previous intuition, while opening up for commercial expansion in the way of future development, marketing, and sale of their vessels. When the customer in the Ulstein case said, 'I want you to build that for me', the statement took place in a living present and became an important event once the encounter was over, and preceding as well as subsequent events became linked to that present, like an unfolding plane.[31]

The temporal agency of a an organizational present relates to its ability to bring to light events or redefine their meaning, and by the same token reproduce, while modifying, the event formation (what Whitehead (1929a) called 'structure of events'). Events reproduce themselves in the mirroring of other events, and past and future events are created and re-created simultaneously by the same operations in the present. The ability of events to connect to other events while reproducing the event formation is what confers agency upon them. Thus, what someone utters in a meeting, the function of a piece of technology somewhere, or a joint discovery of a concept in a certain place and at a certain time are not something that is given agency by itself. Instead agency reveals itself through the mirroring or resonance it has with other, related, events.[32] 'Mirroring' is not to be taken in a passive or objective sense. Whitehead uses the notion of mirroring when discussing events and event formation, but pondering the significance of the term may be useful. Mirroring is first and foremost to be seen as an act and not a mere gaze at a reflected image. In addition to conveying a reflective projection, it means that something is done in the process of establishing the reflected image.[33]

The manifold as described above reflects an event formation as an open, ever-changing, ever-renewed complex of events, which re-generates itself while remaining open to the emergence of novelty. The wholeness of patterns of events enables them to infuse events and bring new events into the manifold. Events and their connecting into patterns are subject to continuous re-interpretation in the present, at which the event formation may begin to take a new direction.

5 Organization, Meaning Structures, and Time

■ SUMMARY

Organizational life is about the coalescence of events into elements, which, when articulated with one another, constitute the processual equivalents of 'organizations'. The elements form part of what in this book is called organizational 'meaning structures'. The word 'meaning' in meaning structures is meant to convey the idea that social actors act on the basis of meaning, and not, for example, from coercion or shared assumptions. Meaning structures become meaningful to actors as they perform acts of articulation of meaning structure elements. Articulation serves to bring the meaning structures to life, which in turn provides acts with meaning. Meaning structures elements are constituted by accumulations of events (encounters with other elements) over time, hence they may be seen as 'event-objects'. Events provide meaning structures with historicity and direction.

5.1 Event-Objects and Delineation of Things

> The traveller who admires a landscape sees a particular image of trees, fields, rivers and peaks, and nearer to his position he hears church-bells ringing and sees villagers walking to attend service. His experience is composed of particular instances of the classes denoted by the terms 'tree', 'river', 'peak', 'church-bell', 'villagers', 'walking' and 'religious service', etc., but when he *reports* the scene he is admiring, his experience will be represented in these general terms, which will not transmit the particular instances that his senses are witnessing. While these experiences will remain his private recollections, his report will convey to its reader merely a conception of the writer's experience.
>
> (Polanyi 1967: 309, 313)

One of the successes—and the problems—of organization studies is the entities it has assumed as constituent parts of organizations. Mainstream works list categories such as people, strategies, technologies, rules, routines, roles, and units, which have become accepted categories from which elements have been scrutinized in many different combinations and from a host of different perspectives. A prerequisite for combination has been that the categories are distinct and separate, which has paved the way for various debates about, for example, human rationality, where writers such as March and others have questioned the tightness of coupling between beliefs, acts, and goals. By taking part in that debate, however, they have also implicitly endorsed the idea that there *are* goals and that they can be seen as distinct from human actors. Once debates take hold, it becomes difficult to question the entities the debates revolve around, as well as the ways in which distinctions are drawn between the entities in question. Even more importantly, the apparent atemporality of categories becomes forgotten, which also explains why a 'categoreal' conception of reality has trouble incorporating temporal thinking.[1]

Categories are useful because they facilitate a certain argument and analysis. They are used like scaffolding to support a building before it can stand by itself. But unlike the construction of buildings, debates may sometimes carry on within the scaffolding and ignore the fact that the scaffolding should be done away with to enable new forms to emerge. An example of a scaffolding left in place is the separation between the human and the material, which is a notable separation drawn to analyse organization processes. Bateson (1972: 318) illustrates the dilemma of distinction by referring to the blind man and the stick:

> If you ask anybody about the localization and boundaries of the self, these confusions are immediately displayed. Or consider a blind man with a stick. Where does the blind man's self begin? At the tip of the stick? At the handle of the stick? Or at some point halfway up the stick? These questions are nonsense, because the stick is a pathway along which differences are transmitted under transformation, so that to draw a delimiting line *across* this pathway is to cut off a part of the systemic circuit which determines the blind man's locomotion.

To say that the man–stick relationship is a pathway along which differences are transmitted under transformation turns an otherwise simple image into a nuanced processual description. Yet it seems more true to describe the blind man and the stick as a pathway than as a composite of two entities. This is not an appeal to express everything as process rather than as composites of things, because the latter is a human disposition. Rather, the force of Bateson's imagery lies in showing how arbitrarily distinctions may be drawn between entities. More precisely, it shows how entities and distinctions may be drawn differently from what has been done previously and how, as distinctions are drawn differently, assemblies of things may take on different meanings. It illustrates how in its brute form the world does not come in ready-made categories and distinctions. On the contrary, it is a tangled maze from which different categories and distinctions may be drawn. Moreover, the act of drawing categories and distinctions is what establishes them. For example, we may articulate an event from the past in different ways. By orally telling a story about the event, the things that made up the event may be present in a particular way. By writing about the event, on the other hand, things may stand out differently in relation to each other than in the oral narration. In other words, the act of delineation of things is what makes the delineation.[2]

Rather than have a substantial status independently of how they are being created, categories and distinctions are established by acts of drawing them. Acts take place at events, and are defined by the events at which they take place. Assuming like Whitehead that things 'are' their historicities and that how an entity becomes constitutes what it 'is' (Whitehead 1929a: 23), the encounters with other entities over time that become inscribed as events in the life of the entity constitute an entity. A piece of pottery, for example, is the result of the events at which it has been shaped and treated by the potter. A piece of pottery, however, is mute to most people. Therefore, to become *that* piece of pottery it is accompanied by stories and perhaps written materials, which serve to give it a distinct identity. Since every reference to entities and encounters takes place at events, delineation from other entities is temporally constructed, which makes it reasonable to refer to entities as event objects, that is, objects (entities) whose identities are shaped by the events throughout their historicities. For example, a strategy is given its particular contents at the various events, including casual chats, formal presentations, meetings, and development sessions. Its historicity not only defines what it is in its actuality, but also confers potentiality upon the strategy in the form of its possible future impact.

A 'thing' is what we can discern as standing out from other things, while at the same time being related to other things. A thing is something we can talk about because we can talk about it as different from other things. In fact, we can only understand relatedness between things that we perceive as distinct from one another. A thing may be a material object, but it may also be a state of affairs, a concept, a person, a role, an organization, or a brand. A thing may be discerned as something in itself, but the nature of this 'in-itself' only makes sense when seen as part of a whole. This 'whole' of which a thing forms part is what Whitehead calls a complex unity; it is an ever-changing yet relatively stable heterogeneous mixture of related things which has no specific composition.

Entities, which I refer to as 'things', are given in such a way that they can be recognized as stable, which should not be interpreted as their having an ontological status of being stable. For example, organizing has typically been defined as involving division of work, which implies that there are types of roles (forms) that are related to each other in a hierarchy of tasks. People are given formal roles to perform, which in most cases outlast the presence of the person. The role of CEO, of foreman, shop steward, head of research, secretary, or budget officer does not change even though people come and go. Thus, formal roles are *principally* independent of their incumbents. However, there are no roles without people to fill them. To be sure, a newly created position waiting to be filled can be seen as a 'neutral' entity. But once filled, the person occupying it gives it a content different from the content that another person would have given it. Hence the combination person–role becomes unique. Moreover, that person–role combination is likely to change as person–role combinations connect with one another to form a larger whole.

Thus person–roles, for example, are bound to change whether someone tries to change them or not. Change is driven by time and, as the world moves on, everything is ultimately affected, but people more than anything else. A new person enters the organization and takes over the formal role of another person. The new person has a different background, different beliefs, and different dispositions than the previous person. Hence, the new person–role invariably becomes different from the previous one. It also becomes different as it connects differently to other person–roles than was the case with the previous person–role, thus modifying the overall formation of things, including the various other person–roles. And, of course, it becomes different because it is contrasted with what was before, while at the same time forming continuity with what was before.

The new person–role, apart from being different in itself, and connecting differently to others, is also different in that it has a different *connectivity* to other things. It embodies a potential, a different propensity for connecting to other things than its predecessor. It is seen as a different possibility of connecting by other actors in the organization. This is what Whitehead refers to as 'proposition', a term that Latour (2005) has borrowed from Whitehead and applied to ANT. Things are not just in themselves and as connected to other things, but also as things—and thus—as connections, *possible*. Possibility for connecting forms part of what a thing 'is' and what it 'becomes'.

We wish to avoid the notion that 'things act', preferring to see things as created through acts, while at the same time avoiding focus on separate things, because things exist relationally. At the same time we wish for them to exhibit connectedness. In organizational life, for example, we do not wish to see the research team as acting, but as acts constituting the research team, while the becoming of the research team is experienced in the light of its 'connecting abilities'. This is what confers a sense of movement upon structure. While the team is in itself a mixture of nouns and verbs, things and processes, then so are the connecting abilities.

Entification (Hernes 2008) of experience comes naturally with the passing of time. Entification is an activity of the mind, and not a reality as such, and the nouns are mere 'nouns-in-the-making', although the acts of connecting may be performed on 'real' things, such as material objects. As events and experiences fade into the past they become related to factors that are seen to have framed them. With time, experiences become explained in terms of events, or acts, framed by certain factors that provide those events or acts with meaning. Even though as individuals we may retain the feeling of an experience, such as our first kiss, our first cigarette, or the taste of a special dish, when social groups make decisions for the future while turning to past events, they communicate with signs (or labels, as Weick suggests) that provide an understanding of the past event that is sufficiently shared among those present to make a decision for future action, or else they look back on a past event with a future projection in mind. Also, when looking forward in time, communication is made of concepts, signs, and artefacts, all of which represent a contraction of experience into something more explicit and synthetic.

This is a point of division between different ways of thinking process, which is of relevance to how one thinks about organizational life. Chia (1999), for example, points out that one problem with capturing the complexity faced by organizers is related to the human weakness of thinking in terms of movement. Chia's argument is that organizational theorists have failed to appreciate the temporal dynamics of organizing felt by organizers through what Whitehead calls 'direct experience'. As much as this is an important point, however, one could argue equally as well that humans both experience things directly and operate with spatial perceptions, and that the relationship between the two is temporally conditioned. The response to Chia, then, is that we are not good at thinking movement, not so much due to our inability to think movement, but because movement cannot be actually thought, but rather is sensed. Thinking movement, however, requires the use of spatial constructs.

While experiencing movement, human actors spatialize the worlds that lie outside their living present. In other words, they think in terms of entities while experiencing flow. In a meeting, for example, past and future events are represented spatially, such as by photos, material objects, maps, plans, budgets, and the like, while the meeting participants interact in a living present of undifferentiated flows. What is undifferentiated is the actual ongoing *experience* of dealing with delineated entities. For example, people may talk about, say, a specific individual as a provisionally defined entity, referring to various events that are significant for describing that person. While referring to the person as a quasi-stabilized entity, their interactions around that entity—their gestures, words—are experienced as ongoing and indeterminate, as illustrated by the example of a wink in the previous chapter. This may go on until the meeting reaches closure, at which time the meeting turns into an event; in other words, it becomes perceived as a spatial entity.

Seen from this perspective, organizing is as much about noun-making as it is about verb-making (Bakken and Hernes 2006), and there is no need to exclude nouns in order to make room for a process view, because the making, remaking, and unmaking of nouns is part and parcel of processes. What matters is how it is done, because, as suggested above, the nouns are defined by the act of articulation. Whitehead, who saw the world as ultimately process, made precisely this point: that we should pay attention to the forming of abstractions from living experience and *back* to living experience. Thus when Weick opposes verbs to nouns Whitehead would say that noun-making is a necessity for human sensemaking because we are not really capable of thinking purely in terms of process. According to Whitehead, letting nouns live their own lives, separated and disconnected from the processes that make them, is erroneous (Bakken and Hernes 2006).³ In this lies two points. First, focus should be on the process from which abstractions (or nouns) emerge. Second, focus should be on their relational character. Nouns and abstractions make no sense in the absence of other nouns and abstractions. It is with these two points in mind that I now begin the discussion of organizations as meaning structures.

5.2 Organizational Meaning Structures

Ethno-methodologists as well as ANT theorists tend to look for the macro structures in micro interactions. Among ethno-methodologists, Bittner (1974: 75) argues that concepts such as organizations, 'must be discovered by studying their use in real scenes of action' (in Gephart 1978: 556). Gephart further suggests that this implies studying how social actors involved in such scenes 'use their everyday constructs to make a variety of everyday events, objects, and activities meaningful' (p. 556). In Hernes (2008) I have cited Latour (1993: 121) on the relationship between micro and macro levels in large organizations, where he suggests that we can study far-reaching phenomena while staying 'local':

> What, for example, is the size of IBM, or the Red Army, or the French Ministry of Education, or the world market? To be sure, these are all actors of great size, since they mobilize hundreds of thousands or even millions of agents. Their amplitude must therefore stem from causes that absolutely surpass the small collectives of the past. However, if we wander about inside IBM, if we follow the chains of command of the Red Army, if we inquire in the corridors of the Ministry of Education, if we study the process of selling and buying a bar of soap, we never leave the local level. We are always in interaction with four or five people; the building superintendent always has his territory well staked out; the directors' conversations sound just like those of the employees; as for the salespeople, they go on and on giving change and filling out their invoices. Could the macro-actors be made up of micro-actors? (Garfinkel 1967) Could IBM be made up of a series of local interactions? The Red Army of an aggregate of conversations in the mess hall? The Ministry of Education of a mountain of pieces of paper? The world market of a host of local exchanges and arrangements?

It makes sense to say, as Latour does, that the organization as an actor is made up of numerous micro-level (inter-) actions. On the other hand, micro-level interactions should be seen as more than merely taking place in the organization: they are constitutive *of* the organization. It is worth paying attention to Heidegger here, that the parts are understood as parts of the whole, and not vice versa, which is where the importance of meaning enters the picture, and why it is useful, if not necessary, to think of 'the organization' as the meaning of micro-level interactions. Such a conceptualization of organization can obviously not be of an entity that can be mapped in its entirety. Still, everything that is said and done is *suggestive* of what the organization may be as a whole, as opposed to what it may not be, what it is becoming as opposed to what it is not becoming.

Acts are not seen to take place within organizations, but to constitute them. Every day there are 'flashes' of acts that are experienced as meaningful through the organizational reality they articulate. As we perform acts we may not be conscious of the meaning of those acts. Differentiating experience implies drawing temporal and spatial lines between entities and is done retrospectively as well as prospectively. Previous acts are given meaning through reconstruction of factors inferred retrospectively to have framed them, just as imagined future acts are given meaning through the imagining of factors that may frame them in the future.[4] For example, the failure of a product to succeed may in retrospect be ascribed to the conditions in the market at the time, aggressive competitors, and inadequate technologies. In this case the market becomes an element in the spatio-temporal ordering that provides meaning to the failure of the product to succeed. Or, in the case of prospection, the act of launching a product in the future may be perceived as framed by expected changes in consumer tastes, emerging consumer groups, or new technologies. The factors that are perceived to frame an act are spatio-temporal in the sense that they are elements associated over a certain duration of time (Whitehead 1920).[5]

It is this spatio-temporal ordering that may be taken as 'the organization', which consists of conceptual, human, or material elements forming interconnected wholes. It is what I refer to as *organizational meaning structures*.[6] The words 'meaning' and 'structure' have been purposely chosen to convey that organizations provide acts with meaning, as acts constitute the organizations, moreover that organizations are structured heterogeneous wholes. Elements of meaning structures are perceived and felt in the present, while they are seen to transcend the present as they become articulated with one another. These elements are the 'nouns-in-the-making' of organizations that are progressively being shaped by acts of articulation. They may be seen as 'event-objects' in the sense that their appearance is the result of their numerous encounters (presents-turned-events) with other entities. A key performance indicator, for example, while being an object shaped through a series of events, also takes part in shaping a number of successive events, both in the practical working environment and during processes of performance assessment.

Elements of organizational meaning structures are not simply signs of representation, but also objects of action.[7] When, for example, a dairy plant processes milk, the milk is a material object in its crude form in the sense that it is extracted, transported, refined, and traded. But it may take on the qualities of a sign when it is referred to in conversation or translated into various schemas, diagrams, statistics, etc.,[8] that is, when milk encounters other actors at organizational presents, which turn into events. And at another level of signification it becomes a symbol, such as when it comes to symbolize life, reproduction, nature, or purity as it encounters actors at other presents that turn into events. Both as an object and as a sign, an element is de facto an accumulation of events at which it experiences encounters with other entities. A chair, for example, is a sign of the various operations that have gone into manufacturing it, its composite materials, their extraction and preparations, etc., just as a bottle of French red wine also constitutes a sign of a certain processing, climate conditions, grape composition, and other factors, signalled by its *appellation d'origine contrôlée* (AOC). Drinking a glass of French red wine is an event at which both the sign, AOC, and the direct experience of the wine as a substance are encountered. What is an object to be touched, smelt, or changed in the present becomes a sign once the presence of the object is no longer felt. A plan may be drawn up on paper in a management meeting, but once the meeting is over, the plan itself is treated in an abstract sense. When it is evoked in successive encounters between actors it may be treated as a sign of the concrete plan that was drawn up in the original encounter. When the plan is referred to it is referred to both as a physical object and a series of events.

Seen as event-objects, elements are provisional outcomes of accumulated events. Any entity embodies the events that made it, and the nature of the entity is distinguished by the events involved in its experiential trajectory. A shoe may be known, on the one hand, as a shoe in the sense of belonging to the category of shoes, but on the other hand, what distinguishes it from other members of the shoe category is the trajectory of events it has experienced. For example a Nike shoe is the provisional output of numerous encounters between material and human actors throughout its history, as it embodies histories of many components, including soles, laces, and tissue, which in turn are products of refined raw materials as well as manufacturing and design. The shoe and its components have their own histories of entangled actors that make up their respective historicities, while at the same time they represent temporarily stabilized patterns of actions and interaction. Thus, when we consider a running shoe, it is not just an output of a production process: it is also an object that has organized processes and actors in time and space while being organized by them in turn. Lately some Nike shoes have featured iPod sensors, enabling the recording of time, distance, and pace while running. As 'organizers', the sensors connect Apple and Nike; they connect runners, who can compare and discuss their trajectories; and they connect those actors who build them into the shoes. This is not to say that human actors do not organize, but to state that when new material actors arrive on stage they form contingencies that influence further processes of organizing. Moreover, those contingencies that influence further developments are created in various encounters between actors, to which they bring their pasts, and from which aspirations for future work are formed. The sensors help shape not only the roles and identities of corporate actors, but also runners and running communities, which serve to shape runners' identities and spur new inventions in turn. On the Apple homepage, <http://www.apple.com/ipod/nike/>, these gadgets are even referred to as 'personal trainers', which may be seen as an attempt to confer human qualities upon them, thus adding complexity to the network of organizing actors.

Meaning is revealed through phenomena as relational wholes, but where the particular derives meaning from the whole (James 1890; Heidegger 1927: 182; Merleau-Ponty 1995; Mead 1938),[9] and not vice versa.[10] Heidegger (2000) uses the example of a school, which may be understood as a meaning structure. We can sense what the school 'is' as the whole of many different parts. We may point at a school and say 'There it is', and others will understand what we mean. We can see classrooms, children playing in the playground, blackboards, teachers, books, pencils, etc. Still, the school as a whole cannot be seen, yet its constituent particulars can only be understood through the whole, much the same way that a novel tone is understood through the tune. A child running, for example, may be interpreted as being late for class or playing during the break. Any one of the two interpretations comes from seeing the totality as a school. In a similar way the constituent parts of an organization (e.g. structural characteristics, human resources, technologies) can be experienced through the wholeness. However, the notion of experience belongs to the organizational present. As the present fades into the past it becomes the object of reflection and takes on characteristics of formation of interrelated elements.

Organizational meaning structures are heterogeneous in the sense that they include elements of different kinds, such as persons, material objects, and concepts (Czarniawska 2004).[11] At Ulstein Group, various elements appear in the stories told during interviews, which in the eyes of the interviewees make Ulstein special. The X-BOW, as mentioned earlier, enabled the group to re-emerge as a leader in its field. The X-BOW is a physical element, but it is also a highly visible and symbolic element that shows how Ulstein is able to transgress boundaries through novel ideas. Still, the X-BOW is but part of the ships Ulstein design and not even integrated into all the ships. Interviewees describe ships built at the yard, which form part of the accumulative outputs of the company's design and production activity. They may speak, for example, of a ship representing a certain series built in the 1970s or another series built in the 1990s. In several narratives the X-BOW exists sometimes as a separate element that signifies their creative capabilities, other times as an integral part of their serial production of ships. Additional elements are other technical solutions that Ulstein sees as making them different from other actors, such as their hybrid technology for ship propulsion.

There is evidently also more to Ulstein, such as the construction yard itself, which works as a laboratory for new designs. The yard is sometimes a contentious issue in internal strategic debate, because it represents a strategic choice between Ulstein being a constructor of unique tailor-made vessels on the one hand (for which the yard is indispensible) or being a producer of series of standardized ship design on the other, in which case the yard might play a different role. Another meaning structure element is human. There is, for example, Idar Ulstein, the founder of what may be called the modern era Ulstein, which lasted from the early 1970s until 1999, at which time he went from being CEO to chairman of the board, before passing away in 2012. In several of the interviews he was clearly seen as being visionary, always looking far ahead, and not being afraid of trying out new ideas. There are also their customers, who play various roles. On the one hand, they are 'normal' customers in the sense of being companies that order ships or have them repaired. On the other hand, Ulstein boasts an almost century-long practice of involving ship owners in design and production. Stories were told during interviews about ship owners or skippers spending time at the yard during construction and repair, which made it possible to both meet deadlines and sometimes improvise new solutions. A frequently actualized element of the meaning structure at Ulstein is the strategy, as mentioned above, which is often brought up. Related to the choice between custom-made design and standardized series is how to collaborate with yards in other countries. Should staff, say, try to transfer their unique skills to other yards, or just consider them suppliers for simpler solutions? The strategy, as presented in the interviews, is not just about the future, but equally about the past. Not only is tradition strong in terms of craftsmanship, but also Ulstein's ability to innovate is associated with past practices and capabilities. Finally, the climate may be seen as a meaning structure element. Ulstein's history, since 1970 in particular, is inextricably linked to the North Sea,[12] and its design capacity is linked to the adverse conditions their ships need to cope with.

The aim is not to attempt a comprehensive description of meaning structures at Ulstein, but to present an outline of some selected elements that appear central to the way people perceive the company. Evidently, none of these elements appear in isolation from any of the others, nor does any element appear identical over time. What is important is the *becoming* of the meaning structure as and when the various elements are articulated with one another. For example, I have suggested that the role of yard becomes important if articulated with the overall strategy of constructing tailor-made vessels versus serial, semi-standardized vessels. Likewise, the particular craftsmanship practised at the Ulstein Shipyard needs to be seen in relation to how their strategy evolves. A strategy that relies heavily on custom-made vessels demands particularly well-developed technical and organizational skills.

It is important not to lose sight of the wholeness of the meaning structure. As mentioned already with reference to Heidegger (1927), elements are perceived from wholeness, and not vice versa. It refers to a more holistic plot or storyline (Hernes 2008: 133–136) that involves meaning structure elements, but is not reducible to them. The plot or storyline says something about the movement, the becoming of the meaning structure, and this holistic impression can only be intuited. Intuition captures a sense of movement, the meaning structure in the making, about the meaning of the organization in the light of its movement through time, experienced in the present. At Ulstein, for example, there are sometimes intense debates about where they came from and where they are heading. The debates tend to be about actionable facts related to meaning structure elements (such as the role of the domestic construction yard in relation to a strategy of expansion) against a background of a holistically intuited meaning structure. In other words, it is important for understanding organization as process to include the meaning structure as a canvas for past and future opportunities. This is how potentiality may reside alongside actuality in the analysis.

What actually makes meaning structures 'meaningful' is the fact that they embody redundancy, in the sense of offering more possibilities than the choices that can be made. Meaning structures will always have to potentially embody more connecting possibilities than can be articulated at any one time. A choice becomes meaningful in view of other possible choices. The X-BOW takes part in making the meaning structure meaningful because it signifies an alternative among various other alternatives. As aptly commented by Luhmann (1995), meaning requires choice between alternative courses of action. In other words, as Luhmann suggests, meaning is the link between the actual and the possible.[13] Choosing a course of action, although it is rooted in the past, will inevitably be made with a view to future aspirations, which means that there is an element of choice between possibilities. As Heidegger (1927: 327) puts it, the being of an entity exists ahead of itself: it reveals itself though its projection onto (future) possibilities. In other words, actors come to understand themselves through their work of articulation of elements between past and future aspirations, being mindful that their aspirations are possibilities among other aspirations. By the same token, any other entities that form part of a meaning structure reveal themselves not just as they are but also through their becoming.[14]

Human actors are able to play on a repertoire of articulations, and while engaging or focusing on some articulations, they are able to keep open other possible articulations. They may, as Polanyi suggests, exercise subsidiary awareness. In fact, Polanyi (1967: 302) argues that it is the subsidiary awareness that provides meaning to the articulation in focus:

It is our subsidiary awareness of a thing that endows it with meaning: with a meaning that bears on an object of which we are focally aware. A meaningful relation of a subsidiary to a focal is formed by the action of a person who integrates one to the other, and the relation persists by the fact that the person keeps up this integration.[15]

Subsidiary awareness may refer to the totality of the meaning structure, as certain elements of it are subjected to focal awareness. This is a way for actors to keep a sense of the overall organization and how it is moving while staying focused on selected elements. For example, Jonathan Ive, chief designer at Apple, describes how Steve Jobs would 'read' the company on an almost daily basis by inspecting models of various products in the design lab:

> When Steve comes in, he will sit at one of these tables. If we're working on a new iPhone, he might grab a stool and start playing with different models and feeling them in his hands, remarking on which ones he likes best. Then he will graze by the other tables, just him and me, to see where all the other products are heading. He can get a sense of the sweep of the whole company, the iPhone and iPad, the iMac and laptop and everything we're considering. That helps him see where the company is spending its energy and how things connect. And he can ask, 'Does doing this make sense, because over here is where we are growing a lot?' or questions like that. He gets to see things in relationship to each other, which is pretty hard in a big company. Looking at the models on these tables, he can see the future for the next three years.
>
> (Isaacson 2013: 346)

The example illustrates how the complexity of the organization may be experienced locally, yet with sufficient precision for acts (such as when a design is altered to better fit the overall strategy of the company) to actually influence the direction of the organization at large. One thing that explains the ability of elements in a local setting to reflect the organization at large is that they embody histories that are significant to actors in the present. In the present, Jobs and Ive are able to apply intuition to grasp not only the complex trajectories of the various gadgets but also their potential for future events. Their simultaneous use of intuition enables them to talk about what to do about those gadgets, and how their actions tie in with other aspects of the organization. They may act upon the gadgets in the present, either by drawing up a different idea, say, on a whiteboard, invite technicians to modify them on the spot, or call a meeting with other people.

Although the term 'meaning structure' has been used in a number of different fields, it has been seen mostly as a representation of reality. It should be quite clear by now that organizational meaning structures, as applied in this book, are not meant as structures of representation, but as performative structures created and sustained through acts of articulation. A car left in the garage and never started may represent a car but is never really experienced as car as long as it does not take us places, just as a piano that is never played may be a sign of music, but does not take part in providing the experience of music.

Performativity, as Butler (2011) defines it in relation to discourse and gender, relates to practices by which discourse produces the effects that it names.[16] In other words, discourse takes part in creating and sustaining the object of its practices. Similarly, organizational meaning structures exist insofar as they create and sustain a certain reality. This implies that their constitutive elements cannot be seen as mere isolated objects that reflect reality by virtue of their relative ordering. On the contrary, they take part in creating and sustaining reality by virtue of the ways in which they interact through practices that instantiate them. Their elements do not, as pointed out by Gherardi and Nicolini (2005), have intrinsic qualities, but they are performed while being reversible and with uncertain *outcomes, no matter* how stable this effect actually may appear at any point in time. They are, as Gherardi and Nicolini point out, effects of operations, manoeuvres, and processes that keep things in place, whether they are scientific facts, societies, technological systems, or symbolic artefacts.

Broadly speaking, a performative view (Austin 1955; Latour 1986; Strum and Latour 1987; Pickering 1995a) assumes that meaning reveals itself through acts or events. In language philosophy, Austin (1955) uses the term 'performative utterances' to underline that saying something was performing an act rather than simply representing reality. In their study of baboons, Strum and Latour (1987: 789) suggest performativity as a way to understand how social structures are created through acts that aim to produce predictable interactions:

Under [a performative definition of society], baboons would not be seen as being *in* a group. Instead they would be seen as striving to define the society and the groups in which they exist, the structure and the boundaries. They would not be seen as being *in* a hierarchy, rather they would be ordering their social world by their very activity. In such a view, shifting or stable hierarchies might develop not as one of the principles of an overarching society into which baboons must fit, but as the provisional outcome of their search for some basis of predictable interactions. Rather than entering an alliance system, baboons performing society would be testing the availability and solidity of alliances without knowing for certain, in advance, which relationships will hold and which will break.

Whereas mainstream works in social science tend to assume a distinction between the worlds of meaning and of structure, it is assumed here that meaning *is* structure, and vice versa. When an act provides meaning to actions, the act is the imagined temporarily completed articulation of elements of the meaning structure. Therefore meaning structures are not merely related to the organization in question: they *are* the organization. They are enacted by being connected and reconnected by actors into meaningful wholes that are de facto the organization as those actors perceive and act upon it. If, for example, Ulstein acquires a company with specialized skills and products, that acquisition changes the ways in which the existing meaning structure elements at Ulstein relate to one another. But the acquisition per se would be but one event and inconsequential if it did not become part of successive articulations.

The status of meaning structure elements as entities relates to the passing of time, and not to their innate qualities. I may, for example, be preparing a budget for an activity. While working on it in 'pure duration' I am engrossed in its complexity and detail; the budget appears an extension and expression of my thoughts and ideas, although constrained. I am interacting with it as a unity that separates, then blends, then emerges as something novel. Instead of myself and the budget being seen as two interacting entities, we may be seen as an evolving situation that eventually comes to closure in the form of the budget as a provisionally fixed entity that articulates in a particular way elements (activities, functions, incomes, etc.) of the organizational meaning structure. Seen as two different entities the budget and I are two entities with our histories that encounter one another in a situation where we form a whole and where we are both elements of the same meaning structure. With the passing of time I will have left my mark on the budget as it was authored by me. With time the budget travels through various encounters in other organizational presents, and with each new encounter the budget forms new connecting possibilities for yet other encounters. The new connecting possibilities represent the potentiality of the budget for connecting. In sum, a budget represents a pattern of events that stretches both backward and forward in time, although at any present it appears as a provisionally stabilized entity.

Another example of organizational meaning structures may be found in the following extract from Chen's (2009) study of the organization of the Burning Man event. Being what Birnholz, Cohen, and Hoch (2007) refer to as a 'seasonal organization', the Burning Man event organization illustrates how past and future events are represented as their members engage in preparations for the upcoming event. Chen's (2009: 25) account shows how organizational past and future are represented as different sets of spatial entities, while staff are engaged in ongoing activities:

At the corner of Third and 16th streets, a gentrifying industrial stretch of the San Francisco waterfront, individuals converge upon the Burning Man headquarters to prepare for the annual Burning Man event. Inside a converted warehouse, posted maps depict the upcoming site for Black Rock City, a horseshoe-shaped series of streets curved toward the signature sculpture of the Man. Displayed artwork, such as oversized photos and hand-painted props, immortalize art projects from previous events. The scattered furnishings demonstrate creative reuse of scavenged materials: a tall vitrine that once hawked watches now displays Burning Man memorabilia; a squat flat file intended for architectural drawings stores art proposals; a dining table supported by a stack of buckets hosts volunteers' meetings.

Amid these reminders of the past and plans for the future, Burning Man members work in offices, conference rooms, and a common area dubbed the 'Zocaló.' In one office, administrative staff process ticket orders mailed in hand-decorated envelopes from around the world. As they sort the mail, they answer phone inquiries about the ticket sales that fuel the organization's approximately $10 million budget. In a nearby room strewn with hardware, information technology (IT) specialists ensure that the

ORGANIZATION, MEANING STRUCTURES, AND TIME   113

server and intranet are up and running. They manage the graphics, content, and Web cam for the Burning Man website, which received almost eight million hits and entries per month during 2005. In another room, human resources administrators gather information on affordable health benefits for the small staff.

While these activities sustain the Burning Man organization, other activities contribute to the Burning Man mission of supporting art and community. In one room, the art curator examines proposals and meets with artists about their progress on large-scale installations and performances. In another area, a volunteer categorizes items for the organizational archives, while an artist, a prominent figure in the San Francisco art scene, finalizes plans for a local event. In an adjoining conference room, the head organizers, who are known as the senior staff, meet to discuss their budget; recruitment and management of members; relations with the media, governmental agencies, and interest groups; and other issues. The limited liability company's (LLC) board members, whose ranks include some senior staff members, also assemble here to decide financial, staffing, and policy matters.

The account shows how various forms of activity serve to articulate the meaning structure, and how artefacts, such as photos, artwork, and memorabilia take part in the work of articulation. Acts of articulation also have a sense of temporality, such as budgets, plans, and proposals being used to set the stage for future events (e.g. posted maps depicting the upcoming site for Black Rock City). No entities, including artwork, represent new categories of entities, but may represent different meaning when seen together. We are looking at elements that are relatively continuous, but may nevertheless appear as changing relational wholes from one present to the next.

Although they are articulated as provisionally stabilized entities, elements of organizational meaning structures are temporal, in the sense that they embody trajectories of encounters with other elements at past events.[17] A piece of technology, although it may be seen as a material substance, is formed by numerous encounters back in time, including with designers, other technologies, concepts, users, measurement systems, etc. Therefore a technology is never just a piece of technology per se, but a provisionally stabilized entity that embodies numerous encounters—actual and potential—over time. As the technology becomes articulated with other meaning structure elements at organizational presents, possibilities are created for future connecting. Lanzara and Morner (2005:86) illustrate this well from their research on open source software (OSS) development:

By plotting the overall stream of threads […], we can appreciate the on-going emergence and disappearance of threads over time. As we have already said, threads are ephemeral entities. Most of them live the life of a mayfly. Robust and durable threads emerge very rarely but the flow of communication is never completely discontinued. The single threads go off and on, but the overall fabric never collapses. At any point in time in the development of the project there is a persistent bundle of active threads that signal and carry on activity at varying degrees of intensity. Agents can go off the stream, but can always re-enter later on. Thus the inter-temporal continuity and stability of the project are assured by a flow of communication along a main stream of development and sensemaking.

While a developer works on a version, he or she interacts with that version. As soon as the version leaves the computer to enter the stream it becomes an entity that the author and other programmers relate to before interacting with it in developing the next version. Hence, modifying the meaning structure implies changing the past as much as changing the future. Most of the time, meaning structures do not change perceptibly, but change may be brought about through disruption in experience (Mead 1938: 347), which also brings to light continuity: 'The break reveals the continuity, while the continuity is the background for the novelty' (Mead 1929a: 239). Disruption may take place in a number of different ways in organizations, such as by external shocks (Garud et al. 2010), breakdown of routines (Feldman 2000), and perceived threats to organizational identity (Schultz and Hernes 2013).

Meaning structure elements, although they may appear as mere spatial snapshots of reality, exhibit temporal stretch in the consciousness of actors via the events they are associated with. They stretch backward and forward in time as event-based trajectories. Thus 'the organization' of Lanzara and Morner's description above may be seen to be the threads of succeeding versions of the software. Those threads are made of entities in the form of temporarily closed contributions. But those contributions are not dead, although they have become part of the thread. We are back to the idea that entities and consequently organizations 'are' their historicities (Heidegger 1927: 20),[18] but in a living sense, and not as mere 'dead facts' (Whitehead 1938: 135). When programmers prepare their contributions to the thread, not only do they see the status quo of the thread represented by the latest update, but they are also aware of the process leading up to that latest update.

A final subtle and yet important point about meaning structures is that that they confer meaning upon acts by *revealing* themselves through articulation (Heidegger 1927; Laclau and Mouffe 1985). Meaning structures are not external context for the acts that instantiate them, but form a seamless relationship with those acts. As Cooper (2014) points out, the act expresses the action of the form rather than the forms themselves. If, for example, I speak of two aspects of an organization, the speech act expresses the action of the form (i.e. the two aspects) upon the speech act rather than the form (i.e. the two aspects) itself. This means that the articulation of a meaning structure is shaped by the mode in which it is articulated. Hence it matters how elements are articulated with one another. It matters, for example, whether a written document is drawn up and includes a plan for the re-structuring of the company or whether things are merely talked about. It matters whether things are evoked frequently or rarely. It also matters who evokes them, where they do it, and when this is done. A strategy may circulate as a document, but it has no real life on its own.

It only becomes a strategy as and when it is related to other meaning structure elements at various events.

5.3 Organizing as Articulation of Organizational Meaning Structures

The meaning structure is the closest we come to the noun-like character of organizations, as their elements may include concepts, physical objects, or human or social actors. The organization does not, however, exist outside the articulations of the meaning structure.[19] Although it may consist of many things that we consider stable and tangible, such as people, technologies, or concepts, it only comes to life through acts of articulation. A railway station, for example, is seen to exist as a railway station (and not as a mere building beside a railway line) as people continue to go through it, ticket counters are operated, trains are running, and announcements are made.[20] Power (1996: 293) makes the point succinctly when he writes about applying a performative view to auditing: 'Making things auditable is what practitioners do when they audit organizations and processes.' In other words, organizations are not objects of auditing per se but become auditable by the work done to them.

Organizations exist as and when their actuality and their potentiality for becoming are kept alive. Unless the open source software community in Lanzara and Morner's study and its practices are shut down and hermetically sealed, it will be sustained—kept alive—by further acts. Those acts are not separate from the structure they sustain; on the contrary, the structures are extensions of those acts. This is also what is meant by organizational meaning structures being performative, in the sense of Butler's (2011) idea of performativity as that which sustains that which it names. Importantly, performativity, as Butler points out, takes place in a temporally structured reality. Consequently, acts are performed in relation to a totality that precedes them and succeeds them, while both changing and sustaining that very totality.

This may be exemplified by Peirce's use of music (1878) to illustrate the bringing forward of meaning by pointing to the act of playing a piece of music, in which each note represents a novel instant or act pertaining to that very note. A note may be present at an instant from which the past and future are both absent. It is different with a tune, Peirce insists. A tune occupies a certain time during which only portions of it are played. To perceive the tune there must be some continuity of consciousness that makes the events of a lapse of time present to the listener. Thus, 'Thought is a thread of tune running through the succession of our sensations' (Peirce 1878: 290). The tune is the meaning that forms the context for the tone, and the tone forms part of the overall meaning. Thus there is an insoluble relationship between the tone and the tune, as between the part and the whole (Peirce 1998). Just as any act, the tone brings to life the meaning structure by making the structure meaningful and making the place of the tone in it meaningful by the same token. The tone articulates the meaning structure by bringing it to life as a harmonic whole. The tune as a meaning structure is not a homogeneous but a heterogeneous formation of elements that the tone articulates. There is also a temporal aspect, since the tune is not quite the same after the tone as it was before the tone was played. The tone signifies a sensation of change. At the same time it signifies a sensation of continuity as it sustains the tune by bringing it forward and projecting it as a possible next tone in the melody. And just as the tone articulates a tune as meaning structure, an act articulates the organization as meaning structure.

Heidegger (1927), Laclau and Mouffe (1985), Foucault (1994), and Latour (1999) have extended thinking about meaning and sign structures to include the idea of *articulation*[21] of elements. Articulation takes place based on a sense of the unit *and* the whole, and, although the acts of articulation are oriented toward the part being articulated, the meaning stems from the whole that extends beyond the units in question.

The term 'articulation' has two distinct etymological roots dating back to the Middle Ages. First, it brings to attention the existence of jointed segments (McKean 2005). HR policies, for example, may bring to attention relationships between management styles and staff efficiency. Such relationships may be of a schematic and general nature, but they only articulate particular organizations when they apply to concrete entities perceived as belonging to the same organizational setting. A particular organizational setting may be characterized by numerous factors, such as specific market segments, technologies, central persons, products, and services. The relationships become meaningful to actors when HR policies articulate relationships between management styles and staff efficiency within the specific setting. Second, articulation brings to attention *how* elements may be related. When someone at a meeting speaks of the relationship between, say, a market segment and a product, two meaning structure elements are being articulated using speech. However, as Laclau and Mouffe point out, articulation may also be done by material means. This happens, for example, when performance measurement indicators are presented in a PowerPoint presentation (Schoeneborn, 2013), or in a paper-based presentation organizational goals or standards are related to organizational performance.[22] At a more general level, articulation may be performed by programmes (March and Simon 1958), product developments (Moorman and Miner 1997), or routines (Feldman 2000).

To articulate does not mean so much linking a priori known parts together as much as it means to indicate and point out (Peirce 1998: 276) connections between parts, or even merely point out a direction among elements. Seen this way, articulating comes close to Deleuze and Guattari's (2004: 112) conception of signifying, making it a question of signification rather than of representation. In other words, an act signifies the meaning structures and becomes significant by the same token. The signifying, however, is not to be seen in a representationalist way, which would suggest that it signifies something immutable that lies there to be represented. On the contrary, it is what makes the structure. This follows from viewing meaning structures as performative. Every act of signification performs the structure. If we follow passengers on their way through a railway station, the station becomes meaningful due to the way they experience its various services, which depends on how the passengers approach those services.

Meaning structures enable meaning by virtue of the variety of articulations between elements that are possible within them. As already mentioned, meaning does not lie in the act itself, but in the projection of the act, that is, that which the act aims towards. Heidegger (1927: 324) defines meaning as the 'upon-which' (*das Woraufhin*) of a projection 'in terms of which something can be conceived in its possibility as that which it is'. Projecting discloses possibilities, according to Heidegger, or more precisely, 'the sort of *thing* that makes possible'[23,24] (*italics* added). But 'possible' implies 'possibility', which again implies some degree of choice. The fact that they exhibit more possibilities than what are actualized is what makes them meaningful to actors. Laclau and Mouffe (1985) use the word 'polysemy' for this: meaning is not confined to what people perceive, but to what they perceive as possible among other possibilities. When I write 'more possibilities' this is not to be understood numerically, as this would suggest a representationalist view of meaning structures. What is meant is that, while taking place, an articulation suggests that other articulations are possible, and its presence suggests the absence of other possible articulations.[25] For example, it makes sense to me to go to work today because I could choose not to go to work or to do something different. If I did not perceive any alternatives, my choice of going to work would not seem meaningful. As we point towards a possibility in the meaning structure it makes sense because, by the same token, we turn away from another possibility. In other words, the making something present and actual makes sense by leaving another option behind.[26] As a matter of fact, leaving another option behind may be said to be as central to meaning structures as those options that are chosen. We are back to the idea of potentiality versus actuality, whereby potentiality is represented by the untried options and actuality by those that were chosen. Untried options may to varying degrees enter the historicity of meaning structures (Hernes and Irgens, 2013) and reside through what will be referred to as tacit articulation in chapter 6.

5.4 Articulation, Time, and Memory

> So, while dead assemblages can be constructed piece by piece from objective parts—that is, from parts that retain their character

> irrespective of whether they are a part of the assemblage or not—living, indivisible wholes cannot. On the contrary, they grow. And in the course of exchanges with their surroundings, they transform themselves, internally, from simple individuals into richly structured ones. In this growth, their 'parts' are in a constant state of change. Indeed, at any one moment, their 'parts' owe their very existence, not only to their relations to each other, but also to their relations to their own 'parts' at some earlier point in time, as well as to their relations to the many different larger wholes within which they are from time to time embedded. So, while existing in space, they are all qualitatively transforming each other through time, and thus the history of their structural transformations is of more consequence than the logic of their momentary structure.
>
> (Shotter 2006: 591)

The idea of meaning structures as assemblages of elements invites questions about the relationship between the whole and the parts, and about their temporalities. Being in the world, according to Heidegger, is about being in time: the existence of *Dasein* is essentially temporal. The worldhood (*Umwelt*) of *Dasein* (that entity which is conscious of its own existence) is seen as a *referential totality* (Heidegger 1927: 123). This referential totality provides significance (meaning) in the sense that its references and assignments provide the means for *Dasein's* self-understanding. *Dasein* is part of the referential totality and it is within the referential totality that *Dasein* experiences being-with (other entities). The word 'worldhood' is not limited to the immediate environment in a physical sense. Entities in the totality may be concrete objects, but they may also be references to other things that are not immediately within reach. *Dasein* reveals itself to itself through its being-with other entities of the totality. Other entities have already been disclosed in their being, which means that being with them provides *Dasein* with meaning. Importantly, the totality defines the entities and not vice versa. According to Heidegger (1927), the referential totality is brought to life by *Dasein* acting within it. *Dasein* acquires self-understanding through its acts, whereas understanding of entities (including itself) comes through *Dasein's* experiencing of the totality. Acting, in the sense of relating to other entities, is key to acquiring self-understanding and understanding of the being of other entities. For example, Heidegger's proverbial hammer reveals itself to us as we use it. It is by using equipment, argues Heidegger, that its specific 'thingly' character reveals itself to us in ways it could not have done if we just stared at it (Heidegger 1927: 69).

Note that entities are not things of 'simple location', as argued by Whitehead. They are their historicities and ambitions, which are trajectories of events at which historicities and ambitions have been played out. Entities 'are' what they have experienced, seen from the present time, including the present time. In other words they 'are' their histories, which they carry with them in an ongoing present. This is an implication of the principle of endogeneity discussed in section 3.3. In the case of organizations this means that when we think about, act within, or act upon an organization, that organization 'is' the choices, experiences, events, and ambitions that make up the organization until now and that are the most concrete facts we have access to. Some might argue that the most concrete impression of an organization comes through what we can perceive instantaneously. However, that is a mere fleeting image extracted through experiential 'point-flashes' (Whitehead 1920). When we experience the individual or the organization, we experience an entity whose experiences are given meaning by the various epochs that individual or organization has lived through.

In the organizational present actors live in the flow of duration in which experiences melt into one another in a 'flowing continuum' (Schütz 1967: 51). In these presents we live within provinces of meaning representing the ready-to-hand reality (Schütz and Luckmann 1973). This does not, however, imply that meaning of past and future acts is not dealt with in the present moment, as it is the interaction that is experienced as a flowing continuum. When we act, we address others; we need their responses, which provide meaning to our acts. We need them to understand our acts; thus we mean what we say while saying it.[27] Upon closure of the temporal present, the meaning of the interactions may be assessed through reflection.

However, we know nothing of what is retained as meaning of the interaction from one moment to the next while simply living in the flow of duration (Schütz 1967: 51) (although not knowing what is *retained* does not mean that no meaning occurs in the flow of duration, it may simply mean that a number of possible meanings are available). On the other hand, if nothing persisted from one present to the next, there would be no way to give meaning to things. Returning to Heidegger, if the hammer breaks there is no way to understand why unless it exists as an integral part of a referential totality of steel, wood, durability, and shape. Similar to Schütz, meaning structures exist as temporally coalesced formations of signs that function as proxies for the temporally situated provinces of meaning, not wholly accessible to actors as they perform in the present, not least because that present is yet to attain closure to become an event.

Searching for temporally informed answers to the question of becoming suggests that becoming refers to the becoming of the past in view of a possible future, and a possible future in view of a possible past. Just like the future, the past represents possibility for becoming. The possibilities of the past are actualized in the present with a view of future aspirations.[28] If we assume that things 'are' their historicities and that how an entity becomes constitutes what it 'is' (Whitehead 1929a: 23), becoming should logically refer to the process by which something comes into being. Similarly, as Whitehead suggests, every new instant adds to what is already, but that presumes that 'something was' already. Every new experience makes an ingression into that which 'is' already and immediately becomes part of its past, together with that which was. Consequently the past is continually changing as new experiences are added with the passing of time. Bergson's (1922: 5) statement, 'Duration is the continuous progress of the past which gnaws into the future and which swells as it advances', illustrates an image of a changing past. The becoming of the past takes place as every new event and experience adds to the past.

The momentary present-past-future dynamics takes place as articulations of a meaning structure reach into time to reveal organizational becoming; they evoke the past by making their way into the organization's historicity while indicating possible futures. It is between the past and future that the potentiality of becoming of the organization reveals itself. For example, Sabel (1993) notes how, based on his studies of forms of cooperation in economic development, in what he fittingly calls 'co-operation in the making', trust may develop as actors review their common histories and interpret conflicts in a new light. When, for instance, conflicts are seen as inevitably developing from fundamental differences between actors, the historical developments may be recast and told as being related to family fights. Modifying the meaning of past conflicts by locating them as situationally generated, rather than brought about by fundamental—and seemingly irreconcilable—differences, enables actors to relate differently to future developments, as potential conflicts are anticipated as possibly resulting from mistakes and misunderstanding. In this way co-operation reveals itself as becoming otherwise.

When reaching into the past, articulation does not produce sameness, but familiarity. Therefore, repeating an act is not, in effect, to do the same again because every repetition means that the number of times it has been done before has changed, however incrementally. But when something is repeated there is a reproduction of something; a reminder that what is repeated is part of a larger pattern. By brushing our teeth we reproduce the hygiene system of our lives. By listening carefully to what our children have to say to us, we reproduce the idea of bringing up children responsibly. This larger pattern, however, spans past, present, and future.

The part of the pattern that stretches into the past reflects remembrance, similarity, and evocation, whereas the part of the pattern that stretches into the future reflects aspirations or expectations. For example, Dodd, Anderson, and Jack (2013), in studying family firms, suggest that the 'familiness' of the family firm may be partly attributed to time in that it exists in the present as past heritage and future dreams. The organizational literature nevertheless locates memory exclusively with the past, for example Walsh and Ungson (1991: 61), who describe organizational memory as 'stored information from an organization's history that can be brought to bear on present decisions', basically representing a view of temporality that considers past and future as discrete periods of time. In contrast, a view of temporality as ongoing considers past and future to be part of the present, thus the evocation of memory cannot be seen as an exclusively retrospective exercise. Therefore, while memory evocation is directed towards the past, memory *making* is a prospective activity oriented towards the future. It may be useful to quote Schütz (1967: 53) who, drawing upon Husserl's distinction between retention and protention writes, 'Protentions into the future are a part of every memory, and in the natural standpoint they are merged with retentions.' Retention is obviously oriented towards the past, whereas protentions are oriented towards the future. Protentions come close to what may be called 'projective memory', just as retentions reflect retentional memory. Experiences and/or inferences from experiences (Levitt and March 1988), if they are to be evoked, inevitably become embedded in some form or other (oral, textual, artefactual) in order to be to be available for future retrieval and interpretation. Thus Husserl writes about fulfilment of protentions, which enables their recollection.[29] Pursuing this line of thinking, it becomes necessary for us to bear in mind the need to follow the process by which experiences become inscribed as memory. It is as memory that later events may connect backward to previous events. In other words, whereas evocation of memory works backwards in time, memory making is a forward process in time.

Evocation is inevitably also an act of looking into the future, just as looking into the future is also an act of evoking the past. Working with memory as both retentional and projective invites direction into the analysis. If memory, as is assumed in works in organization studies, belongs to the past only, its use in the present provides no direction into the future. In other words, memory is evoked for the sake of evoking it. Such an assumption, however, is not adequate for organizational analysis, nor is it practically legitimate. I would, for example, be hard pressed to believe that organizational members ever evoke a past memory without by the same token addressing some future aspiration, however modest it appears. Fairy tales (as far as they represent memory), for example, such as *Little Red Riding Hood*, the ancient tale about the little girl who met the big, bad wolf in the forest, were apparently told to keep young girls from venturing into the woods to meet their boyfriends. Memory, then, is not defined as to whether it belongs to the past or not, since everything that is has a 'pastness' (James 1890; Shotter 2006)[30] about it.

In the above citation, Shotter (2006) emphasizes the importance of temporality in the relational dynamics between elements, pointing out that they owe their existence, not only to each other, but also to their relations at some earlier point in time. Whereas much has been made of the existence of actors in time, it is important not to lose sight of the fact that past as well as future are made of events, constructed in the present. Elements, while being articulated in the present, are perceived as events of encounter in past and future. As already pointed out, what makes an element what it 'is', are the particular events associated with it. Whereas elements derive their temporal existence from a trajectory of encounters, meaning structures derive their temporal existence from event formations that are seen as particular to those meaning structures. As much as events provide historicity and a sense of movement to organizational life, event formations provide historicity and a sense of movement to the meaning structures they are associated with. Acts of articulation take place in the flow of the present, but become events of articulation at the closure of the present, to be constructed as parts of event formations at other presents. Such thinking invites closer scrutiny of articulatory modes, temporality, and agency, couched within a logic of events.

6 Articulatory Modes and Agency

■ SUMMARY

This chapter suggests and discusses five modes of articulation, referred to as intersubjective, practical, textual, material, and tacit. Intersubjective articulation comprises oral and bodily gestures in social interaction; practical articulation refers to practice as in routine-based human activity; textual articulation refers to written texts; material articulation signifies the use of material objects; and tacit articulation resides in knowledge of actual and potential articulatory work. Tacit articulation, in particular, represents intuition and therefore potential for novelty and change. This chapter also discusses how articulatory modes provide for continuity and change in organizational meaning structures, which enables discussion of temporal agency.

6.1 Setting the Stage

The ambition of a process-based organization theory is to better understand the work of connecting actors within organizational meaning structures, which helps better describe a flat, atomistic world where connectedness prevails over size, and where temporality prevails over spatiality. A process-based organization theory aims to extend both the types of actors considered and also the performative work of articulation in meaning structures to transcend that of traditional organization theory. Organizational meaning structures constitute the world in which actors operate, defined by those actors and the meaning attached to their actions, rather than by organizational boundaries. Mobilizing, changing, even maintaining organizational meaning structures, requires work performed by both human actors and material and conceptual[1] actors.

Applied to meaning structures, a performative view implies that the meaning of the various elements is not decided a priori but emerges through the ways in which elements of different kinds are articulated with one another. Elements of organizational meaning structures comprise, therefore, not just virtual signs (Schütz 1967) to be interpreted by actors, as mentioned previously, but also real 'things' to be related to one another by the ongoing work of actors. Importantly, the word 'structure' is not to be seen as stable patterns of related elements that exist beyond the work of actors, as meaning structures have no existence outside the ongoing processes of articulating their elements (Heidegger 1927; Laclau and Mouffe 1985).

Performativity becomes significant from the view of continuity and change because it directs attention to how acts or events articulate the past and the future as part of the present. Structure provides for continuity by enabling options for action and interpretation to be held open over time in such a way that decisions may be repeated with similar expectations of outcomes as if they were made yesterday. Organizational meaning structures (Heidegger 1927; Luhmann 1995; Mead 1934; Schütz 1967) are sufficiently stable to enable coherence of choice over time in such a way that continuity of choice may be to hold recognized options open, which enables change by the same token.

The tone in a melody articulates the tune, and in so doing provides the experience of both continuity and change. It continues the patterns suggested by previous notes, while by the same token changing that pattern. A parallel may be drawn with organizing processes, where an act is experienced as a continuity of the pattern created by previous acts, while at the same time changing that pattern by adding an experience. In most cases the pattern is changed imperceptibly; in others it may be changed significantly. How much a pattern is upheld or changed, however, can only be inferred retrospectively, and even then it is subject to (re)interpretation.

The perception of continuity and change is subject to the duration under consideration. An event may be considered to last an instant, such as when we are asked 'Where were you and what were you doing?' when the planes crashed into the Twin Towers on 11 September 2001?' Whether such an event is an event of reference more than an event of impact, however, depends on the extent to which the event shaped our lives. The numerous reminders of the event in the public debate, the US invasion of Afghanistan that the acts precipitated, and the killing of Osama Bin Laden are what make it significant in ways that it would have been if those acts had not taken place. If we assume a temporal diameter of several years, the 9/11 attacks will stand out as consequential for global politics for many years, whereas the event of witnessing the attacks at an instant, seen in isolation, appears of limited political importance, although it is highly consequential for the individual observers. What makes a difference is the nature of articulatory events and the way they are made to connect.

6.2 Articulation and Modes

> A trader selling a currency in order to take a profit may trigger trading responses in others because of what he or she has done. Even if no direct response is triggered, the signals of others' involvements

continually shape market participants' strategies and attitudes. Some market makers also reflexively use the signalling potential of deals to try and influence the market, that is, price movements and other traders (see also Soros 1994). In all these cases, the reciprocity indicates that global financial markets are fields of interaction: at any point in time, all traders will be watching the same events and one another, but some also interact (trade) and, in doing so, implement a new level of signaling and responsiveness among themselves.

(Knorr-Cetina and Bruegger 2002: 927)

Articulation is the lifeblood of organization. Every act serves to instantiate the organization through articulation of meaning structure elements. For example, within the field of strategy as practice, practices serve to articulate strategies. However, practices are evanescent acts of articulation that would be forgotten if they were not inscribed into more stable forms, such as PowerPoint presentations, Word documents, artefacts, and plans, as well as talked about in various settings. At another level, institutional fields are articulated by various staged events (Moeran and Strandgaard Pedersen 2011), serving to provide them with a foothold in time.[2] What becomes the focus of attention is how certain phenomena, such as practices, institutions, etc., are articulated, as well as how the actual forms of articulation influence their persistence in time.

Every present points towards articulation of some meaning structure. In the trading room described by Knorr-Cetina and Bruegger there is an ongoing stream of actions, talk, and gestures, all pointing towards elements of the 'market meaning structure' (my expression), including rules of conduct, currencies, financial instruments, and traders, including themselves.[3] While in action the traders experience a living present in which texts, actions, words, gestures, etc. form a maze of articulatory processes. As they move from moment to moment they perform their business and act in response to other traders on the basis of experience, intuition, and knowledge. While all these acts serve to sustain the organization of financial markets through articulation, it is of interest to explore, through the lens of articulation and temporality, various modes by which organizations are sustained, changed, or extended. For example, traders operate in a continuous present to facilitate temporal coordination across time zones, but Knorr-Cetina and Bruegger (2002: 929) note:

One way to globally organize such long-term transactions is for option traders at one desk to pass their option accounts every evening to the same bank's option traders at another desk in the next major time zone, who will manage the accounts and add deals during their working hours...[a]s a result, the coordination of consciousness [...] becomes more inclusive, encompassing groups that are not simultaneously present but take sequential and overlapping turns observing and acting on the market; traders coordinate trading intentions and philosophies with the next and previous desks in evening and morning phone calls and electronic conversations, respectively, and the book remains on their mind (and available on their screens) while it is out of their hands.

The temporal experience of traders is summed up and communicated to other traders who, though they may relate intuitively to the experience of the trader who has logged off since they are in the same trade, receive the experiences in abstract form. The experience of the previous traders has been brought to provisional closure and transmitted to others, who interpret the meanings of the experiences through reading and reflection, which in turn enters the experiential world of the traders who are going online. On the one hand the organization of financial markets is upheld through the ongoing articulation of traders. On the other hand, it is upheld by the articulation performed by the reports that circulate. As long as conditions are fairly stable and the types of actors remain much the same, modes of articulation uphold the organization in its current form. As and when important changes enter the marketplace, such as with the arrival of new actors or regulations, the meaning structures change, as alternative articulatory modes are employed. Substantial structural changes are likely to require face-to-face negotiations between back-office managers, combined with written memos and instructions serving to articulate modifications in the meaning structures.

Articulation not only discloses the connectedness of the meaning structure, but also its connectivity. Any act can but disclose a limited section of a meaning structure, leaving many connections in the dark, what Spencer-Brown (in Bakken 2014) calls 'the unmarked state'. The articulation of the meaning structure enables the articulatory act to point towards connections that are not disclosed by the act. Herein lies the potentiality of the meaning structure, in its surplus of connections, as its potentiality accompanies the disclosed connections (its actuality). The two, potentiality and actuality, are mutually dependent, just as pronouncing a word depends on the existence of what is not pronounced, and presence depends on absence. In other words, articulating the meaning structure brings to light what it is in terms of connections and its elements, while suggesting what it is yet to be. That which may potentially become a connection signifies connectivity, which implies movement in time, towards new events. Articulation, in this view, serves both to instantiate the meaning structure in terms of what is disclosed and what is not disclosed. Thus existence cannot be reduced to a simple location, as a finite, finished form (Cooper 2005b: 66); it is, instead, part of a process and becomes a projection in an onward movement:

> Presence is the pre-sense of an absence or gap that invites us to re-cover it as thrownness or projection; it is sense in continuous movement, always supplementing itself in an onward movement of deferral and anticipation. It does not and it cannot appear as a finite, finished form since its thrownness and non-immediacy means that it is neither fully present nor fully absent but forever suspended *between* the two.

Although processes of articulation are in themselves complex phenomena, they may be seen to take place through five different modes, which are considered analytically distinct while empirically entangled. In other words, the modes are more like 'ideal types' (Weber 1968) than realities found in practice. I label the five modes intersubjective, practical, textual, material, and tacit. Intersubjective articulation is manifest in the oral and bodily gestures in social interaction, similar to what Schütz (1964: 29, in Knorr-Cetina and Bruegger 2002: 921) describes as 'a maximum of vivid indications' in face-to-face situations involving movements, gestures, expressions, intonation, and the rhythm of utterances. Practical articulation refers to practice as in routine-based human activity. Textual articulation differentiates itself from intersubjective articulation by the use of structured relations between letters, between words, and between sentences, thus exhibiting a relative constancy of meaning (Saussure 1986: 32). Material articulation signifies the use of material objects that exhibit flexible interpretation, among other things. Finally, tacit articulation refers to that which is socially experienced and acknowledged but not overtly expressed. Tacit articulation exhibits potentiality, as it harbours historically generated perceptions of possibilities.

The notion of 'mode' has a number of different definitions, but we may think of a mode as a style or fashion (the French word for fashion is *mode*), a certain manner in which something happens (*Oxford Advanced Learner's Dictionary*). A mode may be seen as a certain manner that abides by its own logic, which applies, for example, to fashion. A mode comprises selected characteristics of a process that can be followed in time and space. For example, human practice may be seen as a mode of organizational life that may be followed in time and space. The same applies to intersubjectivity, which is a mode that may be considered distinct from practice. Materiality is a mode whose logics is characterized by properties of materiality.

Clearly, any act of articulation is a hybrid of various modes of articulation.[4] The following extract from Weick (1993: 641), where he describes the use of caribou shoulder bones by the Naskapi Indians in setting the direction for hunting, illustrates the tangled nature of modes of articulation:

They hold bones over a fire until they crack and then hunt in the directions to which the bones crack. [...] The wisdom inherent in this practice derives from its ambivalence toward the past. Any attempt to hunt for caribou is both a new experience and an old experience. It is new in the sense that time has elapsed, the composition of the hunter band has changed, the caribou have learned new things, and so forth. But the hunt is also old in that if you have seen one hunt you have seen them all: There are always hunters, weapons, stealth, decoys, tacks, odors, and winds. The practice of divination incorporates the attitude of wisdom because past experience is discounted when a new set of cracks forms a crude map for the hunt. But past experience is also given some weight, because a seasoned hunter 'reads' the cracks and injects some of his own past experience into an interpretation of what the cracks mean. The reader is crucial. If the reader's hunches dominate, randomization is lost. If the cracks dominate, then the experience base is discarded.

In the example we can identify tacit articulation as manifest in the unspoken interpretation of the cracks. Material articulation is manifest in the actual bones and the cracks that develop over the fire. In addition it is likely that gestural articulation is important as the interpretations evolve into collective commitment towards the direction of the hunt. Although the actors present will perceive a partly undifferentiated entanglement of articulatory modes, it is by distilling articulation into ideal types that we may be in a better position to analyse the temporal agency of organizational events. Temporal agency of organizational events is likely to vary with the relative manifestation of the different modes. For example, the mode of practice tends to extend a meaning structure without extensive modification. Deliberate social reflection and intersubjective articulation, on the other hand, may lay the basis for changing the meaning structure, not only by changing the view of the future, but also by changing meanings of past events. Material articulation may provide the seeds of substantial change owing to the immediacy and the compelling nature of touching, feeling, or smelling a material object.

6.3 Events and Agency

An event is a spatio-temporal entity of some duration, derived from the encounter between entities during an organizational present. Reference has been made earlier to James' expression 'bow and stern', which are felt as temporal boundaries of a living present that mark its duration. Duration is not experienced as a linear stretch of time, but what Whitehead (1920: 53) defines as a 'concrete slab of nature limited by simultaneity'. The idea of simultaneity is useful in defining the duration of an event. It corresponds to the idea of encounter between entities 'being there, then' as a point of departure for defining organizational presents as it is done in this book. Simultaneity of the presence of entities is inferred retrospectively as constitutive of the event that emerges from the organizational present. An organizational present embodies an entanglement of articulatory modes, which are experienced as a totality for the duration of the event, and which confer agency upon it.

As the temporal diameter of the present is left behind with the flow of time, it becomes an event that can be 'felt' (to use an expression from Whitehead) by a new present, which becomes an event in turn. The term 'feeling' is appropriate because events cannot be experienced directly as they 'are', but reached towards in a more indirect sense. It is this reaching out and 'feeling' of events which is done through articulatory modes in the present. For example, at a meeting, the problem of absenteeism among staff may be discussed and statistics may be scrutinized to get an idea of the extent of the problem. The discussion brings to attention other events related to the problem of absenteeism in the organization, as well as frames future actions to deal with the problem, for example by planning a campaign, which becomes in itself a series of events. The content of those events will be partly influenced by the scrutiny of the statistics in the said meeting, and the statistics are one material mode of articulating the meaning structure. In this way some articulatory modes make ingressions into events (to borrow a term from Whitehead). For example, the statistics on absenteeism make a particular ingression into the intersubjective process at the meeting, which provides the meeting with temporal agency in the sense of defining other past and future events.

Whereas articulation is ongoing in relation to the meaning structure, events provide the meaning structure with historicity as they become part of the event formation. Historicity is the history that belongs to the entity in question and what 'makes up' the temporal identity of that entity. For example, I was born in a certain place, I worked for a certain number of years with a particular organization, I fell ill at a certain point in time, my children grew up at a certain period in a certain place, etc. Heidegger (1927) makes the point that being is inherently temporal and that the possibility of historicity derives from the temporal state of being in time. In the flow of time, organizational presents mark a difference, as suggested by Mead's (1932: 23) definition of a present as that which marks out and selects what has made its peculiarity possible, while creating with its uniqueness a past and a future. The difference is the emergence of the present marked out by the present, which marks out and selects its past and future. In other words, the present inscribes itself as a difference, thus providing historicity to the process. As Latour (1999: 150) suggests, 'differences are all that we require, at first, to set a lively historicity into motion'. How that difference makes for historicity would depend on how the present enters the organizational reality as an event, which in turn depends on the articulatory modes employed at the present.

The agency of an event relates to its ability to enter the process of historicizing, that is, to be viewed as temporally significant. Historicizing, as Heidegger approaches it, is done from historicity; it makes historicity *intelligible* (Hoffman 2005: 330). Just as historicity derives from a temporal state of being, historicizing derives from the notion of an ongoing present at which the intelligibility of the entity's historicity is continuously subject to reconstruction. This is illustrated in Garfinkel's (1967: 178) account of Agnes, the 'woman-in-becoming', who, through a number of surgical interventions in 1958 was transformed to a woman. What is particularly relevant about the account is his use of historicizing and temporality:

Time played a peculiar role in constituting for Agnes the significance of her present situation. With regards to the past, we have seen the prominence with which she historicized, making for herself and presenting us with a socially acceptable biography. We have already remarked on the fact that the work of selecting, codifying, making consistent various elements of a biography, yielded a biography that was so consistently female as to leave us without information on many important points. Two years of arduous female activities furnished for her a fascinating input of new experiences upon which this historicizing process operated. Her attitude toward her own history required ever new rereadings of the trail that wound off behind her as she sought in reading and rereading the past for evidences to bolster and unify her present worth and aspirations. Before all, Agnes was a person with a history. Or, more pointedly perhaps, she was engaged in historicizing practices that were skilled, unrelieved, and biased.

Much like Agnes' life, organizational life is characterized by the connecting of events. The 'agency' of articulation relates to the production of events past and future, which reproduce and modify the meaning structure by their entry into the event formation. As previously mentioned, the event formation provides a sense of historicity and movement to the meaning structure. In the case of Agnes the event formation is alluded to by the mention of her 'two years of arduous female activity'. The agency facilitates the recursive making of relationships between the making of the events and the mutual relations between events (Whitehead 1920: 167). This is how the meaning structure is set into motion, through the making of events and their mutual relations, thus providing the meaning structure with historicity.

In what follows I will discuss five different modes of articulation in the light of events and agency. It is assumed that each mode may be ascribed certain agentic qualities, which strengthen the possibility of the events at which they are played out to influence other events. It is assumed that the agency of an event depends on the participation of individual actors, but is not reducible to the participation of those actors. Instead, what confers agency upon an event is the articulatory work in which individual actors take part and the ability for the work to connect events during the present associated with that event. The actual process takes place while the event is a living present, which means that it is still indeterminate and open, and that the resulting agency of the present becomes noticeable as it turns into an event, which in turn occupies a place in the event formation, which provides historicity to the meaning structure, and hence, the organization.

6.4 Intersubjective Articulation

> Language does not simply symbolize a situation or object which is already there in advance; it makes possible the existence or the appearance of that situation or object, for it is a part of the mechanism whereby that situation or object is created.
>
> (Mead 1934: 78)

Intersubjective articulation of meaning structures includes exchange of gestures, talk, moods, and utterances between people. Organizational life contains a plethora of micro situations in which meaning structures are articulated through intersubjective processes. It would not be useful to limit the mode to talk, discourse, or language, but to try and include the richness of intersubjectivity that lends agency to a present.[5] Take, for example, the film *The King's Speech*, in which Colin Firth features as King George VI, the stammering heir to the British throne who became king in 1937. The film shows the interactions between the king and his speech therapist (played by Ben Wimsett) as they struggle to enable the king to give public speeches. 'Struggle' is an appropriate word because one of the most striking features of the film is the king's internal struggle as he tries to overcome his speech impediment while fighting childhood traumas and facing the momentous task of being Britain's royal figurehead during a world war. His struggle is as much present in his bodily gestures as in his words, where he expresses boyishness, foolishness, pride, humility, and defiance. Analysing the film based on analysis of the dialogue alone would provide a bleak picture of the process leading up to the king's famous radio broadcast following Britain's declaration of war in 1939, as there are numerous instances in the film where the relationship between the king and his speech therapist might have taken a different course. On such monumental occasions much more than words is exchanged. When, for example, the king dismisses his speech therapist during a walk in the park, he does so with an air of royal authority. At that very instant it is the British royalty as an institution and not him as an individual who is speaking; to understand the full significance of the utterances, both his bodily gestures and words must be witnessed together.

Much organizational research that concerns itself with gestural effects on organizing processes focuses on talk, or the structured exchange of words. Thus, for example, Brunsson and Winberg (1990: 124) write about how organizational reforms get talked into practice; Czarniawska (1997) writes about narrating organizational identity; and Weick, Sutcliffe, and Obstfeld (2005: 409) describe sensemaking as an issue of talk by which situations, organizations, and environments are talked into existence. Less is done, however, on the wider range of behavioural exchange in social settings.

Meaning structures are predominantly created through intersubjective processes in which talk and gestures serve to connect different temporal phases of the social act (Mead 1934: 76). Note that meaning is not attached to one thing or one fact, but is acquired by relating experiences over time through the interrelating of elements of the meaning structure, including the communicating subject. Importantly, the evocative power of social interaction lies in its ability to confer meaning upon past events through mutual sensegiving (Polanyi 1967). The richness of intersubjective processes primarily enables the transmission of meanings of past experience (Blumer 1969) and the possibilities of future experience between people. Transmission by gestures, words, or actions in social interaction (Blumer 1969) provides an extraordinarily rich and instantaneous form of human communication (Suchman 2006).[6] Storytelling (Martin et al. 1983), narratives (Cunliffe, Luhman, and Boje 2004; Czarniawska 1997),[7] rituals (Kunda 1992; Trice and Beyer 1984), and ceremonies (Trice and Beyer 1984), for example, enable the potentially complex relationships between past and present events to be conveyed in a compact and vivid form (Boje 1991).

The experience of intersubjective articulation is characterized by the previously mentioned 'pure duration', in which socially mediated, 'undifferentiated experiences' 'melt into one another in a flowing continuum' (Schütz 1967: 51). The gestures and oral exchange of intersubjective articulation hinge on the meaning creation that takes place as callers' expressions towards their interlocutors arouse the feelings in the callers themselves, corresponding to the responses they aim for (Mead 1934: 73). This demonstrates the importance of social legitimacy in encounters between actors, and in particular how the persuasive power of words, stories, allegories, or metaphors, combined with bodily movement in the intimacy of direct communicative interaction, may hold particular agency in times of change. Putnam and Boys (2006), for example, argue that stories and narratives serve as vehicles of contestation or vessels for conveying corporate meaning. At the same time, as argued by Cunliffe, Luhman, and Boje (2004), narratives have the ability to interweave through many moments of encounters. Put together, these two works suggest that intersubjectivity is powerful as a mode of articulating organizational meaning structures, by virtue of connecting events in time. Importantly, Martin et al. (1983) suggest that stories generate, as well as reflect, changes in organizations, partly due to the rich detail and multiple interpretations enabled by them. Tsoukas (2009) supports this view in pointing out that when participants engage relationally with one another they are more likely to take responsibility for both the joint tasks they are involved in and for the relationships they have with others.

Through the lens of temporality, intersubjectivity adds a particular quality to organizational life by affording selectivity of past and future events. As mentioned previously, meaning structures become meaningful by offering choice. In a conventional sense choice is seen as the ability to select from different opportunities, but provides those opportunities with neither 'pastness' nor 'futurity' (Heidegger 1927). In most works, choice seems to be viewed in an atemporal sense as the choice between alternatives at interlinked, yet discrete moments in time. Whereas a living present is heterogeneous, that is, composed of human as well as non-human actors, it is the human element of intersubjectivity that provides possibilities for selecting patterns of pastness and the futurity of meaning structure elements.

Change requires that the past be consistently redefined over several presents such that past events come to be redefined in the meeting with a changing future. Throughout their conversations, Agnes repeatedly tried to impress Garfinkel with the fact that she was really 'born a woman'. Although the operation provided her with female genitalia and she began to date a man, it evidently remained important for her to impress upon people her 'female' history, even at the point when she was seen as a boy. She would perform this in social interaction by consistently over-emphasizing feminine aspects of her past by talking and gesturing like a woman; for example, when relating past work experiences she would say things like, 'Oh, everything was just so wonderful'; 'It was the best job I ever had'; 'Everyone was so nice; the arrangements were so harmonious'; 'I still correspond with all the girls there'; 'It was just a ball'; and 'Everyone was just bubbling over with friendship and cheer' (Garfinkel 1967: 167).

Garfinkel (1967:167) notes, for example, how such descriptions were emphasized, and more functional—and maybe masculine—aspects underplayed: 'Her specific duties were slighted in her account. When she was pressed, she did not find them "at all" interesting to discuss (she chose what to articulate). Also, as we have seen, the female character of her early history was exaggerated while evidences that she had been raised as a boy were suppressed.' Several other accounts show how she 'managed situations' in social interactions (Garfinkel's expression) to impress people with the idea that she was a 'born woman', and show that this 'situational management' was performed as a means to acquire social legitimacy as a woman in a society which at that time in particular held a binary view of sexuality (either male or female):

> Agnes was self-consciously equipped to teach normals how normals make sexuality happen in commonplace settings as an obvious, familiar, recognisable, natural, and serious matter of fact. Her speciality consisted of treating the 'natural facts of life' of socially recognised, socially managed sexuality as a managed production so as to be making these facts of life true, relevant, demonstrable, testable, countable, and available to inventory, cursory representation, anecdote, enumeration, or professional psychological assessment; in short, so as unavoidably in concert with others to be making these facts of life visible and reportable—accountable—for all practical purposes.
>
> (Garfinkel 1967: 180)

The passage is indicative of the richness of intersubjective articulation and how it serves, at least in the eye of the beholder, to successfully give a different meaning to past events in order to prepare for a different future. It also shows how intersubjective articulation is different from conversation analysis, which maps sequences and structures of signs and utterances in communication. Although sequencing of words and gestures is important (the blink of an eye may carry a totally different meaning at the beginning of an encounter than at the end), sequencing and structuring do not capture the richness and hence the temporal agency of the encounter. Talk can be recorded through the structure of language and can therefore be correlated to outcomes of interaction, such as the balance of power. However, that would mean treating talk as an average situation and it would take out the living 'eventness' (Cunliffe et al. 2014) of talk.

Bearing in mind the centrality of event formations it becomes important to understand the agency of some events to change or to stabilize those formations. Although we do not know until after—sometimes well after—an event if things are changing, an important assumption is still that some events come to be seen as more decisive than others for the overall course of events. This is why the gestures considered need to include more than mere talk and also why it becomes important to understand gestures as taking part in the ongoing stream of interaction.

Given the degree of legitimization, the richness and vividness inherent in intersubjective articulation are a powerful mode for maintaining as well as redefining events and, by implication, the patterns they constitute. Intersubjectivity allows for soliciting, arresting, challenging, questioning, or endorsing utterances during the flow of interaction. By the same token it enables continuation and consolidation of meanings, although, since intersubjectivity is a relatively volatile mode, those meanings are open to change.

6.5 **Practical Articulation**

Ethnomethodologists have traditionally studied how the frameworks of actions are instantiated by actions and, in line with process philosophers, have rejected the idea that processes are framed by factors that are independent of those processes (Boden 1994).[8] In a similar way, the literature on practice has directed attention at the level of actions as a locus of instantiation of frameworks of meaning. A central idea is that organizations are activity systems, where social participation in practices at all levels of organization constitutes what the organization 'is'. Organizations are not seen to have any intrinsic qualities, as pointed out by Gherardi and Nicolini (2005), but they are performed socially through material means. Thus Gherardi (2000: 214) points out that when a carpenter uses a hammer, he enacts 'hammering' and 'carpentry'. Practice studies are concerned about pointing out the inherently social character of practice of organizational life, and point towards the relationship between actions, social relations, and organization. As an example, Orr (1990), who studied photocopier maintenance technicians, observed how they interacted with the technology and each other, using their tacit knowledge to let the materials 'speak'.

Ethnomethodology is one of several schools of thought (such as new institutionalists in organization studies) which, under the influence of Bourdieu and Giddens, consider agency as habitual, repetitive, and taken for granted

(Emirbayer and Mische 1998). Lorino (2014) points out Peirce's definition of practice as an experience-based, socially constructed disposition, which Peirce calls 'habit'. Habit points to the temporal quality of practice, as its repetitive nature directs attention to the historical construction of certain patterns of action. Practice is principally about repetition, and practice in the social realm would imply repetition that both constituted a certain social momentum and 'pointing towards' collective acts. But repetition is not limited to repetition of activity, but repetition of that which has been seen as possible. Thus Heidegger (1927: 391) refers to 'repetition' of the possibilities that 'have been'. Hence repetition brings the organization in touch with itself in view of its past and with possible connections in its external environment through activities that are reproduced. Without repetition, actors fail to be reminded of the organization and its possibilities.[9] A railway station can only exist as long as people continue to go through it; a prison is only upheld as a prison as long as there are inmates and wardens going about their business. The activities remind actors of what the organization is capable of, such as keeping inmates locked away or reforming them.

By practical articulation I mean practice- or work-based articulation. Practice implies bodily activity, which is meaning creating as well as functional. It provides a visual and/or bodily experience of how things are done, how they have been done in the recent past, and how they are likely to continue being done in the foreseeable future. While watching practical articulation is primarily a visual experience, taking part in practical articulation is also a bodily experience that provides understanding through action. The doing is done in socio-material contexts and serves to provide experience-based knowledge of how elements of meaning structures connect. In fact, from his study of the development work of particle physicists, Pickering (1995a) concluded that practice was what affected associations between elements of the culture of the communities and not just of knowledge production.

A question to ask is what characterizes the connecting performed by practice in time. Orr's (1998) study of photocopier technicians is helpful here, because his study contrasts the effects of written manuals with the effects of practice. First of all, he shows how practice works as articulation by pointing out how technicians found themselves 'interpreting machine behaviours, users' actions, and their colleagues' accounts of both, in a context-laden attempt to maintain the equilibrium of a relationship between machines, users, and technicians' (Orr 1998: 450). Machines, users, and technicians may be seen as elements of meaning structures that are articulated by the ongoing practices of technicians.[10] Whereas text in manuals provides reference and codification of practice across dispersed situations, practice enables a situated, bodily, and rich understanding that makes improvisation possible. Practical articulation may address new problems and problems in different contexts in ways that text cannot, according to Orr.

From a different perspective, Schatzki (2010: 214) makes the point that the presence of the past is manifest through a repertoire of actions in the public space that someone can perform without having to do something else. The repertoire, because it is a result of past experience, serves as a reminder of the presence of the past. Schatzki makes the point that the bodily repertoire is closely related to practical understanding, which may be taken as an implication that the past represents other, possible actions. In other words, practical articulation brings attention to a past of other possible articulations. The history of possibilities is what provides awareness of possibilities in the present.

Practice travels with the human body, which, through movement, articulates the meaning of a particular organizational arrangement. The human body and its movements both work as a medium of experience and expression, and as a carrier of meaning. The multi-sensorial experience of practical articulation provides the human body with richness and adaptability in different situations. In living presents, practice points towards multiple quasi-identical past events by implicit evocation, while also pointing towards multiple similar future events.

Practical articulation is therefore highly subjective while being suggestive of large volumes of events, thus making for social momentum in articulation of the meaning structure. Social momentum becomes primordial, as individual performances take place in the public sphere and are experienced as signs of a larger movement of coordinated activity articulating the meaning structure. This is how, for example, a gesture made by one person in an encounter may influence the outcome of that encounter, as it comes to be seen as representative of a much larger social pattern. Moreover, that social pattern may stretch back a long time, which means that it represents a total 'timespace' of numerous actors at multiple events.

6.6 Material Articulation

> It is evident that the future certainly is something for the present. The most familiar habits of mankind witness to this fact. Legal contracts, social understandings of every type, ambitions, anxieties, railway time-tables, are futile gestures of consciousness apart from the fact that the present bears in its own realized constitution relationships to a future beyond itself. Cut away the future, and the present collapses, emptied of its proper content. Immediate existence requires the insertion of the future in the crannies of the present.
>
> (Whitehead 1933: 191)

It is quite remarkable how, when prominent politicians are to be sensitized to the problems of global warming, they are taken to the Arctic to see the degradation first hand. Obviously, once they stand on the ice they feel the ice under their feet; there may be sounds, even smells, that make an impact on their resolve to do something about the threat of global warming. I imagine that when politicians have an intense experience during a visit to the Arctic region the impact relates not only to the future threat of global warming, but also to the contrast (for some at least) with the winters they are familiar with. When I think about the threat of global warming, memories of childhood winters when the snow was a natural playground for months on end lurk at the back of my mind. To most people who grew up with snowy winters, snow represents various different smells, shades of white, textures, and even sounds, all of which relate to sensorial experiences of play, leisure, work or sport. The richness of sensorial experiences of being exposed to a substance such as snow enables vivid bodily evocation, while directing attention towards the future in the present. In the present during which the snow is felt, meaning structure elements, such as policies, are brought to attention. Their significance may be felt through the sensation of being materially present in the substance that is their object.

The kind of materiality we are speaking of here enables vivid evocation. Whether or not it makes a difference for the work of combating global warming, however, depends on how succeeding events are brought into existence and given meaning by the visit. As time moves on, other competing issues enter the stage, which threaten to take away attention and resolve from the environmental cause. For serious work to begin, other actors need to be brought into the work; concepts, and agendas established; and technologies and resources harnessed. Much of that work, however, will be carried out by actors who have not had the privilege of experiencing Arctic decay up-close. Policymakers therefore need to rely on other material means of articulation, such as pictures, budgets, memos, etc. for that to happen (supplemented, of course, by face-to-face events). The question is whether the impetus from the Arctic experience can be kept up through 'dead' materialities as substitutes for the immediate experience of the snow and cold. It is likely to enable a common attitude among multiple actors, but less likely to arouse passion or determination.

Much of the work on materiality focuses on the stabilizing effects of materiality in various socio-material constellations. However, much of the work may be extended through a lens of temporality. The work that material objects perform in the forming and stabilization of organizational arrangements is argued particularly in studies on boundary objects (Carlile 2002; Star 2010; Star and Griesemer 1989). These studies, however, focus on how objects perform bridging functions between different social communities in the absence of consensus (Star 2010: 604), and do not give importance to the temporal roles played by boundary objects, although a notion such as temporal boundary objects could well yield some interesting ideas.

Orlikowski (2006), emphasizing the importance of the social nature of materiality, argues that knowing is always material. Material articulation also enables transcendence of the organizational present in particular ways, by (re)defining past events and anticipating future ones. Materiality, as pointed out repeatedly by ANT researchers (e.g. Latour 1999; Law 2004), enables a particular form of stabilization of organizational life. Whereas ANT researchers focus on how materiality takes part in stabilizing organizational processes through the acquisition of actors' identities, it would also be interesting to see how, from a temporal view, materiality seems to take control of organizational processes. In some cases, materiality may be overwhelming and, by its sheer presence, powerfully and continuously impact organizational life. Such is the case, for example, with large machineries that effectively organize the actors around them, such as the 250-tonne machine described by Lindahl (2005). Lindahl observes how the machine eventually works as an active attributor of important versus less important activities:

> It is true that an engine does not 'draw' cables, pipes and other machines in the full sense of the word, but it 'draws' attention. Performing an installation with an engine as a point of reference means that some actions, or action sequences, become more likely than others. They also become more or less likely if the reference point had been defined as the generation of 30 MW or as the transaction of 600 MSEK.
>
> (2005: 63)

In the above example Lindahl shows how big machines may articulate life around them. Still, the performative qualities of material devices in articulating organizational arrangements over time need further study. A temporal focus might bring out factors less related to size, power, or force than spatial analysis does.

For example, De Laet and Mol show how a material artefact may impact by being fluid, as they show in their study of the Zimbabwe bush pump. The bush pump, they point out, articulates life around it in a variety of ways. They ask, for example, 'For if the bush pump must act, what is it to do: provide water or provide health? Build communities or make a nation?' (de Laet and Mol 2000: 247). In other words, it is a community-building device, a health promoter, and ultimately a nation builder, since it provides access to precious resources. But, as they point out, the articulatory performance of the bush pump is not so much due to the pump as a definite, uniform, clearly identifiable object. It is an assemblage of various (and varying) parts and may take different forms. The elasticity of its appearance and composition enable it to be a 'travelling band' (my expression) performing articulation throughout the countryside. Although de Laet and Mol do not make explicit reference to it, the temporal existence of the pump is likely to matter if the pump is seen as a co-creator of experiential events that in time and space shape an event formation throughout the countryside. The pump forms a natural element of encounters (living presents) at which its role in a broader meaning structure is articulated.

Materiality may make for rich and sensorial articulation, as in the case of standing on the Arctic ice in the face of global warming. It may also provide for repeated, routine-like articulation among multiple actors at different spatial locations and at different times, such as when their activities are coordinated by the use of technology. The first, however, is most likely to exhibit temporal agency in combination with inter-subjective articulation, as in Schütz's (1967) example of the making of we-ness. The second is more likely to exhibit temporal agency in connection with practical articulation, which provides momentum across time and space.

6.7 Textual Articulation

> Thus, texts are not foundational; however, they participate, like other agents, in the daily production of organizational life.
>
> (Cooren 2004: 374)

> The actual text of the contract introduces a series of tangible and intangible elements (concepts, materials, substances, experimental devices, researchers etc.) which help to delineate and structure the frame within which it will be performed. The contract could not be framed and 'fulfilled' without the participation or requisition of each of these elements: they are involved in the same plot, the same scenario; each of them is obliged to play a predefined role. The actions within the frame are prepared and structured by the equipment, the theoretical statements, the skilled persons of the researchers and technicians, the procedures and reports; all these elements ensure that they are not scattered or dispersed.
>
> (Callon 1998: 254)

Mathiesen's (2013) analysis of the making of strategies in a Danish biotech company shows how the materials of what she calls 'strategy work' consist of a range of various written media, including large sheets of brown paper, flipcharts, coloured Post-its, coloured notecards, pre-printed response cards, whiteboards with different coloured markers, and PowerPoint documents. Mathiesen observes the following about a departmental meeting:

A projector shines a large colourful word cloud onto the screen. The words have been collected as descriptors of the department. The twenty or so people present sit back and look up at the visual graphic, digesting that this is what they said. Then they begin to correct the image: they argue that some words should be larger; that two or three terms actually mean the same thing; that something is missing, etc. The PowerPoint slide with the word cloud on it feels very strategy-like. In the meeting, the department uses the cloud as a 'conversation piece' to start a discussion about who they are.

(2013: 145)

Mathiesen makes the point that the visual language of strategy enables those involved to recognize that they are actually doing 'strategy work'. The above quote illustrates how text from the strategy work makes ingression into a meeting and influences its outcome, thus forming precedent and antecedent to events related to the strategy process. I assume that the experience of strategy work engenders event formations with strategy-related issues, at which the production and re-production of texts take part in shaping a unifying image of the organization's strategy. As for most formal organizations, the strategy may be seen as one central element of the meaning structure.

Although they are essentially complex images of a desired future, strategies depend in large measure upon wording, which requires that their performative textual articulation be given attention. Cooren (2004) makes the point that, although there has been a growing interest in discourse in organization studies, little attention has as yet been given to the actual agency performed by texts in organizational life. He argues that text takes organizational research beyond the preoccupation with face-to-face communication and that instead of focusing on what members say, focuses on the oral, written, or iconic texts produced, as well as how these texts span space and time. He also makes the point that texts, such as policies, contracts, and forms, serve the purpose of reaffirming organizational identity and existence. A performative and temporal view of organizations as meaning structures demands precisely that the temporal agency of texts is discussed. Cooren's interesting argument is that studies of texts may invest actors with less agency than they actually possess. The agentic qualities of texts would, from a process view, be manifest in the ability of texts to connect events through articulation of the meaning structure.

The underlying structural characteristics of texts are the regularity of signs and the relations between them.[11] Saussure (1986) points out how text in written form exhibits a relative constancy of meaning over time, which is due to the regularity of signs and the relations between them. Utterances of words in social interaction involve an infinite number of muscular movements, but written texts freeze language into a constant visual image (Saussure 1986: 32). In relation to organization studies, Smith (2001: 160), for example, observes that '[t]exts and documents make possible the appearance of the same set of words, numbers or images in multiple local sites, however differently they may be read and taken up'. In other words, a text may be read in similar ways over spans of time and space. Cooren provides us with an example in his description of how people rely on written notes in their daily activities, because notes have a capacity to do what humans do poorly: remind or recall throughout space and time. The durability of notes means that 'they *last, endure, remain—properties* that human memory lacks' (2004: 378).

Notes and checklists, however, are not to be seen as pure representations of the actions, but as performative devices playing specific roles in the accomplishment of tasks. In the words of Putnam and Cooren (2004: 326): 'texts are not the essence of the organizational phenomenon, but they participate in its daily production and reproduction'. In his essay on framing and overflowing, Callon (1998) points out how texts frame interactions between actors, but without dictating their actions. Negotiations presuppose textual framing, according to Callon, without which it would not be possible to reach agreement, just like playing a game of chess presupposes written rules to which the players submit before they begin to play. In other words, texts may work as articulatory modes that provide rules of the game in such a way that actions may be carried out, while by the same token acting as a resort for resolving ambiguity or conflict. At the same time, the structured nature of texts makes them amenable to contestation (Putnam and Boys 2006), as and when actors with legitimate authority provide justifiable modifications to them. The fact that texts are both authoritative and contestable enables them to play decisive roles in effecting relatively durable changes of meaning structures.

At a different level, texts perform the connecting of dispersed actors in time and space by repeatedly reminding them of the nature of their interconnectedness. For example, in his discussion of the connecting roles of newspapers, Cooper (2005a) points at how they connect through text by assembling information from multiple and distant sources. The assembly, in fact, is what constitutes the newspaper. While connecting information from sources, the newspaper also reveals that there are many sources that are not present in its assembly, what Cooper refers to as 'missing presences' (2005a: 70). Taken together, the connected presences and the missing presences define an encompassing framework of space and time, where the newspaper, by virtue of its texts, occupies a connecting (and hence articulatory) role. Each day of its appearance the newspaper manifests its role as that which connects the disconnected and its roles as defining that which is present and that which is not. The regular reappearance of the newspaper is a reminder that it performs the connecting, which may be seen as the articulation of meaning structures made up of the various sources of assemblage.[12] There is the continuous threat of the paper's disappearance, which is averted through its daily reproduction, which Cooper sees as revealing its underlying fragility and impermanence. Cooper's example points towards the performative role of text in articulating and thereby upholding the organizational reality of media in producing multiple presences at which texts are consumed by readers. While the reproduction of media may be fragile and impermanent as a mode of articulation, it exhibits the quality of expressing meaning in a structured way while reproducing realities across multiple settings.

The regularity and structure of the form of texts that makes their meaning comparable over time and space enables statements to be made about organizational concerns, which lends them authority but also makes them contestable by the same token. Longstanding and ongoing debates about the meaning of various messages in religious texts are a case in point. The form of texts also enables them to be readily de-composed, re-composed, and connected to other texts to change their meaning: in other words, how they articulate meaning structures. The literature on auditing demonstrates the authority that may be conferred upon certain texts. Skærbæk (2009) points out how the idea of 'purification' (Power 2003) in the auditing literature is referred to as showing how audits work as powerful articulatory devices in time and space. Power (1996: 311) relates the production of texts as public knowledge to the legitimacy of those experts who produce them; hence, the process of replication of audits is preceded by consensus on occasions. On the other hand, events also provide the opportunity for the contestation of public knowledge, but only, Power points out, if done by reputable experts. In other words, refutation of public knowledge may take place on occasions characterized by the presence of experts or counter experts. Such events set and keep the meaning structure of the public knowledge in motion. As counter experts contest public knowledge they not only create 'counter' events, but they also shed a different light on those events that endorsed the public knowledge in the first place.

Texts connect over distance; as shown with the newspaper example, they potentially connect many actors, and their authors may be many and anonymous. This makes a text a 'distant' mode of articulation in the sense that it is not associated with certain actors. This is convincingly argued in the organizational literature, where it is shown that bureaucratic devices work to solve interpersonal conflicts in ways that interactive forms do not. Rothschild-Whitt (1979: 510), for example, notes that in voluntary (non-bureaucratic) organizations, interpersonal conflict may be endemic. In more bureaucratic forms, on the other hand, rules embedded in impersonal texts serve as resorts for solving contentious issues. Texts are relied on as resorts, reference, indication, suggestion, or prediction (Cooren 2004: 380), because they have, at least momentarily, stood the test of time and, having stood the test of time, they are legitimate means of linking events in time.

By virtue of their relative constancy, texts may appear timeless in the sense that their origins are not important, although this does not apply in all cases. In US elections, for example, the initial signing of the Constitution in Philadelphia in 1787 by the Founding Fathers is commonly alluded to, especially when it comes to interpretations of basic rights. Still, the temporality of such documents, which are of high symbolic importance, is not representative for most texts that circulate in organizational life. It is uncommon, for example, to bring up the conditions and timing of the making of technical manuals, unless they are considered irrelevant or out of date, in which case they become subject to contestation. The participation of texts at organizational events, such as auditing, happens more or less regardless of the conditions at which the audit was initiated.

While articulating meaning structures, organizational presents not only endorse or refute texts, but produce, revise, and re-produce texts, thereby exercising different agency in relation to event formations and meaning structures. Until a few years ago this chapter would refer to texts that would be assumed to remain unchanged until replaced or revised by people with the authority or legitimacy to revise them. Such texts may be called 'closed' or 'read only' texts. In organizational encounters read-only texts are read, then acted upon. In other words, the closed nature of the texts engenders a sort of bifurcation between the text as medium and the social processes around it. Increasingly, another type of textual media is entering organizational life, generally referred to as social media, such as, for example, Wikipedia.

An emerging area that would aid in better understanding the peformativity and agency of texts is the detailed study of social media such as Twitter, not because Twitter as such is expected to prevail, but because it may yield interesting knowledge about organizing and micro situations where text is used.[13] Recent events, especially in the Middle East, have brought attention to the potential of social media for staging and coordinating political protests. In a commentary, Keller (2010), while suggesting that social media play an important role, questions the potential of Twitter[14] for organizing activity, notably in the case of the Iranian uprising in the spring of 2009:

'The immediacy of the reports was gripping,' reported the *Washington Times*. 'Well-developed Twitter lists showed a constant stream of situation updates and links to photos and videos, all of which painted a portrait of the developing turmoil. Digital photos and videos proliferated and were picked up and reported in countless external sources safe from the regime's Net crackdown.' Journalists even gave the unrest in Tehran a second moniker: the 'Twitter Revolution.' But was there really a 'Twitter Revolution?' Radio Free Europe's Golnaz Esfandiari recently described the idea in *Foreign Policy* as 'an irresistible meme during the post-election protests, a story that wrote itself.' Esfandiari explained that opposition activists primarily utilized text messages, email, and blog posts to organize protests, while 'good old-fashioned word of mouth' was the most influential medium for coordinating opposition. Social media tools like Facebook and Twitter were not ideal for rapid communication among protestors, and utilized more by observers in other countries. 'Western journalists who couldn't reach—or didn't bother reaching?—people on the ground in Iran simply scrolled through the English-language tweets posted with tag #iranelection,' quipped Esfandiari.

Although Keller claims that Twitter failed as an organizational tool, Esfandiari points out that text messages, emails, and blog posts were used to organize protests. Keller, on the other hand, points out that Twitter played an important role in conveying the significance of what was happening to the international media. Three comments are worth making in relation to the example of social media in such a situation. First, social media are significant in the mobilization of many distributed actors, as well as in their coordination. Second, social media act alongside direct social interaction to coordinate the movement. What is not so much known, however, is *how* various media interact in achieving coordination. It is not sufficient to claim that some media are simply less effective than others, because one seemingly ineffective medium might be far more important as a complementary medium than what its apparent effectiveness might suggest, once temporality and the connecting of events are taken into consideration. A point made by Abbott (2001: 25), for example, is that the importance of events should be understood more in terms of their temporal endurance than the size of the social structures they impact on. Alternative questions might revolve around issues such as the impact of the simultaneous occurrence of a blog post and face-to-face meetings in organizing the uprising. Third, when Keller speaks of the organizing powers of Twitter, he refers to the direct impact on actions and interactions. To be sure, if we limit the analysis to actions, the argument may hold. However, organized actions are framed by meaning: they are directed towards the meaning that underlies them. In the case of the Iranian 'Twitter Revolution', Twitter updates communicated to international media gave those media insight into what was going on and helped muster support for the uprising, but those very updates also articulated to those who prepared them the meaning of the actions of those who protested. Therefore, the meanings of the uprising, the medium of Twitter, and the Twitter updates and the actions are linked in time and space in organizing the uprising, along with several other factors.[15]

Textual articulation seems to combine the ability to connect events involving actors in dispersed locations and times, while also offering a nuanced form of articulation. For example, complex phenomena such as strategies are conveyed through texts. As shown, texts also provide sites of authorization and contestation. Whereas conventional ('read only') texts perform temporal agency across time and space, partly due to the structuring qualities of language (Smith 2001), the temporal agencies of media such as Twitter warrant attention, because they have demonstrated the ability to mobilize event formations of considerable momentum.

6.8 Tacit Articulation

Probably one of the least studied aspects of practitioners, and especially of managers, is their ability to pursue certain courses of action while being aware of alternative courses of action. It is as though the urge of researchers to lock human behaviour into mutually exclusive categories has prevented them from fully appreciating that practitioners are able to work with multiple contingent courses of action (Hernes and Irgens 2013). Analyses of management have tended to associate a course of action, such as a strategy, with certain sets of goals or intentions without exploring the alternative courses of action that were present to the actors in question, but which were purposely not pursued. Such assumptions have led to debates for or against rational decision making where, for example, March argues that actions and goals are loosely connected or even sometimes contradictory. But such arguments rest on the assumption that one can analytically relate certain actions to certain goals and ignore the possibility that human actors operate with several contingent sets of goals and actions. Teece (2012: 399), for example, reports that in an interview, Steve Jobs said the following about pursuing possibilities at Apple:

Apple is a very disciplined company, and we have great processes. But that's not what it's about. Process makes you more efficient. But innovation comes from people meeting up in the hallways or calling each other at 10:30 at night with a new idea, or because they realized something that shoots holes in how we've been thinking about a problem. It's ad hoc meetings of six people called by someone who thinks he has figured out the coolest new thing ever and who wants to know what other people think of his idea. And it comes from saying no to 1000 things to make sure we don't get on the wrong track or try to do too much. We're always thinking about new markets we could enter, but it's only by saying no that you can concentrate on the things that are really important.

Shotter argues, based on Polanyi's work, that human actors may well pursue a line of action while being aware of alternative lines of action: 'While being "focally aware" of the responsive whole resulting from us "looking over" what is before us, we have ignored the background structure of anticipations (of which we are only "subsidiarily aware") that guide us as we actively "do" the relating of ourselves to our surroundings' (2006: 597–8).

Whereas Polanyi focused on individual actors, I suggest extending the idea of tacitness to social processes, somewhat in the way that Nonaka and Takeuchi (1995) suggest mechanisms of tacit knowledge development take place between the individual and the social. Nonaka and Takeuchi focus on knowledge transfers and conversion, but the concern here is to understand the tacit processes that articulate organizational meaning structures. Tacitness is taken to mean that which is collectively thought, felt, or implied without being stated in social interaction. In groups, mindful attention is also directed at issues that are not explicitly articulated, although in the research literature focus tends to be given to explicit articulation, which serves as a basis for concerted action. However, it is that which is not explicitly articulated which is what resides in people's minds as to what might be done alternatively, or done differently.

In a study of Hugo Boss, a luxury fashion and style house, Vangkilde (2012) shows how innovation in design is social and distributed, rather than bestowed upon an individual chief designer, and also how it relies on collective intuition and sensing. At Hugo Boss, he argues, many individuals develop a sense of, or intuition about, what is going on in the business at any one time, without this being explicitly articulated. The temporal dimension of articulation is crucial, because the work of sensing includes extending what Hugo Boss is about, which could be seen as a meaning structure (or multiple meaning structures) embedded in the past while pointing towards the future. Vangkilde (2012: 21) cites a creative director as saying:

For me, the thing that I think is right is to create our own identity. Taking the risk—because this is always a risk, at least in the beginning—to be different from everybody else. The risk is that people will say that 'I don't like it' or 'I don't buy it.' But then, on the other hand, the advantage of this is that people understand what you want to do. And that is the most important thing that has happened to us.

Making people in and outside the company understand what it is about takes place through explicit and sometimes tangible articulation, such as through talk, artefacts, surveys, and campaigns. Trend reports, for example, contain data-enabling forecasting of anticipated styles and fashions (and occasionally relate what was anticipated concerning past trends). But, some of the staff whom Vangkilde cites explain that they also rely on intuitive sensing of what is currently going on, or what they call zeitgeist or spirit of the time.[16] This intuitive sensing, which extends well beyond trend reports, while being tacit and difficult to express, nevertheless enables them to determine specific fashion directions to pursue. This is possible only by being highly attentive to the world and knowing a great deal about what is happening in the present. It is, Vangkilde suggests, almost bodily knowledge that is so '[…] profoundly incorporated that you just feel it'. (p. 139). Vangkilde's tentative conclusion is that understanding of the spirit of the time remains to be developed, and that it may tell us exactly how people such as designers and product developers, possessing the spirit, feel able to decide, almost by instinct, what to do (p. 139).

'Catching the zeitgeist' may take on historical proportions, as shown in the following extract taken from Erik Larson's 2004 book, *Devil in the White City*, which describes the preparations for the 1893 world trade fair in Chicago. Until then the famous Paris fair of 1889, at which the Eiffel Tower figured as part of the exhibition, had caused worldwide excitement. Chicago, having suffered a devastating fire in 1871, was in need of establishing an identity as an emerging modern city. Thus was born the idea of creating a world fair that would become historical by its audacity, originality, and sophistication. Daniel Burnham, the chief architect, was one of the main organizers and visionaries of the project, which seemed to overwhelm even the invited architects from New York, who had been invited to prepare drawings of designated buildings within the concept of a white city, evocative of ancient Rome. The following is an excerpt describing the situation at which the architects revealed their respective drawing to one another,

All the architects, except Sullivan, seemed to have been captured by the same spell, although Sullivan later would disavow the moment. As each architect unrolled his drawings, 'the tension of feeling was almost painful,' Burnham said. St Gaudens, tall and lean and wearing a goatee, sat in a corner very still, like a figure sculpted from wax. On every face Burnham saw 'quiet intentness.' It was clear to him that now, finally, the architects understood that Chicago had been serious about its elaborate plans for the fair. 'Drawing after drawing unrolled,' Burnham said, 'and as the day passed, it was apparent that a picture had been forming in the minds of those present-a vision far more grand and beautiful than hitherto presented by the richest imagination.'

As the light began to fade the architects lit the library's gas jets, which hissed like mildly perturbed cats. From the street below, the top floor of the Rookery seemed aflame with the shifting lights of the jets and the fire in the great hearth. 'The room was as still as death', Burnham said, 'save for the low voice of the speaker commenting on his design. It seemed as if a great magnet held everyone in its grasp'.

The last drawing went up. For a few moments afterward the silence continued.

Lyman Gage, still president of the exposition, was first to move. He was a banker, tall, straight-backed, conservative in demeanor and dress, but he rose suddenly and walked to a window, trembling with emotion. 'You are dreaming, gentlemen, dreaming', he whispered. I only hope that half the vision may be realized.'

Now St Gaudens rose. He had been quiet all day. He rushed to Burnham and took his hands in his own. 'I never expected to see such a moment', he said. 'Look here, old fellow, do you realize this has been the greatest meeting of artists since the fifteenth century?'

The situation, although hardly being descriptive of many situations that any of us are going to experience, shows how there may be a collective feeling of something going on that is not made explicit, yet it is felt by actors present. The actors may direct their focal attention on what they are doing (e.g. their respective drawings), while their subsidiary attention may be directed at something far less tangible, yet just as real; the grandeur and impact of the exhibition to be realized.

In social terms, tacitness refers to those articulations that are not visibly pursued through socially committed acts.[17] The social tacitness may be seen to represent articulations that are historically embedded as opportunities in the making, as articulations that might have been different from those made. As organizational meaning structures are subjected to contingent yet relatively stable trajectories of events of articulations, a socially constructed reservoir of possibilities builds up, ready to be articulated when the time is ripe.

Hatch's (1999) analysis of improvisational jazz offers some insights into how processes of tacit articulation operate. She describes how listening plays a major role in improvisation over a theme (which is an open structure characterized by, for example, subtlety, implicitness, and ambiguity). Listening, while expecting that things might turn out differently than expected, challenges musicians to continually make sense out of unexpected sound patterns as they emerge, and rather than try to contain 'wrong notes', they focus on the context of an unexpected note, which may sometimes produce a novel idea. The temporality of improvisational jazz becomes important, as the ability to anticipate and accommodate unexpected moves is experience based. I suppose that for most jazz bands the past is collective, in the sense that certain emergent 'wrong notes' may evoke a shared memory of improvisation and production of novelty, without leaving the 'groove'[18]—that which helps them to feel the structure of the music inside themselves and which enables them to create novelty by departing from predictable patterns (Hatch 1999). In fact, Hatch notes that, 'As the past is invoked with the playing of a head, so too is anticipation of the improvising to come, thus the future is invited into the present via expectation created by recollection of similar experiences in the past' (p. 93). While being a social process, improvising on the basis of past experience appears to rely on tacitness. Hatch illustrates how, with its emphasis on continuous sensory and bodily engagement, jazz shows how novelty can emerge. The engagement, however, is both directed at that which is taking place and that which might take place. In other words, it exhibits both actuality and potentiality. The actuality is what is experienced by the spectators as they listen to the performance, but the potentiality of how it could turn out differently is mainly reserved for the musicians, through their ongoing tacit sensory and bodily engagement.

Tacit articulation may point towards that which is in the making, ready to be applied. It represents socially stored but not necessarily enacted knowledge of historical opportunities. Hence it refers to the not (yet) realized consequences of pursuing opportunities. Tacit articulation represents a richness of understanding that surpasses that of consciousness, because it refers to both the actual and the potential, both to actualized and non-actualized potentialities.

Acting routinely while mulling over other possibilities is actually what managers do most of their time, according to Weick (1984),[19] which is possible as human actors apply subsidiary awareness to provide an 'anticipatory sense' of what is to come next in an ongoing process. I pointed out earlier in the book that meaning structures become meaningful because they offer choice, however forced the choice may appear. Moreover, a process view considers organizational life to exhibit potentiality as well as actuality by assuming that, although a certain course is pursued, things may yet turn out otherwise. Taken together these two points imply that, although a certain course of action is pursued, there are forces at work, accumulated over time, that point out an alternative course of action, while continuity still prevails; in other words, a change in the making. This, I suggest, is the work of tacit articulation, which, although it is not manifest in conscious organizational memory, represents possibilities of the meaning structure being articulated otherwise by enabling novel elements or categories of elements (Jones et al. 2013). Most of the time, tacit articulation takes place in relation to practice represented by repetition.[20] Over time, tacit articulation accumulates knowledge about the actual and the potential, which serves to guide the emergence of change.

Tacit articulation represents accumulation of unrealized possibilities, which means that, although it may be shared in the sense of being similar between individuals, it resides with individuals, which is why innovation tends to be a solitary journey, at least in its initial stages. In the case of Ulstein the X-BOW was a possible, as yet unrealized opportunity, which could only be understood conceptually before it was developed further. It was grasped tacitly as a possibility at several presents before it was finally articulated as a meaning structure element by the people of the Ulstein Group.

6.9 Events and Meaning Structures

In the present, articulation directed towards meaning structures is perceived as undifferentiated, while the various gestures and utterances during that present are made meaningful in the way that they articulate the meaning structure. For example, a colleague may point towards a bullet point on a PowerPoint slide and articulate that point as distinct from other bullet points, and related reactions by others present may make the distinction provisionally determinate and meaningful. It is nevertheless as the living present becomes an event that the processes at the present become provisionally determinate in relation to the broader meaning structures. The meaning structures are organizations, that is, the nouns-in-the-making that take shape for those actors who are involved in articulatory work, and their change and continuity are understood as the ways in which meaning structures are upheld and altered. Events exhibit temporal agency in view of their ability to frame other events (both past and future) so that the organizational meaning structure is upheld and modified.

Although actors experience time as an ongoing present, every present is subject to provisional closure and becomes an event attributed thing-like characteristics with the passing of time. Closure is provisional, as the event enters the event formation, seen as a manifold. Based on a study of how social media take part in shaping the collaboration between Novo Nordisk, a Danish pharmaceutical company, and its stakeholders, Tunby Gulbrandsen (2012: 49) concludes that:

the meaning formation process between the organization and its stakeholders is organized as a collaborative networked bricolage, where individual texts, pictures, videos, links, like's and dislike's are remixed and reassembled by the different actors, both individually and collectively, in ways they at any given time 'see fit'. [...] As such, individual contributions become a collective story about what and who the organization is. Not because the individual contributions always directly relate to each other, nor because they reflect the same attitude or sentiment, but because they are all concerned with the same matter—Novo Nordisk. On an individual level the communicative process may seem fragmented and disparate, but on a collective level, a network level, they converge. The communicative process does not, in other words, play out like a chain of events, but as a networked process.

Seeing events as networked rather than as succession is somewhat consistent with Whitehead's thinking about events[21] and represents an advance from a view of events taking place in temporal succession. More than anything it highlights the fact that events take place in a field rather than as a string of events, a point made by Rüling (2011) in his study of festivals.

Still, the actual work performed in articulating meaning structures while framing other events, both in the past and in the future, remains to be studied more closely. When, for example, in an encounter between different people, elements of the meaning structure are articulated, such as through a discussion of the relationship between a key technology and staff turnover; these two elements—technology and staff—are articulated in the encounter. At the same time the encounter (or meeting) mirrors other encounters. First, the discussion picks up topics and agendas from other meetings and, by the same token, projects topics and agendas for future meetings. Second, the meeting reflects the articulated meanings of other meetings in the past, as well as various other, related events; in so doing, it becomes a meaningful event as well. In other words, the meeting becomes a meeting through its mirroring of other, related meetings and events. Moreover, the ways in which this mirroring is done influences how future meetings are held, that is, how, and around which topics and according to which agendas. Events, seen from this view, become constitutive of one another in the sense of being given the power to establish or give existence to one another while becoming constitutive of one another by reproducing similar basic underlying traits or themes found in the meaning structure.

Events are spatio-temporal, in the sense of being positioned in time while being associated with entities, for example when a meeting is associated with certain people having made a decision around a certain agenda. The event at which the ship-owner CEO said during his meeting with designers at Ulstein, 'I want you to build it for us', set the stage for a whole new company development process. Later events in various parts of the organization both reinforced that event and added to it, while also becoming events in the mirror[22] of that and other related events. The X-BOW came in many ways to represent the meaning of that event. As the organization grew again around the concept of the X-BOW and related concepts (such as energy-saving concepts), other events in and around organizational functions reinforced the initial event while themselves becoming spatio-temporal events. The X-BOW may be seen as an element of meaning of the 'new Ulstein organization', occasioned by the encounter with the customer representative and re-enacted in multiple other settings.

Events also become inextricably intertwined with the meaning structures they articulate. It may be possible, during a living present, to distinguish articulation from meaning structure. For example, during a PowerPoint presentation the relationship between new technology and unexplored market potential may be articulated, and the PowerPoint articulation may be differentiated from the meaning structure elements, such as when oral comments are made as to the relevance or correctness of the data in the PowerPoint presentation. However, with the passing of time, the event involving the PowerPoint presentation and the oral dialogue around it become one bundle of articulatory modes, acts, and the associated meaning structure elements related to that one event. The thingness of the event enables it to be retained in the event formation, and its meaning may be modified as it becomes related to other events.

An event is understood by provisionally fixing the identities of the actors related to the event, during that event. The temporal aspect of the event includes the temporal reach in terms of evocation and projection into the future in terms of other events. However, distinctions between spatial and temporal aspects are likely to disappear with passing time as the event blends into the meaning structure. The actual temporal reach of one event, for example, cannot readily be distinguished from the temporal reach of other events, because as events happen they become entangled with spatial factors. Still, it is possible—indeed useful for organization studies—to analyse how events come to incorporate the articulatory modes and agendas of other events.

As events blend into their associated meaning structures they become constitutive of the spatio-temporal entanglement that is experienced as 'the organization'. As events they are no longer experienced as living presents: they become entities available for re-definition with the passing of time. In Whitehead's vocabulary they become 'data' for later events. As data they take on a status similar to the elements of the meaning structures they are associated with. In addition, as new events articulate meaning structure elements, they articulate previous events by the same token, since meaning structures are de facto accumulations of articulatory events categorised into quasi-stable meaning structure elements (event-objects). A piece of technology, for example, represents the accumulation of events in the form of encounters between actors (material, social, human, and conceptual) around that technology over time. While evoked as taking part in past events, the technology is articulated in the present in relation to a broader meaning structure of quasi-stable elements.

The organization, the nouns-in-the-making, is the becoming of the spatio-temporal entanglement of events and elements. It is not, however, a moving entanglement, but a becoming entanglement. If it were seen to be moving, that would signify that the observer stays in one place from which the entanglement is seen to move. Instead, it is seen in view of its possibilities, just like when we see our careers, we see them as temporally generated trajectories in view of possibilities, past and future. This is what characterizes the organization in the world on the move.

Part III

Process Theory and Selected Aspects of Organization and Management

■ **SUMMARY**

In this part, consisting of three chapters, the framework developed in previous chapters is applied to a few selected topics in organization and management studies. The discussion shows how the temporality aspect of the framework in particular can be used to recast, refine, or redefine some central notions in the selected topics. The topics are organizational continuity and change, management and leadership, and organizational culture, identity and institutions.

7 Process Theory, Organizational Continuity, and Change

■ SUMMARY

This chapter discusses the implications of temporality for organizational continuity and change. Taking an endogenous view of process, as done in the book, enables change to be seen as a change in the experience of becoming of the present–past–future relationship. In relation to the framework of the book, change may be seen as the emergence of novel elements of the meaning structure, occasioned by rearticulation.

> We say, 'The wind is blowing,' as if the wind were actually a thing at rest which, at a given point in time, begins to move and blow. We speak as if the wind were separate from its blowing, as if a wind could exist which did not blow.
>
> (Elias 1978: 112)

> Indeed, the 'change' that is synoptically explained ex post facto is *experienced* by practitioners as an unfolding process, a flow of possibilities, and a conjunction of events and open-ended interactions occurring in time. If we are to understand how change is actually *accomplished* (Eccles et al. 1992), change must be approached from within—not as an 'abstract concept' (James 1909/1996, p. 235), but as a performance enacted in time.
>
> (Tsoukas and Chia 2002: 572)

> Without change there is no history; without regularity there is no time.
>
> (Kubler 2008: 72)

In the mainstream organizational literature organizational change is associated with change in the ways in which things are organized, while implying an atemporal view of organizations as tools. In its most basic form, organization refers to the pure instrumental condition of a task system. The verb 'organize' derives from the Latin word *organum*, which refers to 'instrument'. The Latin word *organa* derives from the Greek word *organon* which relates to implement, tool, musical instrument, organ of sense, organ of the body, related to *ergon*: work (Chambers 1988). The view is parallel to an assumption of 'the in-here versus the out-there' discussed in chapter 2, where the in-here is the cause and the out-there, the effects of the cause. In the example of the blind man and the stick taken from Bateson (1978), the stick would be seen as the effect of the hand, and the line of analysis would be drawn at the skin of the hand. However, that would deprive the analysis of showing how movements of the stick are related to corresponding movements of hand and arm in time. A process view, on the other hand, would regard the coming together of cause and effect, that is, how the stick and the body relate to each other in time. In addition it would focus on actual as well as potentially connecting movements between hand and stick.

Viewing actors as caught in the flow of time implies a world of *continual* movement. Movement, as Bergson insists, is not a succession of displacements, punctuated by imaginary stops. Movement, he points out, is *indivisible* because it takes place in time and time cannot be reduced to a number of stops. Similarly, Mead insists on the experience of the continual emergence of the present as the temporal experience. The feeling of movement related to the present provides a feeling of an emerging present. To Mead, as with Bergson, there are no stops or arrests of movement, because movement is all there is. This is why Achilles will inevitably overtake the tortoise in Zeno's famous parable. Achilles undertakes one continuous movement from the beginning of his race until the end of his race, at which he finishes before the tortoise. His race is not to be seen as an infinite number of stops at which he looks back on the distance run and the distance to run.

As noted above, the idea of meaning structures is meant to capture not just the actuality of things but also their potentiality, translated as connecting possibilities. Studying organizational change would imply studying how organizational practices articulate the coming into being of actors, including technologies, markets, regulations, and institutions, much like studying how the arm articulates the stick. An implication of such a view is that adding a customer group would in itself be an act of change, as it would mean that articulatory practices would be altered. The arrival of a new customer group signals change, not because it necessarily leads to change in the organization itself, but because it leads to change in the ongoing work of connecting. In our study of LEGO, Majken Schultz and I (Schultz and Hernes, 2013) found that LEGO effected important changes by closing down recently developed product lines while expanding their traditional product range. To mainstream customers, not much had changed, since they could still find more or less the same products as previously. Not much tangible change took place within the organization, except for an expansion of production volumes, the addition of production lines in various countries, and a re-thinking of their logistics system. What did change, at least for key actors within LEGO, was the way they related to their own past. The ways in which they articulated their meaning structures changed, resulting in connecting differently with emerging stakeholders compared to previously. In other words, re-articulation meant going back to what they had been doing in terms of product ranges up to that time, while seeing those product ranges in relation to modified meaning structure elements, such as suppliers, storehouses, and wholesalers.

What had changed at LEGO was the overall disposition towards their past–present–future. Seen through the eyes of mainstream change theory the change was unspectacular, but seen through the eyes of those involved, the change was spectacular. What was experienced as particularly important was the fact that many potential avenues were eliminated, such as brand extensions into products more or less vaguely related to the LEGO bricks. What made a difference to those involved was the change in the *becoming* of the organization, not its actual *being*. To them LEGO was revealing itself in the light of its novel opportunities of becoming, including their past. People at LEGO experienced the movement as changing, and not so much its punctuated states. To them, Achilles was overtaking the tortoise.

When the organization is seen as an organon, this conception of change does not readily come across. This is not a problem of the change being unimportant, because it is important to involved actors: no one can contest their experience of the importance of change. Rather, it is the problem of how change is conceptualized, while avoiding the assumption that time takes place as discrete segments of time or periods. Consequently, if such change (and continuity) is going to be accounted for in an organizational analysis, concepts need to be used that correspond to the ongoingness of organizational life.

The assumption of endogeneity and immanence in process thinking might at first sight seem to prevent it from explaining change. Whitehead held that, since the future is immanent in each present occasion, no future occasion can be in existence. He also held that anticipatory propositions are necessarily rooted in the present and the necessities inherent in it (Whitehead [1933]1967: 193). To some people this would not make the theory especially potent for explaining organizational innovation or change. It would seem that the theory is at best able to explain continuous change (Tsoukas and Chia 2002; Weick and Quinn 1999) in a Heraclitian manner, whereby no act or event can be identical to the one that preceded it, due to the passing of time. The idea that process thinking embraces a world of continuous, ubiquitous, and never-ending change comes partly from a need to contrast process theory with its 'adversary', that is, entitative assumptions about the world, according to which the world exists as successive conditions of stability punctuated by change. The abhorrence of such views tends to lead process thinkers to suggest that change is all there is, an idea process thinking can wholeheartedly embrace. Hartshorne (1987: 398) writes, for example:

The argument against the process view has been, 'If there is change, something, X, must have changed from state A to state B.' Very well, suppose the weather changes from wet to dry, does this mean there is an entity, the weather, as concrete as the wet and dry states? Are these in the weather? Surely the weather is in them. Suppose 'public opinion' changes, or 'the situation' changes—is it not obvious that the 'subjects of change' here are relatively abstract entities? Process philosophy generalizes this insight. It treats change as the successive becoming of events related to one another, but also differing from one another in some more or less abstract respects which interest us.

Still, the inevitability of incremental change should not prevent us from examining the possibility of explaining more substantial change from a process theory perspective. The only thing to remember is not to fall into the temptation of speaking about a changing 'thing', such as an organization (Hernes 2008) because that would assume that the organization is viewed as an entity in itself.

In organizational life there are myriads of presents every day at which the pattern of past and future events may be attempted redefined, or redirected. This is what accounts for the omnipresence of change and makes room for Tsoukas and Chia's (2002) argument that change is the rule and not the exception in organizations. In fact, they argue that the pervasiveness of change makes it possible for an organization to appear stable, which is similar to the argument made by March (1988), that organizations are able to keep up an appearance of consistency while carrying out many loosely connected inconsistent acts. This is shown nicely in the imagery that Tsoukas and Chia (2002) borrow from Bateson on the micro movements of a tightrope walker, which for her represent ongoing change, but which appear on the whole as stability when viewed from afar:

> For example, at a certain level of analysis (or logical type)—that of the body—the statement 'the acrobat maintains her balance' is true, as is also true the statement 'the acrobat constantly adjusts her posture,' but at another level of analysis—that of the *parts* of the body. The apparent stability of the acrobat does not preclude change; on the contrary it presupposes it.
>
> (Tsoukas and Chia 2002: 572)

But even this imagery of micro movements, has its temporal aspects. When the acrobat readjusts her posture she makes a change from the posture that immediately preceded it. She changes the 'vector' (i.e. the intensity and direction of a movement) that represented the movements up to the moment of adjusting her posture. She re-directs the vector of her bodily movement so that it points towards the new posture. What she has at her disposal is the mental and physical concentration in the present that enables her to mobilize the muscular movements to ensure a continued posture, readjusting the present past-to-future vector. In a similar way actors in organizations make changes in myriads of 'presents'. Every little change may be seen as a 'bending' of the past–future relationship as actors resort to materials of the present (Schultz and Hernes 2013) to bring forward aspects of the past in an ongoing process of translating them into prospects for the future. Just as with the tightrope walker, however, bending the past requires work.

Seeing organizations as assemblies of tightrope walkers, however, may amount to saying that no consequential change ever takes place. Consequential change comes about, not through myriads of infinitesimal changes, but as streams of related events, not dictated or planned by supreme decision makers, but through contingencies that are partially intended and partially emergent. Using Whitehead's (1929a) term 'prehension', one could say that events 'grasp' for each other,[1] as prehension relates to the propensity of an event to connect to another event with which it has common aims. Commonality of aims, however, is produced by the connecting of events. This is how events achieve some degree of mutual agency, and this is how the mutual making of events may or may not create substantial change.[2] Change takes place, according to Whitehead, as each event takes in all the frozen data from its predecessors and adds novel feelings of its own. For example, in the LEGO case, the move to re-introduce LEGO bricks as the exclusive future strategy came in the wake of a report by MIT researchers that the LEGO CEO had requested that firmly established the virtues of the LEGO bricks over electronic media.[3] The report was referred to in arguing for the new strategy and was considered a strong 'ally' in paving the way for the new strategy. The drawing up and reception of the report may be seen as a decisive event for the preparation of the strategy that fed into its becoming an event-object and element in the LEGO meaning structure.

For something to be experienced as change there has to be a feeling of difference. Mead (1938: 347) refers to disruption, or interruption, as a basis for experience. Without disruption, 'there would be merely the passage of events' (Mead 1938: 346), and mere passage does not constitute change:[4] 'Stating the position generally, until there occurs an interruption in the act such that a certain content in the field persists while other contents shift, there will be no lasting content and no lasting experience' (Mead 1938: 347). If an act is not accompanied by a feeling of difference it means that the meaning articulated by the act is not noticeably different from the meaning articulated by past acts. This is what Mead (1938) refers to as 'timeless spaces' as, with the absence of interruption, there is no sense of time. However, with interruption and the distance from an event created by the passing of time, change is experienced, as it becomes possible to perceive that a change is taking place compared to a past condition. As Mead explains, 'Change involves departure from a condition that must *continue in some sense to fulfill the sense of change from that condition*' (Mead 1938: 332, italics added). At the same time, interruption enables continuity to be experienced. Again, Mead (1929a: 239) argues that 'Without this break within continuity, continuity would be inexperienceable.[5] The content alone is blind, and the form alone is empty, and experience in either case is impossible.' We may infer that the 'break within continuity' suggested by Mead means a break in what 'frames' an act or event and not necessarily a change in the act or event itself. In other words, a change signifies a modification of the prevailing structure of meaning.

The break is not, of course, a break at the time it is experienced, but an event that is seen as decisive when related retrospectively to other events. Yet the break is a necessary imaginary point that works as a basis for the narrative of how a certain trajectory of change took hold and developed over time. In Mead's (1938: 347) words: 'The break reveals the continuity, while the continuity is the background for the novelty.' As pointed by Simpson (2009) in her discussion of Mead's temporality, reflexive thinking may be stimulated when some obstacle arrests or inhibit the flow of action, in which case the objective becomes to find a way of continuing the activity in some form or other. The emergence of something different is not a break per se, except in the minds of some people as a possibility, perhaps as a remedy to a problem that has occurred. It is during the time following an act that the act is given explanatory power in the event formation and takes part in shaping the past of that course of change.

The idea of change in an absolute sense is something like an optical illusion, although a useful one at that. Yet, change is going on all the time. However, the ongoing change is change in the form of intuition more than reflection. Change, being an inordinately complex phenomenon may at best be intuited as it is taking place, intuition being that which best captures the elusiveness of being in time. In the present we may feel that change is happening, but reflecting upon change requires that temporal segments of history are drawn and compared. This brings me back to my point of divergence concerning Chia's statement previously referred to, that we are not good at thinking in terms of movement, my point being that movement is sensed. Change, on the other hand, is a schematized *trompe l'oeil* projected upon the process of experienced change. What needs to be done is to study how the schematized images of change make incursions into the processual reality of actors, what they do to the understanding of the past, and how they influence the expectations of the future.

There is nevertheless an emerging sense of change at the time, which, if it takes hold, slowly generates into a temporarily sustained emergence of change. Emergent change takes place through tentative rearticulation of meaning structure elements that reveals the emergence of novel elements. Seen from a process view, change takes place through the emergence of novel elements, which provide a sense of *changing* (rather than change) of the meaning structure. If they are to lead to change, however, emerging elements require sustained articulation, enabling an event formation that involves the new element, as a constitutive and repeated element associated with events.[6] The emergence of an idea in a meeting, for example, is likely to disappear unless it is used verbally and perhaps materially uses artefacts to articulate parts of the organizational meaning structure. Once it becomes an object of sustained intersubjective articulation over a duration of time, it may qualify as a potential meaning structure element. Becoming an actual element of the meaning structure, however, requires that it acquire an identity as an autonomous element, enabling it to form relationality with other meaning structure elements and to form part of a larger whole. Emergence is more likely to succeed if there is a certain density of concordant events over time at which it is articulated as an element of the meaning structure. The event formation becomes crucial to the sustainability of the novel element by providing its participation in the meaning structure with historicity. Event formations imply precedents and antecedents involving the novel element, and provide it with temporal 'legitimacy' in alliance with other meaning structure elements.[7]

8 Managing and Leading in Time

■ SUMMARY

A practical implication of a temporal view for managers and leaders is that they act in the flow of time, which means, for example, that when they take over a new unit, they need to contend with the present–past–future relationship that people of the unit experience. Managers and leaders have a certain degree of choice of temporal focus in exercising their functions. In certain situations they may feel forced to escape the immediate past to revoke it at a later stage in time. The notion of 'vector' is introduced in this chapter, where leadership is seen as the ability to change the vector of the present–past–future relationship.

> Yet we look forward with vivid interest to the reconstruction, in the world that will be, of the world that has been, for we realize that the world that will be cannot differ from the world that is without rewriting the past to which we now look back.
>
> (Mead 1932: 37)

In his magnum opus *Being and Time*, Heidegger (1927) describes *Dasein* as constituted by time, and he uses the term 'thrownness' to underline that his notion of time is ontological: time belongs to the world, and *Dasein* finds itself as already being in the world. It is as thrown into the world that *Dasein* discloses to itself its own potentiality for being, and hence time is that which actually constitutes *Dasein*. Thrownness is useful for understanding leadership as it happens, because it locates leaders in a flow of time that is not wholly of their own making, but where they still feel that they have to make their mark, notably by articulating how the future makes sense in relation to the past. This, of course, is not necessarily done explicitly, nor are leaders necessarily conscious of doing that. At the Ulstein Group, for example, people told me that their much-respected CEO, later chairman of the board, Idar Ulstein, would repeatedly speak of the importance of looking ahead and of investing in R&D to prepare for the future. When I asked them if he often spoke of the past, they could not recall that he often mentioned the past. On the other hand, he *represented* the past. Most people at Ulstein knew that after taking over as CEO in the 1970s, he had steered the company through rough seas, which had turned him into something of a myth, and meant that his views had become widely known. I infer from the interviews that he was seen as embodying the past, and by virtue of this embodiment, he could articulate the future and thus retain a considerable 'temporal arch' that was meaningful to most people involved with

Ulstein. Whereas his articulation forward in time was explicit, his articulation backward was more implicit and symbolic.

It is rare, however, for leaders to have the privilege to stay long enough to embody a long past while having the possibility to articulate well into the future. When taking over a function, most managers engage with an existing event formation that dates back some time and is already projected upon the future. In other words they step into a temporal stream in which past experience and future ambitions are already carved out. New leaders step into this stream of temporal patterning of the meaning structures and face various choices as to how to act.

When taking up new responsibilities, managers sometimes go through the ordeal of stepping into new and often unknown temporalities, as the unit they receive responsibility for has its own sense of historicity as well as its potential for the future. This creates a dilemma in changing its future (as a manager must often do), where the sensemaking of members refers to the past (Weick 2005). The dilemma is particularly acute as evoking memory is indispensible for making sense of future claims, while at the same time memory needs to be re-interpreted for a different future to take place.[1] New managers have various options open to them, including suppressing memory of certain past practices in their discourse, relying on the past and memory to forge a different future, or redefining the meaning of past experience and memory. The first option is risky, because suppressing memory may lead to reduced commitment among staff to new strategies for the future. This was observed by Krogstad and Unneland (2012), who show how a new CEO who took over a Danish media company partly suppressed existing organizational memory accrued under previous CEOs in an attempt to gain acceptance for a different future strategy. Krogstad and Unneland argue that, as long as the new strategy proved to work, his omissions of organizational memory might not harm his existence as CEO. However, these authors suggest that not paying attention to the organizational memory might cause the new strategy to be received with mere cautious commitment on behalf of the management team. If his strategy for the future were to fail because he had suppressed details of organizational memory, then the lack of commitment from management, partly based on his choice of suppressing memory, might well prove to backfire on him.

In general, the challenge of new managers is to connect events in the past to selected future ambitions in such a way that the patterns are visible and meaningful to those concerned with their management. If the aim is to ensure continuity, efforts might be directed at upholding a current event formation, but if the aim is to stake out a new future, it should entail articulating meaning structure elements in such a way that a different patterning of past events becomes visible. Evoking a certain technology and articulating that technology with a certain skill, for example, would entail articulating the technology with the skills in terms of events of encounter between the skill and the technology.

A manager wishing to stake out an alternative future should articulate encounters between technology and skills different from those normally assumed, in order to connect those encounters to a different event formation going from the past into the future. This would be a different strategy from, say, suppressing the past and focusing solely on the future.

Leadership may be seen as the power to bring to life and sustain belief in a certain event formation stretching into the past and into the future, but there may be times when the need arises to make a break, at least temporarily, with the past in order to create commitment towards a new future. Ødegård's research (in Hernes et al. 2013) suggests how, once Norway deregulated its electrical power market, electric companies quickly began to stake a future free of the relatively drab past with strict regulations and unattractive large-scale mechanical technologies. Harnessed with the verve similar to start-up enterprises, some companies quickly began diversifying their activities into new areas and acquiring new competencies in an attempt to replace the drab past with a more exciting future. Some twenty years later, however, some of the companies that were deregulated in 1991 have begun to take a more pragmatic view of the past they were once eager to leave behind, and look more favourably upon the future potential of some of their old practices. This suggests that what appears to be an unattractive past may not seem so with the passing of time, as events of that past enter an event formation in the era that ensues the break from the past. Events acquire their meaning from the event formation they become part of, which inevitably means that their meaning changes with the passing of time. It is possible that the passing of time, especially in industry, also enables the emergence of new possibilities, and as new possible events emerge on the horizon, past events take on new meanings as parts of the emerging event formation.

In some instances managers may strategically use timing to attempt to enlist events in an emerging event formation. In their seminal paper on power, Bachrach and Baratz (1962) draw attention to the exercise of power through what they call 'non-decision making', which may be done by indirectly influencing the choice as well as the non-choice of decision-making issues, which they referred to as 'mobilization of bias'. Thus they define power as 'the extent that a person or group consciously or unconsciously creates or reinforces barriers to the public airing of policy conflicts' (Bachrach and Baratz 1962: 949). Withholding an issue at one point in time, for example, may have another effect than withholding it at another point in time would have had, just as the duration between two points in time may be significant. In a similar way, Garud, Kumaraswamy, and Karnøe (2010) suggest that temporal agency may be manifest as actors sense appropriate moments to wait or strike, which, they suggest, allows actors to cultivate serendipity. In other words, by letting time pass, other possible events may appear on the horizon that enable a different meaning to be made of events that have already happened.

In so far as agency relates to a certain degree to collective intentions and is described in part by strategies, it becomes useful to employ imagery that includes directionality. I suggest that a useful imagery is that of 'vector'. It may be risky within a constructivist discipline to invoke the imagery of vectors, which in mathematics are depicted as a straight line with an arrow at the end and positioned in a two- or three-dimensional Cartesian system. The vector as a straight, neat line is not, however, meant to be a description of movement, but more like a descriptor of thrust. The vector is meant to serve no other purpose than as imagery in order to describe change within a process view.

The description of any organizational arrangement is done partly with the help of events and their formation, set against the background of its meaning structures. Meaning structures provide the means for living presents to enable both continuity and change, as continuity is provided by repeated articulation of the meaning structure, whereas change is signalled by change in articulation, including the emergence of novel meaning structure elements. Articulations of the meaning structure taking place in the present bring the meaning structure to life and provide it with a sense of movement, or becoming, as its elements and their inter-connectivity become suggestive of possibilities. The becoming of continuity and change takes place as continuous movement, where the meaning structure elements, while serving their structural purposes, take on changing meaning, and the event formation provides the meaning structure with a sense of movement and historicity. This is what constitutes organization in a world on the move.

Using vector imagery we might say that the event formation has a certain direction and intensity. By 'direction' I mean that its overall event formation is produced and re-produced by mutually consistent events. Intensity of the vector, a term I borrow from Whitehead,[2] refers more to the thrust, or the propulsive force of the event formation, reflected by its ability to enrol or convert other possible events into its trajectory. I imagine, for example, that certain institutional logics (Jones et al. 2013), technologies, or doctrines may provide an event formation with a high degree of intensity.[3] In a process view such as this, change means the change in the vector, meaning change in its direction or intensity. Change in direction may be affected by events that redefine the event formation such that a noticeable change in the patterns is felt or observed. Change of the direction of the event formation takes place along with change in the meaning structure; these two modes of change are inevitably linked to one another.

The vector imagery catches the ongoing nature of organizational life, because the vector is always there, in the present, indicating organizational becoming. Whereas the term 'becoming' is almost synonymous with the process philosophy developed by Whitehead, it is also a practical notion. I previously mentioned how, for example, Apple Inc. is valued in its becoming as well as its actual being by corporate analysts. In a similar way a vectorized image of organization may open for a concretization of becoming so it is not confined to the highly abstract notion as drawn from philosophy.

An organizational vector of becoming would in itself be in the making and never end as the finished arrow of direction and intensity found in the mathematical understanding of vectors. An organizational vector of becoming would also be multiple, in the sense of consisting of multiple vectors, each representing a different mode of articulation. The temporal spread of the vector would also be of interest. What is perceived as a straight vector of continuity in one temporal spread might be seen as a turning vector of change in different one. For example, a technology may be seen as changing rapidly within the spread of a few months, but the exhibition of relative continuity is seen within the spread of, say, several years. Intensity seems important, in that certain current patterns of events may be felt as projecting the organization decisively from a far past into a far future (such as Whitehead's experience of the conformation of Einstein's general theory of relativity in 1919), while providing curvature of the meaning of events in the present.

Still, as I have tried to illustrate with the case of Ulstein and the X-BOW, meaning structures may sometimes experience a jolt and the vector begins to take a turn, which is when a novel meaning structure element gets to be associated with certain events. This is when possible events involving novel meaning structure elements are prehended. Given the complexity of prehension I suggest that it is done through tacit articulation, at least initially, which involves observation and the use of intuition. Intuition is a result of experience, and in particular the succession of experiences at which non-realized possibilities are explored. Prehension is the early stage of incorporating a novel element into the meaning structure. The overall process of incorporating an element into the meaning structure may also involve phases of apprehension (making the element fixed) and comprehension (making the element intelligible).

Agency lies with the events created by managers or leaders and not with the person per se. An event may be seen to mark a difference when a new solution, topic, aim, or perspective is brought up. However, the event will not signal change unless it inscribes itself into an event formation that is perceived to be different from previous event formations. It is when the vector—the direction and/or intensity—of the event formation is 'bent' that change is experienced. A singular event may yield a prescient sense of change, like the feeling that something is in the air, but it is when the event formation vector is bent that actual change is perceived.

An interesting question relates to the temporal stretch across which prehension of events takes place. Most of the time events are connected which are within days, weeks, or months from the event in question. At decisive moments, however, events may be evoked that lie decades or centuries into the past. Similarly, a large temporal stretch into the past may correspond to a large temporal stretch into the future. Leaders hoping to leverage the past may sometimes refer to distant events to change the vector of the event formation. Distant events may be important because they have become legendary, for example Dr Martin Luther King, Jr's famous 'I Have a Dream' speech delivered during the March on Washington in August 1963. They may alternatively be important because they lie outside the reach of individual memories and hence be less controversial than if present organizational members had taken part in the event and might hold different interpretations of it. As a matter of fact, Luther King's slogan was seen as a cliché by one of his advisors at the time of preparing the speech in 1963. Events that have taken place so long ago that they are beyond living memory may be more easily 'fitted' into an event formation that points towards a radically different future.

In order to exercise leadership from a temporal view as presented in this book, some aspects of events and event formations may be worth considering. One aspect is that of a combination of articulatory modes. The modes suggested above are, as mentioned, merely ideal types of modes, the purpose of which is to help in the discernment of some basic characteristics when it comes to exhibiting agency upon the event formation in relation to meaning structures. As previously mentioned, events provide meaning structures with a sense of movement and historicity, and their agency relates to their ability to reproduce and modify the event formation related to a particular meaning structure. An example of combined articulatory modes may be found with Sutton and Hargadon's (1996) analysis of face-to-face situations in which prototypes from previous product development processes are used to develop new products. A prototype is typically given fixity, with its composition of sub-parts and technical specifications referred to as 'solidified intellect' by one of their informants (p. 699), into brainstorming sessions. With the added effects of inter-subjective articulation such sessions may prove decisive in generating novel designs based on existing models, as shown by their analysis.[4]

If we take into account the assumption of evanescence inherent in a process view, the question of persistence presents itself. Whitehead's (1925) notion of re-iteration has been referred to above, which does not signify repetition in the sense of sameness. Reiteration is a necessary (although not necessarily sufficient) condition for processual momentum to emerge and uphold itself. Multiple reiterations of certain types of events may make a difference to the temporary consolidation of a meaning structure. By concordant events I mean events that are consistent with one another in how they articulate the meaning structure, which elements are articulated, and how they are articulated with one another.

The proximity in time between events at which a particular meaning structure is articulated may matter. This is not to be taken as density as measured by clocks or calendars, but as experienced density. Any emotional sensation of a present is likely to wane if not re-iterated, and can only be reproduced by presents that come to be associated with that present as events. The mode of articulation that does this almost by default is practical articulation, which articulates meaning structures on an ongoing basis by its sheer momentum and habitual nature, but which may not arouse decisive feelings. It is a different matter with, for example, inter-subjective articulation, which, if it takes part in articulating frequently the same meaning structure elements, may exercise particular agency in terms of arousing emotions around a certain course of action. Managers have the possibility of exercising leadership precisely by arousing emotions at certain times. What is important in addition, is to understand the importance of events that are concordant with those presents at which emotions are aroused, so that 'the message' is experienced at other presents, without the physical presence of the manager. For example, attempts at organizational change tend to be unsuccessful, not because actors fail to see that they are needed or important, but because they tend to fizzle out as the energy and commitment around a course of action is not re-created at successive presents. It is quite striking how seemingly sensible and exciting attempts at staking out and implementing a certain course of action around a strategy wane for lack of sustained emotional commitment, whereas other attempts appear to be sustained. Luther King's memorable speech was given only once, but has been reiterated at numerous presents involving various articulatory modes throughout the world for fifty years. The original event is not seen as a cliché, although anyone trying to emulate it would be susceptible of making a cliché out of it. Still, although the speech was memorable, the process of change that it was meant to energize is far from accomplished.

9 Organizational Culture, Identity, and Institutions

■ SUMMARY

Organizational culture and identity, although deeply entangled with the temporality of organizational life, are not commonly analysed as temporal phenomena. In this chapter some ideas are developed about how the framework in the book may contribute to a temporality-based understanding of organizational culture and identity. A temporal view also enables the dynamics of institutions to be understood differently. Drawing upon an example, the notion of 'stubborn facts' derived from Whitehead is articulated in relation to the framework of the book.

9.1 Organizational Culture as Memory

As described earlier, meaning structure elements constitute tails of historicity stretching into the past. Culture is too large a subject to be treated in any depth in this book. I have earlier mentioned Pickering's use of the term 'culture' as various kinds of elements ('things of science'), such as skills, social relations, machines, instruments, scientific facts, and scientific theories. In organization studies, Schein's (1985) work on culture is foundational. History, learning, and shared experience are the main basis for the formation of organizational culture. Schein makes the point, for example, that stories form around critical events in the history of an organization, which may become shared in the form of stories between members with the passing of time. At a more general level, he points out that cultures evolve around particular technologies and markets. For example, particular divisions of a company may develop their separate sub-cultures following from different and separate historical trajectories over time. Schein emphasizes the importance of what he calls shared history as a basis for culture formation. Actually, his very definition of culture is a 'learned set of assumptions based on a group's shared history' (Schein 1985: 319). Moreover, cultures, according to him, will tend to exhibit varying degrees of strength and stability depending on the length and emotional intensity of their shared history.[1]

A more explicit temporal view of organizational life may serve to bring renewed attention to the actual dynamics by which cultures emerge from experiences in time. The ideas in this book point towards the importance of distinguishing between past, history, historicity, and historicizing. An organization's culture may be seen as a persistent locus of experience from repeated articulation of the meaning structure, which in temporal terms could be called 'memory'. An organizational memory tends to survive over time as a composite 'sediment' from successive articulations that synthesize the very meaning of the organization. Memory is strengthened by particular events and rituals, and involves symbolic acts and artefacts. Memory, however, although it accumulates as a retrospective phenomenon, is applied prospectively in an ongoing present. Schütz' idea of retention and protection is useful here, where retention is oriented towards the past and protection oriented towards the future. In a similar way we may speak of memory being both retrospective in its retrieval and projective in its application, as suggested earlier in the book.

Thus, memory is central to both continuity and change. Bergson, like Deleuze, conceived of memory and past in inner experience as a pure ongoing process not subject to preservation in any artificial form.[2] But memory, even at the individual level, can be very complex, even without the participation of artefacts. As we grow up and leave home, we sometimes face situations in which the wisdom of our parents is not instantly available and we may resort to asking ourselves, 'What would my mother or father do in a situation like this?' Imagining what they would have done is added to inner personal experiences. Likewise with life in organizations, the people who were present at decisive occasions in a distant past may no longer be with the organization, or may no longer be alive. Memory can then only be evoked indirectly. According to Schütz (1967: 209), memory involves using signs to evoke an extinct stream of consciousness:

Since my knowledge of the world of predecessors comes to me through signs, what these signs signify is anonymous and detached from any stream of consciousness. However, I know that every sign has its author and that every author has his own thoughts and subjective experiences as he expresses himself through signs. It is therefore perfectly proper for me to ask myself what a given predecessor meant by expressing himself in such and such a way. Of course, in order to do this, I must project myself backward in time and imagine myself present as he spoke or wrote.

Most memory in organizational life is indirect, in the sense that it refers to the experience of others, which, as Schütz writes, obliges actors to imagine the context of other actors' choices. Hence, evoking memory may take different forms, as shown by Schultz and Hernes (2013). Moreover this process can be carried out more or less consciously. A useful distinction to draw is to view memory as either being unconsciously embedded in organizational actions, routines, or programmes, or as conscious attempts to evoke past experiences (Cohen 1991). The great achievement of organizational life lies in its ability to make it possible for multiple actors to perform coordinated and often complex tasks without thinking about them. Practical articulation is performed almost subconsciously and provides people with what they need to keep doing what they are doing. This is what is referred to by some writers as procedural memory. In organizational life procedural memory is embedded in skills, practices, routines, or programmes. A key characteristic of procedural memory, as Moorman and Miner (1998) point out, is that it becomes automatic or unconsciously accessible. People may be aware that they perform practices conceived in the past, but are ignorant of how and why those practices emerged. This is also why procedural memory refers to process memory or memory of underlying skills for performing tasks (Moorman and Miner 1997).

The counterpart to procedural memory is declarative memory (Cohen 1991; Moorman and Miner 1997; Singley and Anderson 1989), which may be found in facts, events, or propositions (Cohen 1991; Moorman and Miner 1998; Singley and Anderson 1989) that are evoked and thus may become the object of re-interpretation. Declarative memory refers to a conscious search into the past in order to understand the context of past experiences[3] and requires intersubjective articulation. Occasions of evoking declarative memory are likely to become decisive events as they both provide a mirroring of events in a way not previously done and become by the same token perceived as central to a changing event formation. Whereas procedural memory provides for continuity of a certain culture, declarative memory may enable change, because it allows for reflection upon articulatory practices that give rise to the prevailing culture. Change requires conscious efforts to evoke experiences in order to make way for the modification or addition of meaning structure elements.

9.2 Organizational Identity as Spatio-Temporal Distinctions

The idea of becoming as opposed to being is slowly emerging in mainstream organization studies. For example, in the organizational identity literature, where temporality naturally becomes an issue, writers have suggested that rather than ask 'Who are we, or who have we been as an organization?', pertinent questions revolve around 'Who are we becoming as an organization?' (Corley and Gioia 2004; Gioia et al. 2000). Asking 'Who are we?' mainly means expressing who are we as opposed to the others, which may be other organizations, but also institutions or various stakeholders, such as customers. To ask 'Who are we?', is to assume that identity is a state of affairs at a given point in time and space. However, asking 'Who are we?' risks assuming the sort of one-to-one relationship with the external environment referred to earlier, which locks the actors into comparing their organizations at corresponding instants of time.

The idea of organizational identity offers considerable potential as a way of thinking about organizations, and not least for understanding their temporal dynamics. On the one hand, organizational identity provides ways to further develop process theorizing of organizations, because it brings attention to the drawing of distinctions. Zerubavel's (1993) point about the ways in which sense is made by carving up the world in delineated islands of meaning that form the basis for what we do, is important. However, the ways in which distinctions are drawn is more arbitrary than what tends to be assumed in mainstream organization theory. Identity refers to how distinctions are drawn among elements in organizational meaning structures. Moreover, because organizational members, and especially leaders, are concerned with the position of other organizations (such as competing firms), they will try and compare their own meaning structures with those of other organizations. This means that organizational meaning structures can be observed from different angles and positions, which is a point that has not yet been discussed in this book. It means, for example, that the part of a meaning structure that consists of strategies and technologies is seen differently by actors within the organization than actors within another organization. When the term 'within' is used here, it means in a temporal sense, not a spatial one. Being within an organization means to be concerned with the flow of time of that particular organization represented by its meaning structure. A focus on identity invites reflections on how lines of distinction are drawn, not just between meaning structures, but also within them.

On the other hand, the organizational identity literature may develop further by drawing upon insights in process thinking. The assumption of heterogeneity offered by meaning structures brings attention to the fact that organizational identity is about more than social identity and organizational form. For example, the organizational identity literature pays little attention to distinctions drawn between the technologies of different organizations. It would seem natural to assume, for example, that to people at Microsoft the distinction drawn between their software and Apple's is an integral part of their sense of identity. One explanation why the organizational identity literature has been somewhat mute on the heterogeneity of identity is the strong focus on social identity, exemplified by the question repeated in several works, 'Who are *we*?', or 'Who are *we* becoming?'. The idea of meaning structures offers a clarification of organizational reality through various distinctions, while maintaining a notion of coherence.

This brings up another element of the debate in the organizational identity field, which goes back to Albert and Whetten's (1985) definition of organizational identity as the central, distinctive, and enduring nature of an organization, a definition which has led others (e.g. Gioia et al. 2000) to question if identity should not be seen as changing rather than enduring. Such criticisms risk being somewhat misplaced from a process viewpoint, because identity, if it is to have any sense, would be seen as central, distinctive, and enduring, but without the assumption that identity approaches any stable, tangible form. To assume centrality means to assume that there is something unifying, which, in effect, allows the heterogeneous nature of identity to be appreciated. To assume distinctiveness is to invite consideration of where and how lines of distinction are drawn, and to assume endurance means to assume that certain aspects of the organizational identity are associated with extension in time and are reproduced across events.

The perspective taken in this book lends focus to the ongoing identity work taking place in time, and how identity is subject to the ongoing work at organizational presents, where the focus is on distinctions between meaning structure elements. Identity becomes interesting as a concept when actors, while articulating 'their' meaning structure elements, observe and draw distinctions to what they observe as other, or alternative, meaning structures in space or time. 'Other' meaning structures may be a past meaning structure of their own organization or a contemporary meaning structure associated with another organization, such as a competing firm. Assuming that a meaning structure may contain elements such as strategy, technology, structure, and routines, identity becomes a salient dimension, since it implies the drawing of distinctions to other meaning structures with similar types of elements. Strategy, for example, becomes a question of identity as and when it becomes an object of comparison with another strategy, either in the history of the same organization, or with a contemporary organization. The enduringness referred to by Albert and Whetten (1989) is subject to the persistence of the work of drawing distinctions in time and space.

Identity work could usefully be seen as 'distinction drawing operations' (von Foerster 1991). Events may be characterized by the distinctions drawn by the actors present as they observe the organization and the environment; alternatively, their own organization is brought forward from the past. Distinction drawing operations are self-referential in the sense that they are oriented towards the organization's self-productive features. At the same time, however, the distinction drawing enables alternative possibilities for connecting within the organizational meaning structure to be considered. This 'dual' situation is where actors observe not only the possibilities for reproduction, but also the possibilities for connecting to something different.

It would be opportune to see identity as both a temporal and spatial phenomenon. In a process view identity may be seen as established in time and space, but not as two separate dimensions. Instead temporal and spatial distinctions may be considered drawn at certain events. In an ongoing study Laurila, Paalumäki, and Hernes (2013) analyse how a Finnish company, which started as a subsidiary to a service corporation, tore away from the parent company and set up as an independent company in the cleaning services industry. With its unique cultural features, expressed through artefacts, company values, and visual identity, the company rapidly became successful in Finland after being established as an independent company (Paalumäki 2000). The event of tearing away from the parent company, the swift establishment of its own identity as compared to competitors, and the rapid and successful growth became seen as an essential aspect of its early history. With time, while still operating in Finland, less explicit attention was given to the early phases of the company, while more attention was given to comparison with national competitors in the relatively familiar landscape of Finland (Hernes et al. 2013). In other words, a spatial view took precedence over a temporal view of its identity. However, when the company expanded beyond the borders of Finland and set up a subsidiary in the Baltics, where the business landscape was much less familiar, the attention changed from being spatial—looking at competitors—to being temporal—looking back at their early past and its projection upon the future in the Baltic market. Somehow, when they set up in an unfamiliar region, they felt they had to become more explicit about their origins some fifteen years earlier. This example illustrates how identity, seen from a process view, may be understood both spatially and temporally. The point is, however, to locate identity work in time and establish both the spatial and temporal dimensions of the events that comprise the identity work.

9.3 **Institutions as Stubborn Facts**

On 21 October 1962 the coastal steamer *St Svithun* sailed up the Norwegian coast from the town of Trondheim.[4] With forty-nine crew and forty passengers on board, the ship had reached Folla, one of the most exposed sea crossings along the Norwegian coast, by evening. The sea was rough, as it often is on that stretch, especially in autumn and wintertime. Numerous underwater reefs combined with violent weather make Folla a particularly treacherous sea crossing. At the helm was a 17-year-old helmsman who had just been given the job after having served on ships in international waters. Also present on the bridge were the pilot and first officer. At one point the pilot gave the order to switch to 335 degrees north, which they had the habit of referring to as 35 degrees. The young helmsman, having sailed in international waters, was not aware of this abbreviated form and put the ship on a 35-degree course, which meant the ship was 60 degrees off course. With the rough weather and autumn darkness the bridge crew only had lighthouse signals and their familiarity with the contours of the rugged mountains and islands to navigate by.

All seemed right to the crew on the bridge (but their perceptions effectively deviated 60 degrees from one another); since they had faith in the correctness of the course and were even able to 'recognize' the landmarks they had passed on numerous previous occasions, they did not consult the radar. Down on the passenger deck a local fisherman became doubtful about the direction of the ship. His knowledge of local weather conditions indicated that the direction of the wind at that time of the evening should have been coming from a different angle. Intuitively, he felt that something was wrong, and after some hesitation he decided to climb the companionway to the bridge.

At the top of the companionway he saw the officers on the bridge through the window and suddenly lost his confidence. Not only was the bridge forbidden area for passengers, but the sight of the uniformed officers with their rank insignia in front of their instruments probably overwhelmed him, and he decided to suspend his own judgement and trust theirs. As a result he turned around and descended the companionway to the passenger deck. For one brief moment he might have intervened and the misunderstanding that reigned between the pilot and the helmsman might have been resolved. Some minutes later, however, the ship ran aground on a reef and subsequently sank; it was way off course. The landmarks the officers had been looking at resembled those along the correct itinerary, but they were not the same. Not having double-checked the interpretations of the course, they both assumed that technically speaking they were on the right course, thus leading to their faulty recognition of the landmarks.

The fateful moment when the fisherman was standing outside the bridge and decided not to intervene had dramatic consequences. In his own personal trajectory of events, his perception of institutional authority led to a decisive moment, where the overwhelming material articulation (such as the uniforms, the helm, the instruments, and the bulkhead hatch), all sediments of institutions, prevented him from intruding.

This story illustrates how institutions can permeate processes with their own facticity. Mundane occurrences, such as technological innovations, need sustained articulations to make their way into organizational life, but institutions, in contrast, have a remarkable ability to penetrate organizational life of their own accord. A view, such as the one taken in this book, opens up for reflections of how institutions actually make ingressions into organizational life. How this happens has not been extensively dealt with in institutional theory applied to organizations, although also here there are attempts at engaging with the fluidity of organizational life. Lawrence, Suddaby, and Leca (2011), for example, make the point that those myriads of day-to-day instances where agency is played out in the face of fluidity and uncertainty are missing from institutional accounts. They suggest that institutional creation, maintenance, disruption, and change are played out during instances of this nature.

One problematic aspect of institutional theory is that analyses tend to reaffirm the power of institutions rather than investigate how they actually take part in the making, sustaining, or dismantling of other phenomena. While the above story illustrates how institutions may powerfully permeate processes, it directs attention to how their influence may or may not take place during certain presents. One issue that arises is how to describe the presence of institutions in such a way that their ingression into processes becomes available for analysis. Institutions are obviously complex phenomena; in view of the framework proposed in this book they may be seen as powerful meaning structures that lie beyond the organization in time and space and which are articulated into its activities as condensed structures in the form of 'facts'. I suggest Whitehead's notion of 'stubborn facts'[5] to describe the ingression of institutions into organizations. As suggested by Hosinski (1993: 23) in his analysis of Whitehead's work, stubborn facts cannot be evaded: they are what they are. In the form of a stubborn fact, an institution, once it becomes articulated into the organizational meaning structure, becomes a non-negotiable element, simply because it 'is what it is'. Hence the present experience 'becomes' in reaction to the stubborn fact as it has been encountered, while adding itself to the stubborn fact, rather than shaping the fact through articulation with other meaning structure elements. The insignia on the officers' uniforms on the bridge of *St Svithun* were signs of powerful institutions that lay outside the organization of *Saint Svithun*, but which nevertheless made an ingression into the present at which the fisherman hesitated about entering the bridge.

As stubborn facts, institutions may be subject to attempts to exclude or ignore them, or they may be enrolled as powerful actors through acts of articulation. In Hernes (2005) I report on a university recruitment process for a political science department that was shown to be consistently lopsided, in the sense that the same 'wrong' candidate was consistently ranked first by the successive decision-making bodies of the university (the department, faculty, and university boards); *post ante*, however, the university president recognized the inherently faulty treatment of the candidate. One explanation for the lopsidedness of the process was how the internal actors articulated various external institutional actors in relation to the case, such as by stating that the candidate was not 'political science' enough, thus invoking the field of political science as an institution.

Stubborn facts are powerful because they represent compact symbols of complex relations accumulated over considerable time and space (neither time nor space being seen in a linear sense), which accounts for their irreducibility. Their pervasiveness makes them unavoidable, to the extent that even if they are rejected, their rejection confirms their presence. In other words, their absence becomes a presence. For example, not to consult the trade union (if there is one) in a process of restructuring and lay-offs is to ignore trade unionism as an institutional member of the process and with the passing of time the restructuring process may come to be seen as an event where trade unionism was ignored. On the other hand, soliciting the trade union is likely to enable a different event pattern than if it were ignored.

10 Some Thoughts on Studying Process

> What really *exists* is not things made but things in the making. Once made, they are dead, and an infinite number of alternative conceptual decompositions can be used in defining them. But put yourself *in the making* by a stroke of intuitive sympathy with the thing and, the whole range of possible decompositions coming into your possession, you are no longer troubled with the question which of them is the more absolutely true. Reality *falls* in passing into conceptual analysis; it *mounts* in living its own undivided life—it buds and bourgeons, changes and creates
>
> (emphases in the original. James 1909, in Tsoukas and Chia 2002)

The aim of temporally based process research is to come to grips with the making of an organization in time, which implies engaging with the ongoing temporality of organizational life. An ongoing view of temporality implies deciphering how actors cope in a continual present, which, for purposes of thinking and acting, requires that the stream of experience is carved, re-composed up, and made sense of. In a nutshell, it is about being in the presents when events are made up of those presents. A question that immediately presents itself is that one cannot be there all the time and one is not at all likely to be there when important things take place, moreover it is not given that even if one is there, that the importance of the event is clear to the actors present. The fear of not being there at the right time, however, arises from a different logic than ongoing temporality. Because an ongoing view assumes that things are continually in the making, there can be no event that stands as decisive on its own. If it is to have impact, an important event will have to be mirrored in other events, including the ones that succeed it, otherwise it is not likely to be a significant event for the study of process.

Take, for example, the X-BOW event at Ulstein. When initial interviews were conducted at Ulstein, the X-BOW had been around for six to seven years. The likelihood of a researcher having been present when the first client ordered the first X-BOW is miniscule and, even if one had been present, there is no guarantee that the import of the event would have been realized. The significance of the event through the events that followed, including the model testing of an X-BOW model, served to silence critics both within and outside the company. In the eyes of some people at Ulstein the silencing of the external critics may be almost as important as the events that initiated the development of the design. The implication is that, even if the event was captured as it took place, the actual agency of the event could only really be assessed in the light of subsequent developments. This is what happens in real life: events are not critical in themselves, but are made critical with time. This point is consistent with Whitehead's insightful argument that the cause lies, not in the source, but in the effect. It is not just about re-interpreting the meaning of an event, but acting upon it so as to make it more critical than it would otherwise have been; allowing it to play out its eventfulness.

Studying process is about being within and without what is going on. It is about stepping into the stream of experience and stepping out of it, just as organizational actors do. It is about following actors in their presents and reconstructions as events; the making of eventness (Cunliffe et al. 2014) of those presents. Capturing the stream of experience requires being there in the present. Stepping out of that stream requires access to the processes of the spatialization of experience performed by those same actors. As pointed out previously, spatialization takes place as events are associated with the entities present, and simultaneity corresponds to the idea of the encounter between entities 'being there, then' as a point of departure for defining organizational presents. Simultaneity of the presence of entities is inferred retrospectively as constitutive of the event that emerges from the organizational present.

An obvious challenge is to capture the ongoing experience of individuals and to avoid representing their experience as a linear sequence of discrete moments in time, which would imply that researchers are outside the time they wish to study (Cunliffe, Luhman, and Boje 2004). At the same time, researchers can only hope to catch glimpses of the 'subject's' ongoing experience of time. This can partly be helped by enquiring not only about what happened and when it happened but about how past and future events were evoked/enacted/framed at certain moments in time. Asking about how events were evoked may enable respondents to think carefully about the processes of re-construction of the past and the future, and about how that reconstruction harboured possibilities of continuity and change. Part of the challenge lies in getting respondents into the 'temporal mode' of thinking and recall.

Organizational research gains access to organizational life through experience expressed by the acts of people in interaction with other people or with artefacts or texts. The idea of endogeneity of process or the organization in its own time means that acts are given meaning by the experience of the actors involved. This experience need not be direct, in the sense of a personal experience. In fact, most experiences that lie at the basis of acts were first-hand experiences for someone, whereas others have access to them through memory forms (Schultz and Hernes 2013), such as oral storytelling, artefacts, or written texts. As Sonenshein (2010) points out, narratives exist at both the individual and collective levels, which invites what he calls 'composite narratives', which involve the researchers' construction of an event on the basis of a group of individuals' narratives about that same event.

Composite narratives may reveal how entities are brought into contact with one another through their respective historicities. People in a boardroom experience the organization through the dynamics of the boardroom, socially speaking a micro-level phenomenon. This is also the case for those who experience it from the factory floor. People in the boardroom interpret macro-level data about the organization through the mangle of their socio-material dynamics. Likewise, actors on the shop floor experience the acts of the boardroom through the socio-material dynamics of the shop floor. The mutual effects of the two, however, can only be marginally understood by looking at how they perceive each other, because their data is neither raw nor simply interpreted for use by the actors in a single act. Instead they enter into the actors' (the board's, the shop floor's) history, a history that may extend from seconds to decades through a mixture of continuous impressions and distinct events. Whatever data they have about each other only begin to matter as and when the data begin to form part of their respective histories. What then becomes the focus of investigation in organizations is how data, or information, become translated and made into experience, which then becomes the respective historicities of the actors, which they draw upon for their own historicizing. The shop floor, the marketing department, the trade union (if there is one), management groups, consultants, families, stakeholders, customers, and authorities shape one another over time as they interact through various forms, sometimes directly, but most often indirectly. As each actor projects future intentions based on history, those intentions enter the experience of other actors.

Aims, actors, technologies, artefacts, texts, etc. are elements of meaning structures that form a tangled mass stretching into the past and the future. Different actors find their ways into their respective meaning structures. But meaning structure elements cannot independently take on temporal proportions, even though they may be seen as event objects, that is, as objects made of events of encounters with other objects. As pointed out already, what provides meaning structures with historicity are events, which connect into event formations. Meaning structures relate to event formations by providing them with recurrent themes. To understand the temporal dynamics of meaning structures a study of events becomes necessary, because they provide the structure with temporality. They provide an idea of how the meaning structure has evolved through articulations in the past and how it might evolve in the future.

The serendipities of organizational life, however, cannot be readily obtained through systematic recording. When things take an unexpected turn, linear data tend to become obsolete. Not only is it improbable that things take a surprising turn when research is going on, but *discovering* serendipities retrospectively is also unlikely. Actors tend to want to present changes as being part of a plan, not as emerging unexpectedly, and only exceptionally as undesired developments. It may take time and patience to tease out developments that arose unexpectedly, demanding that researchers go into a 'dwelling mode', as pointed out by Nair, Burt, and Chia (unpublished manuscript), which requires an orientation that is open, pragmatic, dispersive, and opportunity seeking. It also requires that researchers apply intuition while engaged in the sort of withness thinking suggested by Shotter (2006). A similar point is made by Alvesson and Kärreman (2007), who suggest that what they call mysteries and breakdowns in organizations are achieved through studies that are processual, emergent, and open, as well as empirically varied and rich. This, they argue, makes it more likely that established frameworks will break down and new, tentative, explanatory frameworks emerge. In referring to Merton and Barber's work on serendipity Alvesson and Kärreman refer to the need to take systematic advantage of what Merton and Barber (2006: 210) call serendipity or 'the art of being curious at the opportune but unexpected moment'. Studying process relies on looking out for serendipities, not just serendipities that occur for the organizational actors under study, but also serendipities in the research process. This is a condition imposed by temporality, whereby seemingly insignificant events from a distant past may emerge as significant for what is going on in the present and for the future that is being shaped.

11 A Plea for Mystery

> In reaching after what 'is' the case, we often ignore how mystery always remains, no matter how detailed our formal lines become; no matter how tight the framing into which things and events are parsed and then organized.
>
> (Holt and Mueller 2011: 70)
>
> There is no holding nature still and looking at it.
>
> (Whitehead 1920: 14–15)
>
> Small structures and short moments can have large consequences.
>
> (Weick, Sutcliffe, and Obstfeld 2005: 410)

Compared to other scientific disciplines, such as astronomy, physics, biology, social anthropology, and religion, the field of organization studies seems bedevilled by a lack of mystery. The problem is that organizational researchers rarely discover much that is experienced as exciting. Astronomers may claim to have discovered new galaxies, physicists work towards theories that confirm or disconfirm the beginning of the universe, social anthropologists may explain enigmatic rituals, and scholars in religious studies strive to uncover hidden meanings in scripts. Compared to some other disciplines, what organizational researchers do seems rather mundane, even when it is dressed up with terms such as complexity thinking, strategizing, practice studies, or process theory. The main explanation for this state of affairs is that what we study is—well—mundane. But then, to the scientist who spends thousands of hours looking through a microscope, it presumably also seems mundane most of the time. The difference (or similarity) between studying organizational life and, say, microorganisms, lies in the ways that the mundane is given meaning and how that meaning is expressed to say something interesting about the world. The mundane does not need to be uninteresting or inconsequential, the point being to unlock the mundaneness of the mundane, relate the seemingly mundane to broader, unexplored issues of interest for society and explain the unexpected, the 'absent'.

The absent is that which holds potentiality for revealing itself. Importantly, absence is not the same as 'nothingness'. On the contrary, absence is highly suggestive of opportunity, or potentiality, as held in Chinese philosophy, notably in the ideas of Laozi (Barbalet 2014. In fact, there is no presence without absence, as observed by Cooper (2005a: 1695), who quotes Levinas (1969: 25) as referring to absence as 'essentially hidden', which 'throws itself toward the light, without becoming signification. Not nothingness—but what is not yet'. Still, organization studies are somewhat reluctant to engage with absence. As pointed out by Helin et al. (2014: 7), we typically consider 'absence with aversion: a hole to be filled, a territory to be claimed and occupied, a wasteland to be made productive, a darkness to be lit, rather than go along with it, treating it as a provocative ally of analysis'. But absence should be treated as the counterpart to presence; that which 'is' derived from that which is not. The absence of a physical voice may be compensated for by the presence of modes of articulation that do not include that voice, such as materiality. Curiously, absence may be more powerful than presence, because it relies more on imagination, which suggests that it may be a better idea to treat absence as an ally rather than an enemy to be avoided.

Absence relates closely to mysteries and vice versa. They may be represented by what Callon would call externalities to organizational acts. Although Callon applies externalities principally to economic behaviour, they apply perfectly well to organizing. Callon's (1998) concept pair of framing and overflowing allows us to translate absences, represented by externalities, into a framework for thinking about organization in a world on the move. Framing (which Callon borrows from Goffman) and overflowing describe the contingent, tentative, and indeterminate nature of organizing in a world on the move. Callon's argument is that all activity creates externalities, as everything is principally connected. It is impossible to understand, much less anticipate externalities, partly because they supersede the causal effects related to actors' spheres of understanding and influence, as actors operate within an omnipresence of connections with the outside world that produce irrepressible overflows (p. 249). Callon provides an example from economics where a chemical company fails to account for the costs its emissions incur upon neighbouring farmers in its calculations because the effects, in spite of penalizing the farmers, remain external to the sphere of economic transactions in which the company operates (p. 245). In a world of externalities actors try to make their existence predictable by means of framing, constituted by the attempts to identify and contain overflows associated with externalities. Actors operate with intentions and models, which lie behind their attempts at framing. Framing relates to those overflows that actors may identify and try to contain. In Callon's conception, framing inevitably produces overflows; in fact, overflows are necessary for framing to occur and help shape the framing that takes place, although a one-to-one relationship cannot conceivably exist between overflows and framing. If we consider framing as temporally structured, it logically relates to previous experience, without being a repetition of that experience, which helps explain why it can but with difficulty contain new overflows; and, hence, why it needs to be seen as incomplete and ongoing.

Something that has kept mystery away from the study of organizational life is that organizations have been assumed to be readily coupled entities that remain stable until some exogenous force hits them and forces them to change. As a result, some of the most interesting changes are in the form of economic performance, organizational culture, or business strategy. Therefore a plea for mystery would go hand in hand with a plea for instability, or at least an assumption of instability rather than the assumption that the organization moves into another form of stability (I owe this point to Steve Woolgar). As I hope to have shown in this book, the very term 'stability' is too static to do justice to the dynamics of organizational life. I much prefer the term 'continuity', which underlines the interdependence of experience over time, while leaving open the nature of the interdependence. Moreover, continuity always has to be reconstructed, which is not implied by stability, that requires work, sometimes hard, itself likely to create dynamics causing dilemmas and challenges for organizational actors. The work may also reveal absences and consequently serve to actualize potentialities. Continuity demands more creativity than commonly assumed.

In order to make the field of organization studies more exciting and more relevant to organizational practice (which *is* exciting) and give it at least some chance of mystery, we would do better to speculate more openly about how organizational logics may lead to various types of phenomena, some of which may be what Weick (1974) calls absurd. One question to ask is how events can connect into different kinds of organized patterns? Rather than assume order, it is potentially more interesting to marvel at the emergence of (any) organizational order from potential or apparent disorder. And rather than just looking at the 'big orders', we should look at how seemingly trivial orders emerge, and accept, along with Whitehead (1929a: 5), that it 'requires a very unusual mind to undertake the analysis of the obvious'. March, who seems to think in similar terms and who directs his focus at explaining the emergence of coherence from seemingly disconnected and incoherent actions, events, and entities, describes a glimpse of organizational life as follows:

Many things are happening at once; practices, forms, and technologies are changing and poorly understood; preferences, identities, rules and perceptions are indeterminate and changing; problems, solutions, opportunities, ideas, situations, people, and outcomes are mixed together in ways that make their interpretation uncertain and their connections unclear; decisions at one time and place appear to have only a loose tie to decisions at others; solutions seem to have only modest connection to problems; policies are not implemented; decision makers seem to wander in and out of decision arenas and seem to say one thing while doing another.

(1994: 177)

One question to ask is what creates coherence out of a seemingly stochastic state of affairs. A multitude of theories exists to enable description of how coherence emerges amidst incoherence (e.g. culture, values, routines, leadership, discourse, power, incentives), but the ability to explain how some orders emerge from multiple possible orders is lacking, and most theories do not enable this either. One way to explain the emergence of coherence in relation to the seemingly disparate actions in the above quote is to study how they are directed towards broader structures of meaning, which are themselves subject to change. The question to be addressed is how articulatory processes enable coherence and hence the emergence of organizational ordering, given that there are multiple possible ordering patterns that may emerge. Once a pattern of ordering is underway, the question becomes how it can reproduce itself or plant the seeds of its own change. This is what I have tried to develop in this book, being perfectly aware that it may not contribute towards a heightened sense of mystery in organization studies, although it may contribute towards better explanations of how multiple possible orders may come into being.

Absences may be found in the past as well as in the future. Mintzberg and colleagues (e.g. Mintzberg, Ahlstrand, and Lampel 1998) have shown how strategies for the future may grow like weeds in the garden, emerge from anywhere, and merge and develop in unexpected ways. In other words, seemingly absent strategies may emerge. Applying the kind of temporality used in this book, there may be absences in the past. Historicizing, which is about making history intelligible (Heidegger 1927), may be seen as the constant weaving and re-weaving of temporal threads of events. Over time the threads of historicizing become institutionalized and alternative threads fade into the background. They become absent to conscious minds eager to make their mark on the future while continuing their work of articulation.

If we stick to the idea that organizational actors are always in the present, looking towards the future while looking back and into the past while looking to the future, we will be better at uncovering treasures of the past, not as dead facts but as lived experience ready to spring to life in unexpected places and at unexpected times. Sometimes, even seemingly mummified experiences might spring to life in extraordinary ways. For example, Hatch and Schultz (forthcoming) report on how the Carlsberg Groups' motto *Semper Ardens* (Latin for 'always burning') was engraved in stone by Carl Jacobsen, the son of the group's founder, who had taken it from a group of artists in Rome in the 1880s, because he felt that it applied to his own passionate philosophy of brewing beer. More than a century later the discovery of the engraving coincided with the effort of Carlsberg's brewers to establish a motto for themselves. I use the word 'coincided', because they discovered the engraved motto and the history behind it after having come up with the same motto. Naturally, finding the motto engraved by the founder strengthened the story of the founding, but also the re-launching of the motto. What started as an engraving by the company's second-generation founder has successively become translated into beer recipes and an electronically inscribed motto for a now multinational corporation. The story of *Semper Ardens* highlights at least two potentially interesting aspects of materiality and historicizing in the flow of time. First, it underlines the shifting nature of materiality and associated modes of dissemination. The lasting engraving in stone was a unique materialization that stayed in the same place to be retrieved a century later, whereas later electronic inscriptions may be disseminated and used as a business slogan in a distributed global corporation. Second, the story draws attention to the robust yet serendipitous journey of an inscribed symbol that different generations of actors came across while looking for ways to articulate an identity for the future.

The institutionalized finitude of ideas, caused partly by the framing performed by scholarly journals and partly by the structuring of conference tracks, tends to set limitations for organizational analysis. Institutionalized finitude, combined with the infinitude[1] of organizational possibilities, prevents mysteries from surfacing in organization studies. While embedded in a scientific field, we may interpret what we see of the field around us as its outer limits. Comforted by the idea that we see the outer limits, we risk approaching what Douglas (1966) calls the margins and unstructured areas of society. Margins are, according to Douglas, dangerous places, but also areas of transition and energy. Therefore, embracing the infinitude of possibilities can energize the field of organization studies, because doing so opens for mysteries in the form of the absent and unexpected.

Organization studies have traditionally favoured factors such as apparent size, impact, power, and level, but we should increasingly ask questions such as what is the combined power of a tweet, the blink of an eye, an order, a rule, a routine, or a machine. Inviting mystery into organizational analysis necessitates letting go of traditional ideas of fixity while still maintaining some basic rules of the game. What gets in the way of letting go of them is probably an excessive degree of Cartesian anxiety and a corresponding dread of intellectual and moral chaos, or madness (Bernstein 1983; Varela, Thompson, and Rosch 1991) that might grip the organizational field in the absence of these and other assumptions. Such assumptions, however, prevent the field from achieving greater empirical and analytical understanding, not just among scholars, but also among practitioners. The point is that the field of organizational analysis will not fall apart if we were to leave what Varela et al. (1991: 140–141) call the 'enchanting land of truth where everything is clear and ultimately grounded'.

Paying more careful attention to the flow of time may enable a different focus on the more elusive, and hence mysterious, sides of organizational life. It seems fitting to conclude with some reflections on mystery by Whitehead,

The theory I am urging admits a greater ultimate mystery and a deeper ignorance. The past and the future meet and mingle in an ill-defined present. The passage of nature, which is only another name for the creative force of existence, has no narrow ledge of instantaneous present within which to operate. Its operative presence which is now urging nature forward must be sought for throughout the whole, in the remotest past as well as in the narrowest breadth of any present duration. Perhaps also in the unrealized future. Perhaps also in the future which might be as well as the actual future which will be. It is impossible to meditate on time and the mystery of the creative passage of nature without an overwhelming emotion of the limitations of human intelligence.

(1920: 73)

ANNEX THE THEORETICAL FRAMEWORK IN BRIEF

The following contains a brief description of some of the key terms that form the underlying basis of the framework developed for this book.

- **A world on the move**. This does not refer to moving things, but to the perishability of any perceived stable arrangement in the flow of time. The essence of persisting in a world on the move is not change (as change goes on all the time), but tentative ongoing stabilization of past experiences and future possibilities in view of their possibilities of becoming otherwise.
- **Ongoing present**. The framework is based on the assumption that actors are continually in the temporal present, in which past and future are enacted. This means that the past, present, and future are not seen as periods distinct from one another.
- **Organizational presents**. Although experience is continuous for each actor, there are temporal presents in which encounters between actors take place. Actors may be of different kinds; therefore an encounter may be, for example, between two types of computer software, between two or more persons, or between a social unit and a concept. Actors do not exist prior to encounters, but are defined through acts at the encounters, referred to as articulation (see below).
- **Living presents** are indeterminate experienced durations that remain open until achieving closure in the form of events. A particular type of organizational present is that of 'living presents' that involve human actors in intersubjective processes. Living presents are not confined to humans alone, but involve them in an intersubjective mode. Living presents exhibit a fluid experience characterized by temporal float, which implies that acts are temporally reversible. When living presents attain closure they become events, to be related to other events.
- **Events.** As organizational presents attain provisional closure, they become events. The passing of time enables actors to ascribe meaning to events, including their temporal extension, actions that took place, associated actors, intentions and outcomes. An event is a generic description for any occurrence of duration and is not to be confounded with staged events, marker events, or epochal events, although some events may take on such proportions.
- **Event formations**. Events may be causally connected to one another in what is referred to as 'event formations'. Event formations include the interconnecting of multiple events around a recognizable pattern. They

are created through prehension (Whitehead) between events. Event formations provide a sense of historicity to meaning structures.
- **Organizational meaning structures**. Meaning structures are heterogeneous wholes of elements that provide the meaning of acts as they are articulated in living presents. Meaning structure elements may be concepts, social or human actors, or technologies. Meaning structures are not seen as schemas that lie between actors and a constructed reality. On the contrary, they *are* that reality, and actors are part of the meaning structures. Actors operate within and upon meaning structures, and not through them. Although they are perceived as distinct enduring entities, meaning structure elements are provisional outcomes of accumulated organizational presents of articulations at events over time. A particular technology, for example, is seen as such on the basis of the numerous encounters with other actors over time. When it is perceived as that particular technology it is due to the accumulation of encounters over time. In other words, it may be seen as an 'event-object'.
- **Articulation**. Organizations in the form of meaning structures are not seen as things in themselves, but as the emergent wholes of connected elements enacted through articulation by actors. Articulation, which constitutes acts of organizing, takes place in living presents, at which meaning structures are instantiated through the relating of elements. Articulation consists of various combinations of modes. This book focuses on five different modes of articulation, referred to as material, intersubjective, practical, textual, and tacit.

NOTES

Preface

1. Thomas Friedman's (2010) description of a small start-up company called EndoStim runs as follows: 'Here's the short version: EndoStim was inspired by Cuban and Indian immigrants to America and funded by St Louis venture capitalists. Its prototype is being manufactured in Uruguay, with the help of Israeli engineers and constant feedback from doctors in India and Chile. Oh, and the C.E.O. is a South African, who was educated at the Sorbonne, but lives in Missouri and California, and his head office is basically a BlackBerry.... This kind of very lean start-up, where the principals are rarely in the same office at the same time, and which takes advantage of all the tools of the flat world—teleconferencing, e-mail, the Internet and faxes—to access the best expertise and low-cost, high-quality manufacturing anywhere, is the latest in venture investing. You've heard of cloud computing. I call this "cloud manufacturing".'

2. By focusing on temporality, the process view proposed in the book enables the dichotomy between the so-called 'strong' and 'weak' process views suggested by previous writers (e.g. Chia and Langley 2005; Van de Ven and Poole 2005; Langley and Tsoukas 2010) to be overcome. A strong view, according to Chia and Langley (2005), deems actions and things to be instantiations of process complexes. According to a strong view of process, actors are not prior to process, but rather are created and changed by process. If anything, they are what Rescher (2003: 53) refers to as 'manifestations of processes' (Bakken and Hernes 2006). A weak view, on the other hand, treats process as important but ultimately reducible to the action of things (Chia and Langley 2005), which in a sense serves to objectify process. A related distinction is drawn by Langley (1999) between what she calls 'variance theory' and 'process theory'. The strong–weak dichotomy does not consider temporality per se, however, or the role that structure plays in temporal construction.

3. Atomism has existed at least since Aristotle. Whitehead, however, subscribed to the atomism proposed by Lucretius (90–55 BC), although Whitehead replaced Lucretius's spatial atoms with temporal events (See Hernes (2008, 2014) for a fuller discussion). Rubino (2002) makes the point that, 'The world of Lucretius is a world of motion, not rest, and it is a world in which complexity and indeterminacy play a fundamental role (Prigogine and Stengers, 1984: 303–5). It is the *clinamen* that makes our universe possible.' The clinamen signifies the deviation of processes without any observable reason for change, and which leads to the emerging formation of an object. The formation of an object (man, tree, rain, mountain etc.) serves to attract other atoms to the process of formation. What takes place is the becoming of "one" (the object) from multiple possibilities.'

Chapter 1

1. Take, for example, the world of fashion, which, according to Bourdieu and Delsaut (1975: 17) rests 'on a temporal distinction between "the modern" and "the outmoded," "the fashionable" and "the old-fashioned," which necessarily calls for a break with the preceding years' canons' (Vangkilde 2012: 5).

2. I purposely use the word thinking *about* process rather than *thinking process*. I was alerted to this subtle yet important difference by Ward Egan. Thinking process is what practitioners do. Thinking about process is what those do who study those thinking process.

3. Mead (1932: 57) is explicit about the point that the past is a past in the present, continually moulded in the present: 'It is of course evident that the materials out of which that past is constructed lie in the present. I refer to the memory images and the evidences by which we build up the past, and to the fact that any reinterpretation of the picture we form of the past will be found in a present, and will be judged by the logical and evidential characters which such data possess in a present. It is also evident that there is no appeal from these in their locus of a present to a real past which lies like a scroll behind us, and to which we may recur to check up on our constructions. We are not deciphering a manuscript whose passages can be made intelligible in themselves and left as secure presentations of that portion of what has gone before, to be supplemented by later final constructions of other passages. We are not contemplating an ultimate unchangeable past that may be spread behind us in its entirety subject to no further change'.

4. With some exceptions (e.g. Tsoukas and Chia 2002; Van de Ven and Poole 2005; Bakken and Hernes 2006), the word 'process' is used merely to emphasize that movement and flux are taken into consideration. Sometimes a processual twist is performed by merely changing terms, such as replacing 'strategy' with 'strategizing', drawing inspiration from Weick's urge to replace 'organization' with 'organizing'. Such attempts serve to sensitize readers to the idea that things move and change rather than stay in the same place, unchanged. Adding 'ing' to a noun, however much it turns the noun into a verb in linguistic terms, does not much influence how we conceptualize process or how we formulate all the important questions that come with that conceptualization (Hernes 2008).

5. Whitehead (1929a) considered creativity to be one of his key concepts. Creativity, in Whitehead's thinking, applies to the one and the many, and the ongoing process of unifying the many into one complex, intelligible unity (Sherburne 1966: 218).

6. However, Heidegger's (1927: 326) temporality gives primacy to the future: 'This letting-itself-come-towards-itself in that distinctive possibility which it puts up with, is the primordial phenomenon of the *future as coming towards*.'

7. Still, Bergson's focus was on individual experience. As Polkinghorne (1988) points out, he saw individual experience as private and incommunicable through a language of concepts, which should signal some caution when drawing upon Bergson's ideas in understanding organizational phenomena that do not escape social interaction.

Chapter 2

1. An example is Lanzara's account of ephemeral organizations that arose in the aftermath of an earthquake in Italy in 1980. It is worth quoting at some length, because it shows the transition whereby an organization emerged and then disappeared:

   The first day after the quake, in a corner of a shattered village 'piazza', a young fellow had set up a really basic coffee shop with rudimentary equipment, consisting of a small desk, a portable gas stove, two gas containers, three coffee machines, coffee packs, sugar, plastic cups and spoons, matches and tanks of water.... The place was crowded: people met there and rested, exchanged information, told stories to each other, made plans and got organized. The third day nobody was there. The coffee shop had been dismantled. Why? The Army had militarized the area and had established checkpoints to control access to the village. To get in and out, an official permit released by the local authorities was needed, and for private individuals and non-sponsored groups, it was extremely difficult to get the permit and go through the checkpoints. (Lanzara 1983: 71)

Lanzara's story suggests that his coffee stand became a sort of hub of ad hoc knowledge exchange and planning. However, the emerging context created by the young coffeemaker was quenched when the public rescue teams moved in with their formal systems regulating access to and from the disaster area.

2. By 'atemporal' I do not mean that it is without time, but without temporality. Temporality is time with history and future, where the passing of time continuously challenges the making of history and the future as well as their interplay.
3. This can be seen in more recent works, as well as, for example, work on complexity and organization, which consider the human system as distinct from the material system. Stacey (2001), for example, considers there to be a non-human environment that impacts on the social world of gestures, feelings, and language. According to this line of thinking, the social world produces tools and artefacts that become part of the material world. Stacey, in spite of leaning on Mead's work on social interaction and temporality, seems to misinterpret Mead's notion of 'the object' which to Mead is not placed outside human inter-action, but forms an inextricable part of it. To Mead, language, for example, could be seen as an object.
4. This conception of organization comes close to the type of temporal connectedness suggested by Knorr-Cetina and Bruegger (2002) in their study of how micro-orders in financial markets connect into global networks. Still, their conception remains within economic sociology involving market-driven transactions, while the conception I suggest for organizational analysis may involve various forms of non-financial transactions. An example is given in Hernes (2008), which is pursued by Nayak and Chia (2011), of terrorist networks that are latent formations of a religious, social, ethnic, and economic character.
5. This coincides somewhat with Martin, Knopoff, and Beckman's (1988) study of The Body Shop, in which they argue that a 'bounded emotionality' is present in The Body Shop due to their relatively high proportion of women in managerial positions. When it comes to their conclusion, however, they relate their findings to the characteristics of the organization as a particular system among other systems.
6. In Whitehead's (1938: 6) words, 'We must be systematic; but we should keep our systems open. In other words, we should be sensitive to their limitations. There is always a vague "beyond," waiting for penetration in respect to its detail.'
7. Correspondence is a point of discussion in linguistic philosophy and, notably, in the works by Wittgenstein and Searle.
8. The idea of correspondence relates closely to the idea of representation, since both assume that there is something to which something may correspond, or something there that may be represented, either as being the same or similar, or as being different from or in opposition to. The idea of reality being representative of something is a critique that Deleuze (2004) makes of philosophers, including Aristotle, and his assumption of categories. If we reduce things to categories, as is done from a representationalist viewpoint, we lose sight of how things *become* different, to take an example, such as in the case of species (Williams 2003).
9. Luhmann (1995: 25) writes, 'There is, in other words, no point-for-point correspondence between system and environment', and in organization theory March and Olsen (1975) suggested that 'We need a theory of choice that articulates the connections between the environmental context of organizations and their actions in such a way that neither is simply the residual unexplained variance for the other' (March and Olsen 1975: 153).

10. Simpson (2009: 1332) points out that, 'This problem has been well recognized in Giddens' theory of structuration, and Bourdieu's notion of habitus, both of which critique the dualistic separation of the individual and the social.'
11. Weick (1979) did in fact point towards relationships between verbs and nouns, notably referring to Mead (1934).
12. In philosophy, as in science, according to Whitehead (1938), abstractions are indispensible, even to living experience, and the role of science is to translate sets of abstractions into laws. But at the end of the day what matters is that the abstractions return to concrete, living experience. The journey from living experience via 'dead' abstractions back to living experience, although it is indispensible, is also a journey of reduction and distortion. As Whitehead (1938: 124) points out, 'The return may be misconceived. The abstraction may misdirect us as to the real complexity from which it originates' (p. 124). The procedure of working via abstractions cannot, according to Whitehead, be rejected, provided that we remember that this is what we are doing. The point is that the totality of what we are trying to describe escapes our conceptual abilities; hence, in the absence of mindfulness about the building of abstractions we run the risk of building abstractions that are misplaced when it comes to framing living experience.

    As a matter of fact, Whitehead (1925b: 200–201) lamented, following work by Smith, that the shaping of organizational life fell prey to misconceived abstractions: '[…] the science of political economy […] riveted on men a certain set of abstractions which were disastrous in their influence on modern mentality. It de-humanised industry. This is only one example of a general danger inherent in modern science. Its methodological procedure is exclusive and intolerant, and rightly so. It fixes attention on a definite group of abstractions, neglects everything else, and elicits every scrap of information and theory which is relevant to what it has retained. […] Accordingly, the true rationalism must always transcend itself by recurrence to the concrete in search of inspiration. A self-satisfied rationalism is in effect a form of anti-rationalism. It means an arbitrary halt at a particular set of abstractions.'
13. Based on research on collaboration between scientists, Star (2010: 604) strongly refutes such an assumption for organized systems:

    Many models, in the late 1980s and continuing today, of cooperation often began conceptually, with the idea that first consensus must be reached, and the cooperation could begin. From my own field work among scientists and others cooperating across disciplinary borders, and two historical analyses of heterogeneous groups who did cooperate and did not agree at the local level, it seemed to me that the consensus model was untrue. Consensus was rarely reached, and fragile when it was, but cooperation continued, often unproblematically. How might this be explained?

14. Callon (1998) succinctly makes the point as follows, 'Let us start by considering the concept of embeddedness first put forward by Polanyi (Polanyi 1957) and subsequently taken up by Granovetter (1985). This does not so much represent yet another expression of the implacable hostility between sociology and economics, as an affirmation of the omnipresence of overflows. Friedberg (1993) rightly highlights the habitual misinterpretation of this concept. Its significance, which is both profound and radical (and incidentally the main theme of Granovetter's celebrated article) centres on the hypothesis that the objectives, intentions, interests, and projects of a given actor, and indeed his or her will, are not simply a set of attributes that define his or her own personal, unchangeable identity which the actor could simply by intellectual application, access or express—even unconsciously—if he or she were given the opportunity (this being the meaning of the expression "to reveal one's

preferences"). Nor are they the result of values, norms, or institutions which reduce the actor to the status of the "cultural dope" so justifiably ridiculed by Garfinkel. In fact, they cannot be dissociated from the network of interdependencies in which the actor is enmeshed and to which he or she is continuously contributing (Burt 1992; Callon and Law 1997). In short, the actor's ontology is variable: his or her objectives, interests, will, and thus identity are caught up in a process of continual reconfiguration, a process that is intimately related to the constant reconfiguration of the network of interactions in which he or she is involved.'

15. For example, drawing upon Greimas' semiotics, Barley (1983) demonstrates in his study of a funeral home the cognitive aspect of meaning by showing how the dead are made as lifelike as possible for the wake, thus signifying a naturalness of death. At pragmatic level he describes how staff at the funeral home at a practical level acted to relate real things to one another, such as by embalming, replacing the corpse's blood with a preservative fluid or dressing it. These, and many other actions, are routinized actions that draw upon material means to relate elements to one another. Elements of meaning structures, therefore, are not just virtual signs (Schütz 1967) to be interpreted by actors, such as implied in works in the hermeneutic tradition (e.g. Geertz 1973), but they are 'real' things to be related to one another by the ongoing work of actors. In other words they are 'actor-worlds' (Callon 1986a) in which actors perform their 'world-making' (Chia 1999).

16. Freezing in time and space corresponds to Whitehead's allegation that philosophers have leaned towards what he called 'simple location', whereby objects are simply seen as occupying a unique location. A piece of matter would thus be seen as a self-sufficient object. Such a view implies that a bit of matter can be described without any reference to how it came to be what it is, which runs counter to a process view. When we segment time–space, we simultaneously introduce boundaries that are transcended by the division that we introduce. According to Whitehead (1938: 140), [...] 'any division, including some activities and excluding others, also severs the patterns of process which extend beyond all boundaries'.

17. Schäffner and Hendrup (2012) illustrate the importance of institutional labels in sensemaking processes in their study of outsourcing of tasks within an MNC.

18. There is a certain parallel between Weick's conception of the processes linking individual and collectivity, and Mead's (1934) discussion of the creation of meaning in social interaction. In Mead's framework, a sense of the social and the individual is created through gestures. In order for thought (sense) to exist, according to Mead, there must be symbols, vocal gestures that arouse in the individual the response that he or she calls out in the other, and in such a way that the response may enable the caller to direct his or her conduct in turn. The process of human interaction establishes common expectations, giving rise to the notion of the 'generalized other', which enables identification of the individual to a broader social system.

19. An exception is found in Luhmann, who, although he works with the notion of social systems as distinct phenomena, takes a processual view by which he does not assume that they exist as given and naturally enduring entities. On the contrary, Luhmann assumes that social systems may at any time break down, and therefore they have to reproduce themselves through communication. In fact, social systems are seen as improbable. A feature of Luhmann's view of social systems is also that they are highly contingent in nature. Furthermore, his idea of contingency is not about necessity for something to take place, but rather that which enables the improbable to become probable.

20. Abstracting knowledge processes from individual actors has been done, however. For example, Douglas' (1986) idea of 'thought worlds' evokes a spatial image of knowledge, but

without locating it at the level of individuals. Whereas several others (e.g. Fiol 1995) have borrowed the term 'thought world' from Douglas, Douglas herself derived it from work by Fleck ([1935] 1979), who used 'thought collective' (*Denkkollektiv*). The location of thought worlds in relation to the individual and collective dimensions is an important question that Douglas brings up, and an underlying issue is the interaction between the cognitive and the social. Moreover Douglas relates the social to thought, but without pinning thought to distinct and identified social entities. In so doing, she draws upon Fleck's conceptualization of cognitive spheres and social relations.

21. This assumption gets questioned by Fligstein's (1985) study of the diffusion of the M-form in firms between 1919 and 1979, in which he suggests that the spread of the M-form is partly explained by strategy, but also by imitation. In other words, managers structure firms as a 'best way' to pursue strategies, but they may also do it by observing and adopting what other firms do successfully.

22. The point is made succinctly by Bergson (2007: 133), who states, 'Suffice it to say that the intellect represents *becoming* as a series of *states*, each of which is homogeneous with itself and consequently does not change.'

23. 'To tell the truth, there never is real immobility, if we understand by that an absence of movement. Movement is reality itself, and what we call immobility is a certain state of things analogous to that produced when two trains move at the same speed, in the same direction, on parallel tracks: each of the two trains is then immovable to the travellers seated in the other' (Bergson 2007: 119).

24. Organization and management theory has, however, largely overlooked the fact that continuity is intrinsic to organizational change. Much of the blame for this has to be taken by the tendency to take what Cooper and Law (1995) refer to as 'distal views', which they oppose to 'proximal views'. Cooper and Law (1995) use the terms 'distal' and 'proximal' to describe macro- and micro-level analysis respectively. The distal refers to form: the results, the outcomes, the 'finished', the ready-made. Organization viewed distally is structured order with clear boundaries that distinguishes it from the environment. The proximal, on the other hand, denotes the emergent, the relational, and the detailed. Viewed from afar over time any system will be seen as either continuous or changing, or both. What is seen as continuity by the external observer is unlikely to be felt the same way by those actually involved in organizational activity.

25. Flaherty (2002: 380) notes that, 'Regrettably, the micromanagement of temporal experience has not been a topic of central concern in the sociology of time.'

26. Future events, though, are not foreseen as future events as such, but they are seen as future necessities for the present, as pointed out by Whitehead (1933: 195): 'But there are no actual occasions in the future, already constituted. Thus there are no actual occasions in the future to exercise efficient causation in the present. What is objective in the present is the necessity of a future of actual occasions, and necessity that these future occasions conform to the conditions inherent in the essence of the present occasion.'

27. See, for example, Gell's (1992: 55) concept of temporal cultural relativism, which he suggests consists, in an ethnographic sense, of 'the differential sets of contingency beliefs, held by different cultures and sub-cultures, as to the historical facticity and anticipated possibilities of the world'. According to Sorokin and Merton (1937), Nilsson provided a well-researched account of socially constructed time in 1920.

28. Clark employs the following four categories to describe how time may order activity differently in different organizations: sequences and signifiers, temporal units, durational differentiation, and orientation to the past/present/future.

29. The linear conception of time has attracted criticism, notably in the critical management literature, which argues, for example, that organizational life has been dominated by clock time (chronos), which again has enabled the exercise of power and exploitation since Taylor's (1911) measurement-based models of scientific management. Hassard (2002), for instance, discusses time as a commodity, as found in modernism, epitomized by Taylor's scientific management; then time as socially constructed, such as is found in workplace ethnographies; and finally time as seen from a post-modernist perspective where instantaneity and time–space compression (Harvey 1990) distort historically established boundaries of speed, rhythm, distance, and experience.

30. An early contribution exemplifying how different temporal logics may be at odds with one another and lead to destructive conflict is in Gouldner's (1954) well-known description of a wildcat strike at a gypsum plant. The gypsum plant was established near towns settled a century before and where the men had led a semi-rural life of farming, hunting, and fishing. With the arrival of the plant, many of them became employees of the plant. The plant was lenient and allowed workers to balance their seasonal logistics with the work at the mine. For example, fewer employees showed up during the hunting and planting seasons and they were able to use certain materials and tools belonging to the plant for their private use. In some ways, the practices were the antithesis of Weberian bureaucracy, which is based on a separation between work life and private life. When a new manager arrived who imposed stricter adherence to administrative time logics including elements such as record keeping, introducing productivity standards, reinforcing rules, and eliminating extra-organizational prerogatives, a strike erupted that led to further degeneration of activity.

31. Their contribution comes close to Bourdieu's (1977) well-known sociological treatise based on his study in Kabylia, which precisely aimed at dissolving the objectivist–subjectivist dichotomy through the lens of practice. Bourdieu (1977: 72) recommends that we abandon ideas whereby social order is seen through the lens of 'statistical regularity or algebraic structure' and that we engage in observing how orders are actually produced. Rather than observe the world as if it consisted of a dichotomy between macro-level structures and human actions, he suggests a recursive view, such as the way that he views the structuring of the 'habitus'. The habitus produces practices which in turn influence the habitus. Recursivity, rather than being mere reproduction of patterns of practice, reveals new horizons of opportunity, what Bourdieu (but also Whitehead 1929a) refers to as 'potentiality'. Hence, recursivity signifies reproduction, but also change.

32. Similar to what Castells (1996) calls 'timeless time'.

33. It has actually been a long time now since James (1890) criticized what he referred to as the string of beads (or serially connected) sensation of time.

34. The view of temporality comes close to that of historians' view of temporality, which Sewell (2008: 517–518) describes as their seeing '…time as fateful, as irreversible in the sense that a significant action, once taken, or an event, once experienced, irrevocably alters the situation in which it occurs. The conceptual vehicle historians use to construct or analyse the temporal fatefulness and contingency of social life is the event. Historians see the flow of social life as being punctuated by significant happenings, by complexes of social action that somehow change the course of history. They constantly talk about "turning points" or "watersheds" in history and spend much of their conceptual energy dividing the flow of history into distinct eras that events mark off from one another.'

35. There are nevertheless notable exceptions. See, for example, Mackay and McKiernan (2004) for a review of the use of the past in psychological decision-making research.

36. The philosopher John McTaggart (1908) theorized two conceptions of time, which he called the A series and the B series respectively. McTaggart's A series describes time as consisting of past, present, and future. The A series reflects what Gell (1992) calls a dynamic view of time, where the present changes and the past and the future change with it. McTaggart's B series, on the other hand, draws the distinction between before and after, which Gell calls a static view of time. An A series has ontological differences between past, present, and future, but in a B-series the three tenses are not seen to be different. Whereas the A series pays importance to whether an event takes part in the past or the future, the B series emphasizes the actual order of occurrence of events. For example, an A series view would regard the recruitment of a new manager according to whether things changed from before to after the recruitment. A B series, on the other hand, would regard the recruitment according to who was recruited before that manager, and who was recruited after. To some extent the A series reflects what I will refer to as ongoing temporality, while the B series reflects a temporality frequently employed in organization studies.

37. Bergson charged that time had been subjected to the same analytical assumptions as those underlying space. Hence time could be represented by the space of the clock, such as by the regular ticking of the clock's mechanism. This imagery obviously imposes symmetry between past and future on time, since the ticking of the past will carry on into the future; and wherever we step into time, the same regularity of the ticking will be experienced. However, considering process to take place in time precludes symmetry between past and future because it assumes that the future is not known.

38. On the basis of their discussion of the need for addressing organizational learning under continuity, Hernes and Irgens (2013: 263) suggest that the 'notion of temporal agency be more explicitly addressed in the organizational learning literature, because it addresses the situated nature of management, where decisions need to be made in the flow of time, with continual adjustment of past and future in view of the needs of the present'. The argument ties in with Emirbayer and Mische's (1998: 963) view of agency, in which they argue that 'the agentic dimension of social action can only be captured in its full complexity if it is analytically situated within the flow of time'.

39. As Mead (1932) points out, while there is a certain irrevocability about the past and an event that has passed cannot be changed, it does not preclude changes in the meaning attributed to the event.

40. Related to this criticism is the one-sided futurity implied by the idea of strategizing.

41. Shotter (2006: 592) articulates this point particularly well:

> We then only too easily reduce the differences between the past, present, and future merely to *differences of position*, with 'past' events being thought of as lying to the left of a point representing the 'present', and 'future' events on the right. Thus solely spatial arrays, wrongly, suggest that successive moments do not have to struggle to come into existence; the fact that *unique, irreversible, creative* changes with their own *unique character* are taking place is lost. Instead, we act as if the observed differences of position are merely movements into positions that were in fact already in existence, and thus any pastness or futurity attached to them is merely accidental, and not crucial to their very nature.

Chapter 3

1. The becoming–being distinction should not be taken as an absolute ontological separation. Hartshorne (1998), for one, argues that it is a misconception to suppose that process

philosophy, although it builds on becoming, rejects being. Hartshorne suggests instead that process thinking is a doctrine of *being in becoming*, whereas philosophies of being are doctrines of *becoming in being*. Bakken and Hernes (2006) use the imagery of the 'pseudopod' inspired by von Foerster and Weick to illustrate how the relationship between becoming and being can be seen as a seamless transition.

2. When Whitehead (1929a: 254), for example, wrote that 'apart from the experience of subjects there is nothing, nothing, nothing, bare nothingness', he referred to the subject (such as an organization) as the process of attaining unity in front of the perishing of time while embodying the past of its many constituent experiences. Hence 'becoming' should be seen as a wholly temporal experience.

3. In process philosophy the subject is the outcome of processes rather than their creator. Whitehead, for example, sought to avoid the human-centred view that he criticized Kant and Descartes for. Whitehead presented his process philosophy as the inversion of Kant's philosophy. Kant saw process as flowing from subjectivity towards apparent objectivity, whereas Whitehead tried to explain process as moving from objectivity towards subjectivity (Sherburne 1966: 152). Whitehead's project is about understanding how facts emanate from flux, from a tangled world in which material and social factors operate. He argues, for example, that 'The doctrine that I am maintaining is that neither physical nature nor life can be understood unless we fuse them together as essential factors in the composition of 'really real' things whose interconnections and individual characters constitute the universe' (Whitehead 1938: 150; 1929: 18–20).

4. 'Time is known to me as an abstraction from the passage of events. The fundamental fact which renders this abstraction possible is the passing of nature, its development, its creative advance, and combined with this fact is another characteristic of nature, namely the extensive relation between events. These two facts, namely the passage of events and the extension of events over each other, are in my opinion the qualities from which time and space originate as abstractions' (Whitehead 1920: 34).

5. Heidegger posited the past as a precondition for anticipation of being. 'Only in so far as Dasein *is* as an "I-*am*-as-having been," can Dasein come towards itself futurally in such a way that it comes *back*. As authentically futural, Dasein *is* authentically as *"having been."* Anticipation of one's uttermost and ownmost possibility is coming back understandingly to one's ownmost "been." Only so far as it is futural can Dasein *be* authentically as having been. The character of "having been" arises, in a certain way, from the future' (Heidegger 1927: 326).

6. Stabilizing is done by actualizing the potentiality in the situation; creatively unifying the many into one complex, intelligible unity (Sherburne 1966: 218).

7. This is also relevant to the realities of modern organizations. Tryggestad, Justesen, and Mouritsen (2013) show, for example, how the temporalities of frogs' lives, including their reproductive timing, influence their impact on a construction project.

8. In fact, it does even worse than that. By seeing activities as taking place over time in a chronological sequence, each state, condition, or stage is treated as separate, yet as a natural extension of that which precedes it, just as the succeeding one is considered a natural extension of the current one. Importantly, each state, condition, or stage can be understood without reference to what precedes or what follows from it. This type of separation in time is what Whitehead (1929a) referred to as 'simple location', which refers to separation whereby objects are simply seen as occupying a unique location. A piece of matter would thus be seen as a self-sufficient object. Such a view implies that a bit of matter can be described without

any reference to how it came to be what it is, which runs counter to a processual world view. Importantly, when we segment time–space, we simultaneously introduce boundaries that are *transcended by the very division that we introduce*. According to Whitehead (1938: 140), '[…] any division, including some activities and excluding others, also severs the patterns of process which extend beyond all boundaries'.

9. March (1999b: 2) argues that, 'The past is uncertain, not because it still remains to be realized but because it is dimly, inaccurately, or differently recalled. The past is experienced in ways that affect both its interpretation and the memories that are retained about it. History is a story, and storytellers of the past appear to be as variable as the storyteller of the future.'

10. A case in point is Pettigrew's (1997) discussion of process analysis in organization studies. First, in summarizing process perspectives, he refers to Van de Ven's (1992: 169) definition of process. Van de Ven argues that process was used in three ways in the literature: (1) as a logic used to explain a causal relationship in a variance theory; (2) as a category of concepts that refer to activities of individuals or organizations; and (3) as a sequence of events that describes how things change over time. Pettigrew singles out the third way (a sequence of individual and collective events, actions, and activities unfolding over time in context) and uses it as his working definition of process analysis. Acknowledging that process is an analysis of flows of events he then moves on to elaborate the role of context: 'If the process is our stream of analysis, the terrain around the stream which shapes the flow of events and is in turn shaped by them is a necessary part of the process of investigation' (Pettigrew 1997: 338).

A limitation of Pettigrew's analysis is that time plays no active role in it. The water in the river may flow past a point in the bank again, but there is no remembrance, neither in the bank, nor in the water of what has happened. Instead we are left to observe a gradual erosion of the bank from a distance caused by the ever-flowing water. Time has no agency other than the linear notion of more time leaving room for more erosion. This view leaves little causal power to the process of flowing water. Instead it privileges the relative immutability of the banks, because they visibly change; although they change through erosion they still determine the flow of the water.

11. This is also one of the tenets of ANT. Latour (1993: 121), for example, suggests that even with large organizations with hundreds of thousands of people in them we never really leave the local level of a few people interacting, because these micro-actors make up the organization as a macro-actor.

12. 'The object is there in its immediate resistance to the effort of the organism. It is not there as an object, however, that is, it has no inside. It gets its inside when it arouses in the organism its own response and thus the answering response of the organism to this resistance' (Mead 1932: 27–28). Mead writes (1934: 134):

Mind arises in the social process only when that process as a whole enters into, or is present in, the experience of any one of the individuals involved in that process. When this occurs the individual becomes self-conscious and has a mind; he becomes aware of his relations to that process as a whole, and to the other individuals participating in it with him; he becomes aware of his relations to that process as a whole, and to the other individuals participating in it with him; he becomes aware of that process as modified by the reactions and interactions of the individuals—including himself—who are carrying it on.

Importantly, as Joas (1997a: 183 in Flaherty 2003) notes, Mead's social psychology assumes that the individual's selective attention is 'constitutive of the environment, and not an epiphenomenon to the environment', contrary to what is assumed in behaviourism and its deterministic temporality.

13. The full extent of this point may be found in Luhmann's (1995) autopoietic theory, where entities are seen to interact with their own historically produced states, interacting cognitively with their own interpretations of the external world, rather than with the external world per se. Since interpretations are formed over time, systems are formed by their own historicity as past choices and the effects of those choices interact to constitute their identities.
14. Latour's (1999: 306) formulation of history versus historicity is useful here. History may tell us how contexts have evolved. Historicity, on the other hand, tells us about the significance of history in the present. Giddens (1984: 374) provides a similar idea of historicity versus history, suggesting that historicity involves a particular view of what 'history' is, which means using knowledge of history to change it.
15. The view corresponds somewhat to Smircich and Stubbart's (1985: 726) view of enacted environments, when they write, 'In an enacted environment model the world is essentially an ambiguous field of experience. There are no threats or opportunities out there in an environment, just material and symbolic records of action. But a strategist—determined to find meaning—makes relationships by bringing connections and patterns to the action.'
16. There are several threads of influence between pragmatism and process thinking. Whitehead, for example, was influenced by James, who owed many of his ideas to Peirce. Bergson, whose thinking on temporality corresponds with contemporary thinking in pragmatism, was one of the sources of influence of Deleuze.
17. See Schatzki (2010) for a discussion of teleological aims, notably his critique of Joas' notions of teleology, where Schatzki argues that Noas holds a narrow conception of teleology.
18. Czarniawska (2004: 781) articulates her view as follows, 'A network assumes actors who make contacts, whereas action nets assume that connections between actions produce actors: one becomes "a publisher" because one publishes books, but, for books to be published, there must be somebody writing them; a "writer" is somebody who writes books, not someone who has a business card with this word printed on it.'
19. For example, in a study of a Danish ferry company Skærbæk and Tryggestad (2010) show how accounting practices took part in shaping corporate strategy. Their findings suggest that accounting performed a role in relation to the following elements: (1) strategy formulation (they found that rather than accounting devices being adopted and adapted to fit strategy in a subordinate role, the strategy adopted by the company was in fact adopted and successively adapted to and mutually constituted by the accounting device); (2) the identity of the key strategic actor (a common assumption is that the key strategic actor is the CEO and that the role of the budget is as intended by him or her, but their findings suggest that the identity and intentions of the key strategic actor are highly dependent on the accounting devices); and, (3) the constitution of strategy and strategic change (they found that accounting participated in the actual (re)formulation of corporate strategy).
20. Thinking about how practices participate in the making of strategies is no doubt an important element in organizational theorizing. However, as mentioned above, a strategy is but one (although maybe persistent) aspect of organizational life, and actions cannot be seen to be oriented towards the strategy alone. This touches on old debates in the social sciences and perhaps most notably Schütz' critique of Weber's conception of meaningful social actions. It is in this critique by Schütz that I find a useful point about the conceptualization of actions and meaning.
21. 'Once materialized, the state of affairs brought forth by our actions will necessarily have quite other aspects than those projected. In this case foresight is not distinguished from hindsight by the dimension of time in which we place the event' (Schütz 1959).

22. Heidegger's view was also that 'repetition hands over the past as a past with *meaning* or *sense*' (Schrag 1970: 289) (italics in original).
23. As Knorr-Cetina and Bruegger (2002) point out, Schütz departs from any attempt to base social relatedness on the assumption of the shared content of experience or on any real understanding of other minds, instead basing his theory on the sharedness of experience, of being there, at the same time. Hence, as they point out, '[...] according to Schütz, was the contemporaneousness of an event, the subject's experience of it, and the indications of the other's attentiveness to it: "Since we are growing older together during the flight of the bird, and since I have evidence, in my own observations, that you were paying attention to the same event, I may say that *we* saw a bird in flight"' (1964: 25).
24. They draw on Husserl for the expression 'polythetic' experiences, i.e. experiences that combine into a structure by virtue of their plurality while at the time sharing some characteristics. Once a total experience is to be made sense of, however, it becomes subject to monothetic recall in which experiences are categorized by virtue of similarity or temporal occurrence.
25. The point bears resemblance to Bergson's (1910) discussion of the counting of sheep referred to in chapter 2, where counting one sheep is not a recurrence of counting an earlier one.
26. The definition is in principle similar to the way in which the identity of actors is conceptualized in ANT, where actors' identities are conceptualized through processes of mutual translation. However, the elements of temporality and the assumption of choice in temporal existence prevent process theory from taking the principle of human–nonhuman symmetry as far as ANT does.
27. 'We talk to nature; we address the clouds, the sea, the tree, and objects about us. We later abstract from that type of response because of what we come to know of such objects. The immediate response is, however, social; where we carry over a thinking process into nature we are making nature rational. It acts as it is expected to act. We are taking the attitude of the physical things about us, and when we change the situation nature responds in a different way' (Mead 1934: 184).
28. For example, as in Callon (1986a: 14):

> The scallops are transformed into larvae, the larvae into numbers, the numbers into tables and curves which represent easily transportable, reproducible, and diffusable sheets of paper.... Instead of exhibiting the larvae and the towlines to their colleagues at Brest, the three researchers show graphic representations and present mathematical analyses. The scallops have been displaced. They are transported into the conference room through a series of transformations.

> On the other hand, Latour (1999: 100) suggests a framework to describe the flows of the becoming of scientific facts, which comes close to a process view as suggested in this book, although it is not explicitly temporal. In this framework he works with four rings or cycles, referred to as mobilization of the world, autonomization, alliances, and public representation. The rings are connected by links and knots to illustrate their ongoing as opposed to sequential nature.

29. ANT studies take time into consideration, which does not, however, imply that temporality figures strongly in their accounts. Time is taken into consideration in the sense of ordering of activities. For example, in his analysis of the efforts of scientists to effect the domestication of scallops in St Brieuc Bay, Callon (1986) describes the order of their acts. He describes how the scientists started out with a visit to Japan and then went on to initiate their project

in St Brieuc Bay. Next they went through successive stages of enrolling fishermen, larvae, and other researchers in their project. The story would have appeared differently, though, if there had been a stronger emphasis on temporality and the various stages had been given temporal agency, in the sense of how strongly or weakly their project intentions connected backwards and forwards in time.

30. Connectedness essentially implies the readiness of various heterogeneous elements to interact with one another and thus to create a coherent whole. As suggested above, an exogenous view treats organizations or environments as contexts for interaction. A different view is being put forward by an emerging group of theorists who seek to transcend the limits of organizational theorizing by interpreting organization as the process of connecting heterogeneous elements. This conceptualization sees organizations as evolving from a more eclectic basis of factors such as artefacts, technologies, and human or institutional actors. Czarniawska (2004) speaks of 'connection' and suggests that connecting is the central activity in organizing processes. Chia (2003) presents an argument for organizing as 'world-making'. By world-making he means how organizing involves combining heterogeneous factors that all work to stabilize actions in time-space. Law (1994) adopts a similar stance regarding organization as a heterogeneous mix of materials, technologies, texts, and humans gathered together in a single entity, the formal organization. According to Law a 'pure' social organization would not last very long: it is by building a network of heterogeneous elements that an object becomes more or less stable. Such conceptualizations help us to understand the way different elements interact, or are made to interact, thus forming a stabilizing configuration.

31. Incidentally this may be compared to Latour's ANT version of herding sheep, which focuses on the spatial stabilization performed by material actors translating the role of the (sleeping) shepherd:

> As a common shepherd all I have to do is delegate to a wooden fence the task of containing any flock—then I can just go to sleep with my dog beside me. Who is acting while I am asleep? Me, the carpenters, and the fence. Am I expressed in this fence as if I had actualized outside of myself a competence that I possessed in potential form? Not in the slightest. The fence doesn't look at all like me. It is not an extension of my arms or of my dog. It is completely beyond me. It is an actant in its own right. Did it appear all of a sudden out of objective matter ready to crush my poor, fragile, sleepy body with its material constraints? No, I went folding myself into it precisely because it did not have the same durability, duration, plasticity, temporality—in short the same ontology as me. By folding myself into it, I was able to slip from a complex relationship that demanded my continual vigilance to a mere complicated relationship that didn't demand any more of me than padlock the gate. Are the sheep interacting with me when they bump their muzzles against the rough pine planks? Yes, but they are interacting with a me that is, thanks to the fence, disengaged, delegated, translated and multiplied. There is indeed a complete actor who is henceforth an actor who is added to the world of sheep, although it is one that has characteristics totally different from those of bodies. Any time an interaction has temporal and spatial extension, it is because one has shared it with non-humans. (Latour 1996: 239)

32. But not different, as in the case of actuality, whereby things may be considered to turn out differently than expected. Potentiality is oriented towards the future and its possible impact on the present.

33. A parallel may be found with Deleuze's (2004) distinction between the virtual and the actual. The actual may be observed as the qualities of an entity as experienced. We may, for example, view an iPhone as exhibiting certain qualities, including its weight, its functions, its battery

life, etc. But entities also have their virtual side, which includes the experienced ideas they represent, including the processes that 'made' them. Virtuality signifies intensities (or pure becomings) in the encounter with human sensations (Williams 2003: 6). Thus an auditing department, for example, beyond performing auditing operations (actuality) is perceived as representing the idea of auditing as acts of 'purification' (Skærbæk 2009), which represent the historically produced virtual side of auditing. Intensities signify depth and multiplicity (Deleuze 2004: 305) in the process of individuation. Hence intensities cannot be general, but can only be individual to the entity in question. An important point is the dynamic interplay between virtualization and actualization, since the individuation process consists of ongoing actualizations of the virtual. In its virtuality an iPhone, for example, expresses a multitude of intensities as they are experienced by the individual; and in the process of individuation the intensities expressed by the virtual aspects of the iPhone are actualized. The ongoing actualization of the virtual is innate to Deleuze's line of thought, which takes place when virtuality is translated into action.

34. This is what Husserl (1991: 62) refers to as memory of the present, durations up to the actual present now, i.e. experience that belongs to the past while forming part of the present, but which is not seen as past experiences remembered.

35. 'Repetition in the eternal return never means continuation, perpetuation, or prolongation, nor even the discontinuous return of something which could at least be able to be prolonged in a partial cycle (an identity, an I, a self); on the contrary, it means the reprise of pre-individual singularities which, in order that it can be grasped as repetition, presupposes the dissolution of all prior identities' (Deleuze 2004: 252).

36. This is why Luhmann, for example, does not treat process as isolated from structure, but considers structure and process as complementary terms (Luhmann 2000: 340). Structure and process become related to one another through *events* at which selections are made. Events, as compared to structure, do not keep options open, but mark irreversibly the choice of some options over others. Because systems depend on being both reversible and irreversible (keeping options open while also making selections), both structure and process become important to systems (Hernes 2008).

37. Contingency is defined here in line with Luhmann's (1995) definition as that which is neither necessary nor impossible, but rather that which enables the improbable to become probable: 'If everyone acts contingently, and thus everyone could also act differently, and knows this about oneself and others and takes this into account, it is, for the moment, improbable that one's own action will generally find points of connection (and with them conferral of meaning) in the actions of others; self-commitment would presuppose that others commit themselves and vice versa. Along with the *improbability* of social order, this concept explains its *normality*; under the condition of double contingency, every self-commitment, however accidentally arisen or however calculated, will acquire informational and connective value for the action of others' (Luhmann 1995: 116).

Chapter 4

1. This applies to evocation as a basis for socially coordinated action, and does not necessarily hold for individual introspection.
2. On the LEGO Group official site: <http://aboutus.lego.com/en-us/lego-group/the_lego_history/1930/> (accessed 13 November 2013).

3. According to Kline (1986: 215), Einstein once declared that 'for us...physicists...the distinction between past, present, and future is only an illusion, even if a stubborn one'.
4. Nor did Deleuze (2004) see past and future as having a 'real' existence, but rather as existing as dimensions of the present.
5. One consequence is that the distinction drawn between the present and the past becomes arbitrary, an observation borne out by Bergson (2007: 152): 'The distinction we make between our present and past is therefore, if not arbitrary, at least relative to the extent of the field which our attention to life can embrace. The "present" occupies exactly as much space as this effort. As soon as this particular attention drops any part of what it held beneath its gaze, immediately that portion of the present thus dropped becomes ipso facto a part of the past.'
6. Boden, however, works from an ethnomethodological perspective that emphasizes configurations of verbal utterances, but without considering the influence of ongoing temporality. Mead's well-known work in his 1934 book, *Mind, Self and Society*, should also be mentioned, as it represents a particularly profound contribution to situated social interaction and the creation of meaning through the ongoing balancing act between the 'I', the 'me', and the 'generalized other'.
7. Although not meant to be synonymous with Heidegger's notion of *Dasein*, the definition is inspired by how it explains two aspects of being in the world. *Dasein* derives from a combination of two different German words and may be taken to mean two things depending on which words it is seen to originate from. The combination of *da* (there) and *sein* (be) translates as 'being there', or what may be understood as being there in the world, while the combination of *das* (the) and *ein* (one) translates as 'the one' and is seen as an entity, but not an entity with substance, such as a physical body. Joined together, the two different combinations may be taken to mean 'the one' 'being there'. *Dasein* as a unity is constituted in time, by being in the world, and not by virtue of having enduring physical substance.
8. *Le ferment de l'acide lactique change son histoire au contact de Pasteur et de son laboratoire. Il est bien réel, mais sa réalité historique le met à parité avec le chercheur et le laboratoire dans lequel il se mêle* (Latour 1994: 11).
9. Such a view of temporal agency is somewhat similar to that of Emirbayer and Mische (1998: 970), who from a temporal view define human agency as 'the temporally constructed engagement by actors of different structural environments—the temporal-relational contexts of actions—which, through the interplay of habit, imagination, and judgment, both reproduces and transforms those structures in interactive response to the problems posed by changing historical situations.'
10. As pointed out by James:

    Perceptual flux means nothing...(I)t is always a much-at-once, and contains innumerable aspects and characters which conception can pick out, isolate, and thereafter always intend....[O]ut of this aboriginal sensible muchness attention carves out objects, which conception then names and identifies forever—in the sky 'constellations,' on the earth 'beach,' 'sea,' 'cliff,' 'bushes,' 'grass.' / (T)he intellectual life of man consists almost wholly in his substitution of a conceptual order for the perceptual order in which his experience originally comes. (James 1996: 49–51, from Weick 2011: 10)

11. Asymmetry between past and future represented as difference between the particular and the specific is illustrated in Weick's (1979: 196–197) account of experiments on people concerning how they reason differently, depending on whether they refer to a hypothetical past

or a hypothetical future. In the experiment one group of people was asked to describe an accident that had taken place, whereas another group was asked to describe an accident as if it were to take place. Curiously, even though both the past and future accidents were hypothetical, the content of the descriptions differed. The descriptions of a past accident tended to be very explicit, providing details about the inhabitants of the car and their injuries, while the descriptions of a future accident tended to be more general, with less attention to detail, particularly when it came to personal injuries and car damage. More attention was given to explaining broader consequences of the crash, such as the involvement of other cars.

The asymmetry is also an issue of philosophy, summarized by Hartshorne (1987: 7) as follows: 'Experience exhibits a contrast, one of the most basic of contrasts, between the actualized happenings of the past and the possible or probable but not actual happenings of the future. Particulars are all past; there are no future particulars. To think the future is to think in more or less general terms; for there is no other way to think "future events." The becoming of events is the particularization of more or less general plans, purposes, tendencies, potentialities. There is no such thing as a fully particularized plan, purpose or potentiality. Always much is left for the future to further define or determine. The very meaning of plan or purpose implies this. Futurity and generality are two aspects of the same basic mode of reality. How few are logicians or metaphysicians who have clearly seen this! Aristotle, great logician, seemed to see it. Did Plato see it? Probably, to some extent. Do most logicians see it today? I gather that they do not. But Peirce (and his disciple W. P. Montague) saw it, and Whitehead saw it. James, Dewey, and Bergson all with some clarity saw it.'

12. How active it is may be better appreciated by paying attention to Bergson's (1911: 194) observation that:

In the fraction of a second which covers the briefest possible perception of light, billions of vibrations have taken place, of which the first is separated from the last by an interval which is enormously divided. Your perception, however instantaneous, consists then in an incalculable multitude of remembered elements; and in truth every perception is already memory. Practically we perceive only the past, the pure present being the invisible progress of the past gnawing into the future.

13. Whitehead (1920) refers to an event as the temporal experience that presents itself as a temporal unit in which sense-awareness is exercised.

14. The indeterminate and unsettling, yet intriguing feeling of being in the flow of speech may be obtained by reading text without punctuation (such as the last part of James Joyce's *Ulysses*, which explicitly uses stream of consciousness when describing the thoughts and sexual fantasies of Molly Bloom.

15. In a sense this situation may be compared to Heidegger's notion of play, where time is left open and the interaction is indeterminate. Bakken, Holt, and Zundel (2013: 20) sum up Heidegger's notion of play as follows:

'A play is without a "why" (*warum*); the "why" dissolves in and is entirely absorbed by (*versinkt*) the game' (Heidegger 2006/1957). Here, all that remains is play—the highest and the deepest ground for being—the same. Being as play, he suggests, plays being and ground to us. The question is thus: whether and how we, while hearing the sentences of this play, engage in the play and adjust (*fügen*) ourselves into the game.

16. I think that Bakhtin's work has much to say at this point, as indicated by this passage from Cunliffe, Helin, and Luhman (2014) in their reference to Bakhtin's idea of self as dialogical, unfinalizable, and always in relation to others. The authors add that, 'While we may

conceptualize life as a whole, Bakhtin argues that we experience it as both given and yet-to-be-achieved in once-occurrent events' (Cunliffe, Helin, and Luhman 2014 (page numbers not yet allocated)).

17. It is not necessary to enter into the discussion about whether, say, machines or plants under some conditions are able to act more or less like humans, because virtually every act in organizational life is essentially socio-material in nature. Even if communication between two persons was hypothetically considered devoid of materiality (e.g. no spatial factors were considered), their gestures may be considered in part material because they are performed with bodily parts, which, apart from being made of material substances, also have their own response patterns enabled by the communicative systems between the cells. The example of the wink of an eye illustrates how an inter-subjective moment of 'living presence' is momentarily objectified by the movement of the eyelid and becomes an event. The eyelid may also be considered material substance distinguishable from the 'human' system, yet not meaningful if not seen as part of a composite socio-material whole.

18. Organized action falls into this category and therefore cannot be reduced to inner experience. Garfinkel's (1967: 114) argument that social action takes its point of departure in accountability is borne out in his study of jurors, where he observed how the decision of the jury was justified and explained in retrospect as the jurors went back and found the 'why' of the decision.

19. Huff (1988), for example, makes the point that decision points, such as budget and planning meetings, are regular opportunities for people, solutions, and problems to meet. She suggests that it is an achievement by organizations to create recurring decision points, i.e. inter-subjective events where different interests, needs, solutions, and problems can meet. Huff (1988: 88) also points out the political aspect of meetings, namely that not only are meetings seen as political arenas, but the timing and structuring of meetings also serve political agendas.

20. This view relates to the assumption of endogeneity of process discussed above, whereby the past is immanent in every occasion. This is a logical implication from the assumption that there is no exogenous structure that frames the process, but rather that structure is part of the process just as process is part of the structure.

21. The reasoning goes as follows. Every act enters our experience with the flow of time, which means that every present act embodies all previous acts. This is what Whitehead calls the principle of immanence; the fact that each outcome, each situation, or each state always necessarily incorporates and absorbs the events of its past (Chia 1999: 220). Hence the act in the present becomes past to a new present with the flow of time. Because the 'present' present becomes part of the 'new' present's past, the new present becomes the past of the ensuing present, and so on; every present will have a different past while including the pasts of every previous present. In other words, the passing of time signifies an accumulation of pasts, with every present embodying a different past. Mead (1934: 36) makes the point as follows:

It is idle, at least for the purpose of experience, to have recourse to a 'real' past within which we are making constant discoveries; for that past must be set over against a present within which the emergent appears, and the past, which must then be looked at from a standpoint of the emergent, becomes a different past.

Still, the reality experienced is always in the present. As Mead (1929a: 235) emphatically states:

The actual passage of reality is in the passage of one present into another, where alone is reality, and a present which has merged in another is not a past. Its reality is always that of a present. The past as it appears is in terms of representations of various sorts, typically in memory images, which are themselves present.

22. In Deleuze's (2004: 97) words, 'The role of the imagination, or the mind which contemplates in its multiple and fragmented states, is to draw something new from repetition, to draw difference from it.'

23. It also means that to understand processes as patterns of events does not suffice if it is not understood how events mutually recreate each other as each others' pasts and futures.

24. Weick's sensemaking framework may be criticized for overemphasizing retrospectivity. Although temporal experience is asymmetrical (i.e. only past experience may be reflected on as having taken place), past and future are entangled in the present and may seem inseparable from the view of temporality as an ongoing projection of past experience upon a possible future. In fact, as pointed out above, Heidegger, for one, gave ontological primacy to future over past, and Schütz worked from the idea of 'future perfect', whereby he reversed the order of past-present-future.

25. There are interesting signs that temporal agency is becoming an issue in the design of workplaces. In a newspaper article, Lindsay (2013) reports on 'engineering serendipity', which means that organizations arrange workplaces to make innovation more probable. At the centre of this thinking is the idea of serendipitous encounters, which may spur innovation. For example, he mentions a study at Arizona State University where they used sensors and surveys to study creativity within teams, and where one of the findings was that people felt most creative on days spent in motion meeting people, not working for long stretches at their desks. Naturally, the challenge is to design the dynamics of social life in such a way that events or encounters spur other encounters.

26. 'Witnessing a historic moment is such an odd and exhilarating thing. It is hard to register the full scope of it because you are chest deep in it' (Blow 2013).

27. It also has to do with the high level of focus on structure, the main body of which is still influenced by Parsons' ideas of systems in equilibrium, which gives agency to space rather than to time. Accordingly, Emirbayer and Mische (1998: 965–966) find that temporal agency was largely overlooked by Parsons: 'In none of his writings, ... did Parsons elaborate a fully temporal theory of agency (or, indeed, of structure): agency remained "outside" of time ... while structure remained a spatial category rather than (also) a temporal construction.'

28. In the 'key' to Whitehead's book *Process and Reality*, Sherburne (1966: 10) schematically shows how an experiential event, A, is in the immediate past of experiential event B; B 'reaches out' to include A in B through prehension. Prehension, however, is a selective process, which means that it is not event A that becomes included in B as event A, but rather it is the 'A-ness' prehended by B, thus constituting the becoming of B. Whitehead saw the importance of showing the difference between what he called 'dead facts' and 'feelings'. He saw the transition from facts to feelings as necessary for what he called the 'creative advance' of the world, as feelings make dead facts come alive and enable novelty. Temporal agency relates to the ability of events to actively reach out to other events through 'feelings'. If we classify events by the use of mere descriptions of what takes place at the event, we may lose out on the connecting power of the event to other events; in other words, its temporal agency may be lost with regard to the analysis.

29. On this point Whitehead's view was shared by James, who rejected a serial conception of events which he called a 'string of bead-like sensations and images' (James 1890: 607).

30. Although the main person behind the design was this particular designer, the idea came up amid special sessions called 'extreme thinking sessions' that an external consulting firm had run for the designers.

31. Whitehead points at the internal relatedness between events as 'prehension', by which he means that each durational unit 'prehends' other events. Thus, as Field (1983: 270) notes, even though the units are discrete, they are not insulated from one another, and the qualities of one unit pervade the constitution of other events, past and future.
32. This is why Whitehead, for one, thought that events should be granted 'mind-like' properties in order to account for the potentiality of process. For example, he writes 'an event has anticipation' (Whitehead 1925a: 72). Here lies an important contribution to process philosophy and organizational analysis in that it distinguishes itself from a substance-based philosophy while avoiding the rejection of the existence of physical objects.
33. One can think of at least three ways in which mirroring may be characterized to comply with these criteria. First, it signifies distortion. What is 'seen' in another event is not the same as what is experienced in the present. Second, it signifies selection. What is projected and observed is a selected portion of the overall picture. Third, it signifies recollection. What is 'seen' strikes a chord of resemblance with that which is going on in the present.

Chapter 5

1. There are exceptions, though. Jones et al. (2013) show how categories, while powerfully shaping understanding of institutional phenomena, such as architecture, change as they become subject to contestation, leading to reconciliation and re-drawing of category boundaries.
2. This is consistent with, for example, Foucault's (1972) idea of the formation of objects through discourse.
3. In fact, Stengers (2008: 3), in a constructivist reading of Whitehead's book *Process and Reality*, treats abstractions similar to the way they are treated by mathematicians, which is to treat them as lures rather than as generalizations: 'To define abstractions as lures, and not as generalizations, is something any mathematician would endorse. For a mathematician abstractions are not opposed to concrete experience. They vectorize concrete experience.... In order to think abstractions in the constructivist sense I am presenting, we need to forget about nouns like "a table" or "a human being," and think rather about a mathematical circle. Such a circle is not abstracted from concrete circular forms, its mode of abstraction is related to its functioning as a lure for mathematical thought, luring mathematicians into adventures which produce into a mathematical mode of existence new aspects of what it means, to be a circle.'
4. Hutchins (1995), for example, writes, 'In giving an account of how to do a task, the performer must assume a world (perhaps more correctly, the report must presuppose a world) in which the described actions make sense.'
5. See, in particular, his discussion of the obelisk Cleopatra's Needle, pp. 165–171.
6. The concept of meaning structures is used in semiotics (Peirce 1998), phenomenology (Heidegger 1927; Merleau-Ponty 1995) and philosophy of language (Austin 1955). It has also been extended to sociology (Cerulo 1988; Dahlberg 2006; Mohr 1998), and organization studies (Beckert 2010; Hernes 2010; Levitt and March 1988; March and Olsen 1989; Meyer and Höllerer 2010).
7. A parallel is found in Greimas and Courtés' notion of actants. This replaced the term 'character' with the term 'actant' (Czarniawska and Hernes 2005): 'that which accomplishes or undergoes an act' (Greimas and Courtés 1982: 5) because it applies not only to human beings but also to animals, objects, or concepts.

8. It is not obvious how one distinguishes a sign from an object, except, perhaps, the sign may be seen as an object not physically present, which is how Knorr-Cetina (1999) deals with signs in her study of laboratories. Laboratories are interesting sites because, being obliged to reduce the complexities of the natural world to the confines of the laboratory, they engage in systematic sign production. Knorr-Cetina observes from her study that different cultural systems construe the world differently according to where they place their bets—between signs and non-signs, i.e. objects or substances, and that they may upgrade or downgrade the role of signs. Molecular biology practice, for example, favours experiential knowledge over sign-mediated practice (Knorr-Cetina 1999: 80). Drawing a distinction between sign and object based on whether or not the object is modelled may work for the study of scientific knowledge and laboratory practice, but it is less certain that it works in organizational life, where distinctions between what is socially constructed versus scientifically constructed seem more ambiguous. Performance-measurement systems, for example, are methodologically constructed using mathematics and they consist of various material artefacts activated by practices. On the other hand, they also constitute important signs, even symbols. As March (1987) reminds us, rational decision making is a celebrated myth in modern society. In other words, decisions are made partly because decision makers would like to be seen as—or see themselves as—rational decision makers. On the one hand, we may speak of a sign of an object when it is manifestly a representation of an object that is not physically present, although it could be argued that physical presence is not in itself a precise indicator. What happens, for example, when a team of surgeons operate on a person thousands of kilometres away via robots? On the other hand, although an object is physically present it can also be said to constitute a sign.

9. James (1890: 621) is explicit on this point: 'But a movement is a change, a process; so we see that in the time-world and the space-world alike the first known things are not elements, but combinations, not separate units, but wholes already formed. The condition of *being* of the wholes may be the elements; but the condition of our *knowing* the elements is our having already felt the wholes as wholes'. Similarly Irgens (2011: 17) points out how Cassirer made much the same point, 'Cassirer believed that in the true synthesis of consciousness, the relationship between the parts is fundamentally surpassed by the relationship of the "whole" to the "parts."'

10. Lorino and Mourey (2013) also refer to Dewey and Follett when making the point about parts deriving from wholes: 'For we never experience nor form judgment about objects and events in isolation, but only in connection with a contextual whole. This latter is what is called a "situation"…an environing experienced world…in which observation of this or that object or event occurs…with reference to some active adaptive response to be made' (Dewey 1938/1993: 73). Follett (1924: 12), too, emphasizes that a fact does not exist in isolation but only through its connection to other facts within a situation and that the whole is not a matter of adding but of interweaving: 'The same activity determines both parts and whole (…). The reciprocal activity of the parts changes the parts while it is creating the unity' (1927/2003: 193–194).

11. As Czarniawska (2009: 156) notes, words are things, not the other way around; and as things they can be used to construct or destruct. I also follow Pickering (1995a: 3) and his concept of scientific culture as including human skill, relations, machines, and instruments, as well as scientific facts and theories. Finally Star (2010: 213) concedes, although reluctantly, that boundary objects may also be words, 'For instance, when archaeologists and classical scholars collaborated to interpret particular words from the Rosetta stone, it would seem likely that a small group of words (or even a single word) could form a boundary object based on the nature of their work relationships'.

12. The Ulstein Group signed a contract with a Singaporean ship-owner company in September 2013 for delivery of two vessels of their PX121 series. On the Ulstein website, where the contract was announced, the following quote appears: 'The first vessels are operating in the harsh waters of the North Sea, and feedback states that the vessels are working brilliantly. Operators are reporting that the vessels have higher regularity than comparable vessels due to their capabilities both in terms of station keeping and transit speed in foul weather. The crews are very impressed with the X-BOW® performance, saying they wouldn't have believed it if they hadn't experienced it. A quote from one of the crews: "No rolling, no spray, just pure fun."' <http://ulstein.com/Kunder/ulstein/cms66.nsf/pages/newslista.htm?open&disp_key =1CCFBBA1E575519EC1257BE1004AAE4A> (accessed 14 November 2013).

13. 'There is always a core that is given and taken for granted which is surrounded by references to other possibilities that cannot be pursued at the same time. Meaning, then, is actuality surrounded by possibilities. The structure of meaning is the structure of this difference between actuality and potentiality. Meaning is the link between the actual and the possible; it is not one or the other' (Luhmann 1990: 83).

14. A parallel to this thinking in organization studies is Kogut and Zander's (1992) idea of 'combinative capability' of firms, which they defined as a firm's ability 'to synthesize and apply current and acquired knowledge' […] which 'correspond to a combination of current capabilities and expectations regarding future opportunities' (Kogut and Zander 1992: 385).

15. Some might argue that Polanyi's ideas, focusing on individual knowledge, do not apply to collectivities such as organizations. True, one should always be careful with transferring phenomena ascribed to individuals to diffuse things such as organizations. For example, treating organizational memory analogously to individual memory could lead to reductionist analysis of organizational memory. Still, as Tsoukas (2005) points out, there is no reason why we should not translate Polanyi's individual-based thinking to organizational theorizing, provided that we do it at a sufficient level of abstraction.

16. In past years performative views have been applied in a number of works in organization studies (e.g. Feldman and Pentland 2003, 2005; Cooren 2004). Feldman and Pentland (2003, 2005), for example, apply a performative view to organizational routines, which they contrast to an ostensive view. Whereas an ostensive view considers routines in their abstracted, summarized form, a performative view considers them as the specific activities that constitute the routine.

17. Giving structure a temporal dimension, Giddens (1984: 377) suggests that 'Structure exists only as memory traces, the organic basis of human knowledgeability, and as instantiated in action'. However, Giddens leaves out the future as part of temporality.

18. Applying Heidegger's terminology to organizations more precisely would be to say that organizations are their 'historicalities'. The state of being involves 'historicality'. *Dasein* 'is' its past. It is, as it were, 'pushing itself along "behind" it' (Heidegger 1927: 20).

19. It is also useful to repeat Bourdieu (1977), who argues that what he calls a 'theory of practice' is necessary to counter the often reductionist view reflected in methodological objectivism. Bourdieu makes precisely this point about history and time, i.e. that methodological objectivism has worked from the idea of human practice being reified in structures that lie outside individual history and group history. In order to offer an alternative to such reductions, Bourdieu (1977: 72) recommends that we abandon ideas whereby social order is seen through the lens of 'statistical regularity or algebraic structure' and that we engage in observing how orders are actually produced.

20. Schatzki (2006: 1864–1865) makes a similar point when he suggests that 'An arrangement helps constitute an organization as something that houses human activity, that is, because it and the entities composing it (1) are referred to or used in or (2) causally support the organization's practices. An example of an arrangement that causally supports many practices is a department or university computer system. Hence, a third aspect of the happening of organizations—in addition to performance and governance—is the material world being taken up in and supporting the performance of the organization's actions.'

21. Although the notion of articulation is not a common term in organization studies, it has been associated with work coordination processes since the 1980s in works by sociologist Anselm Strauss and colleagues (Strauss et al. 1985; Gerson and Star 1986; Strauss 1988), and pursued in the Computer Supported Collaborative Work (CSCW) field (Schmidt and Bannon 1992). This work, although highly relevant to the understanding of organizing and organizations, has not been widely cited in the field of organization studies. Nevertheless, articulation and the associated assumptions about organizational life are significant to a process view of organization. According to Strauss (1988), articulation forms part of a 'negotiated order'. Articulation of that order (which is what I suppose Strauss calls 'the articulation process') helps task systems to function even though parts of the system are not aligned. At the same time it enables decomposition of local problems as they become aligned through more system-wide articulation (Gerson and Star 1986).

22. Schoeneborn (2013) provides an interesting discussion of the dynamics of using PowerPoint presentations among consultants, pointing out how communicative events using PowerPoint may serve to constitute professional or organizational identities.

23. 'Taken strictly, "meaning" signifies the "upon-which" of the primary projection of the understanding of Being. When Being-in-the-world has been disclosed to itself and understands the Being of that entity which it itself is, it understands equiprimordially the Being of entities discovered within-the-world, even if such Being has not been made a theme, and has not yet even been differentiated into its primary modes of existence and Reality. All ontical experience of entities—both circumspective calculation of the ready-to-hand, and positive scientific cognition of the present-at-hand—is based upon projections of the Being of the corresponding entities—projections which in every case are more or less transparent. But in these projections there lies hidden the 'upon-which', of the projection; and on this, as it were, the understanding of Being nourishes itself' (Heidegger 1927: 324).

24. A parallel to Heidegger's understanding of meaning may be found in Mead's (1934: 75–76) definition of meaning as the response to a gesture: 'Meaning arises and lies within the field of the relation between the gesture of a given human organism and the subsequent behavior of this organism as indicated to another organism by that gesture. If that gesture does so indicate to another organism the subsequent (or resultant) behavior of the given organism, then it has meaning.'

25. The distinction between present (or actual) and absent (potential) articulations is far more complex in reality, because, as Luhmann (1995: 76) points out, articulations also contrast indeterminate possibilities with other indeterminate possibilities: 'Thus the point of departure for a factual articulation of meaning is a *primary disjunction*, which contrasts something as yet indeterminate to something else as yet indeterminate.'

26. In Weick's work on sensemaking he also points out choice as a prerequisite for sensemaking. Organizations, he points out, 'resemble puzzling terrain because they lend themselves to multiple, conflicting interpretations' (Weick 2001: 9). If organizations work this way, it means that there is an element of choice in processes of sensemaking and that the presence

of choice is what makes the organization meaningful. Choice implies the ability to perceive alternative courses of action. In Weick's (2001) words, sense may be constructed from an indefinite number of plausible possible maps. The totality of articulations, some of which are actualized, others of which are open as possibilities, provides a level of meaning that transcends local connections in a network. Weick's idea of an infinite number of possibilities, however, becomes subject to moderation once temporality enters the equation. Temporality inevitably involves the limitations of past experience, and past experience, although it may in theory offer an infinite number of possibilities, is in most cases limited by the labels that actors have come to allocate to experience over time through habit.

27. I owe this passage to Philippe Lorino (private communication).
28. Heidegger (1927), for example, referred to history as being authentic when it is seen as a recurrence of the possible (Carlisle 2005: 140).
29. 'These protentions were not only present as intercepting, they have also been intercepted. They have been fulfilled, and we are aware of them in recollection. Fulfillment in recollective consciousness is refulfillment' (Husserl 1991: 76).
30. James (1890: 605) writes, '…many things come to be thought by us as past, not because of any intrinsic quality of their own, but rather because they are associated with other things which for us signify pastness.… To think a thing as past is to think it amongst the objects or in the direction of the objects which at the present moment appear affected by this quality. This is the original of our notion of past time, upon which memory and history build their systems.'

Chapter 6

1. Greimas and Courtés replace the term 'character' with the term 'actant', i.e., 'that which accomplishes or undergoes an act' (1982: 5), because it applies not only to human beings but also to animals, objects, or concepts. As Czarniawska (2009) notes, words are things, not the other way around; and as things they can be used to construct or destruct. I also follow Pickering (1995a: 3) and his concept of scientific culture as including human skill, relations, machines, and instruments, as well as scientific facts and theories.
2. Moeran and Strandgaard Pedersen (2011: 10) point out that 'Fairs, festivals and competitive events provide a venue for the (re)enactment of institutional arrangements in a particular industry's field and for the negotiation and affirmation of the different values that underpin them.'
3. Knorr-Cetina and Bruegger (2002: 925) point out that, 'As they take positions (i.e. as they buy and sell currencies for their own accounts), traders become part of the market, and, as a consequence, market events in general and their own position within them is of intense interest to them.'
4. In the words of Cooren (2004: 377) 'A focus on nonhuman agency paves the way to recognizing hybrid agency; that is, the way humans can appropriate what nonhumans do. They exchange properties with each other: the gun is different in a person's hand, just as the person is different with the gun in his hand. Knowledge of this hybrid relationship helps us understand the role that texts play in structuring organizational settings.'
5. Laclau and Mouffe (1985) point out how the theory of speech acts outlines their performative character. They refer to Wittgenstein's (1983) point about language games, that they 'include within an indissoluble totality both language and the actions connected with it: "A is building with building stones; there are blocks, pillars, slabs, and beams. B has to pass the

stones, and that in the order that A needs them. For this purpose they use a language consisting of the words 'beam,' 'pillar,' 'slab,' 'beam.' A calls them out; B brings the stone which he has learnt' (Laclau and Mouffe 1985: 108).

6. Research on face-to-face group behaviour, for example, suggests that people develop collective transactive memory systems where they fill in for one another on the details and locations of past occasions (Boje 1991; Wegner 1986; Weick and Roberts 1993). The act of filling in observed in face-to-face group behaviour bears out the argument from symbolic interactionists that social interaction facilitates meaning.

7. Another example is provided by Tsoukas and Hatch's (2001) interpretation of the temporal role of narratives, taken from Ricoeur (1984). Their discussion brings attention to the powerful role of narratives, which, they argue, serve to organize the continuous flow of experience into sequences of events with beginnings, middles, and ends. Central to narratives and emplotment is, they point out, the '*three-fold* present of our experience (the present of the past, the present of the present, and the present of the future)' (Tsoukas and Hatch, 2001: 1005, italics added).

8. In her analysis, Boden (1994: 205) concludes, 'actors create and re-create their organizations. Their talk [...] is the centre of their coordination.'

9. In a way it reminds actors of how the organization exploits (March 1991) its opportunities.

10. Practical articulation may perform differently in relation to organizational arrangements depending, for example, on the degree of repetition. Referring to Sydow and Staber's (2002) work, Scarbrough et al. (2004: 1583), for instance, point out that 'Unlike communities of practice, project practices tend to be non-repetitive and time-bound, and are often loosely coupled to multiple organizational contexts through subcontracting or supply chain relations.'

11. According to Whitehead (in Stengers 2008) writing gave us, 'increased powers of thought, of analysis, of recollection and of conjecture'. Whitehead's guess, according to Stengers, was that 'before the advent of writing, speech could not be separated from the interfusion of emotional expression and signalling, always entailing an immediate situation' (2008: 12).

12. From Hernes (2008: 129).

13. As I work to complete this book I discover the unit of measurement 'tweets per minute' (TPM) and an argument by Charles Blow in the *New York Times* that although President Obama's speech at the Democratic National Convention did not quite match Democrats and other followers' expectations, what matters is comparing the amount of Twitter activity during the Democratic National Convention with that of the Republican National Convention. According to log.twitter.com/2012/09/dnc2012-3-million-tweets-and-counting.html, First Lady Michelle Obama's speech peaked at 28,003 TPM, more than double that of candidate Mitt Romney. Whether or not tweets can make up for, say, declining economic and labour figures, however, remains to be seen and will require sophisticated analytical approaches. On the other hand, such observations open debate on how large numbers of micro-encounters between messages (tweets) and human actors can affect sensemaking in organizational life, and not just in politics.

14. 'Twitter is often understood as a derivative or miniature version of the regular blog—i.e. a microblog, consisting of "short comments usually delivered to a network of associates"' (Jansen et al. 2009: 2170). Larsson and Moe (2011: 730–731) write, 'By sending short messages—tweets—of up to 140 characters each, Twitter users share these updates to a network of followers.'

15. A social medium different from Twitter, which explicitly invites discussion about temporality, is that of search engines and interactive texts (such as Wikipedia), where contributions

are added and old information can be deleted with the passing of time. With Wikipedia the ongoing editing and corresponding timing is to some extent available for scrutiny, but this does not apply to search engines. Wouters, Helsten, and Leydesdorff (2004), for example, argue that search engines are unreliable tools for data collection for research that aims to reconstruct the historical record, because they delete documents without warning, leading the authors to conclude that 'both Google and Altavista systematically relocate the time stamp of Web documents in their databases from the more distant past into the present and the very recent past. They also delete documents. We show how this erodes the quality of information. The search engines continuously reconstruct competing presents that also extend to their perspectives on the past. This has major consequences for the use of search engine results in scholarly research, but gives us a view on the various presents and pasts living side by side in the Internet' (Wouters, Helsten, and Leydesdorff 2004: 1).

16. 'So, you have to have this feeling for this time spirit in a way, because then you know basically what people are going to like in maybe one year... If you know a lot about what is happening in the world, you can also already imagine what could be in one or two years' time. There are a lot of trend reports and things like this, but it is not only this. You have to kind of feel it or take it in' (Catherine, fashion designer, in Vangkilde, 2012: 138).

17. Weick (2001) views acts, interacts, social commitment, and committed interpretation as elements of sensemaking processes. Social commitment signals commitment to social inter-acts, and forms a bridge to the stage of committed interpretation at which broader structures are invoked to justify acts and inter-acts.

18. 'Once the groove is found, the drummer or bass player can play ahead of, or behind, the beat to create tension by either pushing the tune forward or holding it back, ever so slightly. Without a strong sense of the groove, the practice of playing ahead or behind the beat would lead to rushing or dragging, but with groove, this practice heightens the emotional content of the performance and helps give the music a distinctive feel' (Hatch 1999: 82).

19. 'When managers act, their thinking occurs concurrently with action. Thinking is not sandwiched between activities; rather, it exists in the form of circumspection present when activities are executed' (Weick 1984: 223).

20. This is similar to the point made by Antonacopoulou and Scheaffer (2013), i.e. that practising as a form of repetition harbours the existence of both the known and the unknown.

21. 'This long discussion brings us to the final conclusion that the concrete facts of nature are events exhibiting a certain structure in their mutual relations and certain characters of their own' (Whitehead 1920: 167). In other words, events become constitutive of process as and when they have relevance for a broader set of relations. By being relevant, events may not just reproduce or reinforce existing relations, but they may also change them.

22. Whitehead (1925a) points out that events *mirror* themselves with past, contemporary, and future events. 'Mirroring' is not to be seen as synonymous with becoming identical, but conveys a symmetry of mutual creation. Thus events are nothing in themselves, nor are they causes of other events. At best events have 'anticipation', making for their own becoming, by creating, or 'feeling' another event.

Importantly, following from Whitehead's atomist stance, whereby he would not adhere to a serial conception of time, events instead take the form of a 'manifold'. In this manifold, events can 'feel' other events, which take place at the same time, as well as events that have passed into history and future events, or 'antecedents-to-be' (Wallack 1980: 167). For example, a management meeting, although it takes place after other management meetings and before others, mirrors events that take place at other locations.

Chapter 7

1. The *Oxford English Dictionary* suggests 'grasping' and 'seizing' as synonyms of prehension.
2. Events, however, should not be seen as closed and determinate, but rather as suggestive, open, and propositional. Garfinkel (1967: 40) makes the point that, 'The events that were talked about were specifically vague. Not only do they not frame a clearly restricted set of possible determinations but the depicted events include as their essentially intended and sanctioned features an accompanying "fringe" of determinations that are open with respect to internal relationships, relationships to other events, and relationships to retrospective and prospective possibilities.'
3. Schultz and Hernes (2013) do not mention this point in the paper.
4. At the same time Mead makes the point that bare continuity cannot be experienced: 'But bare continuity could not be experienced. There is a tang of novelty in each moment of experience' (1929a: 239).
5. 'Passage is pure continuity without interruption. Change arises with a departure from continuity. Change does not, however, involve the total obliteration of continuity—there must be a "persisting non-passing content" against which an emergent event is experienced as a change' (Mead 1938: 330–331).
6. This is more complex than it might seem, though. In their discussion of the emergence of *de novo* categories in architecture, Jones et al. (2013) point out how there are different views as to how novel categories emerge, including re-combinations of existing categories and the re-labeling of existing categories. They also point out how distinctions between categories may be graded rather than dichotomous. The authors suggest that novel categories may also come into existence through theorizing, thus enabling the combinations of previously unavailable materials and symbols.
7. This discussion draws inspiration from Latour's (1999) discussion of the becoming of scientific disciples, where he portrays the process as consisting of automization, alliances, public representation and mobilization of the world.

Chapter 8

1. This may be particularly delicate if parts of the memory relate to failures, or even negligent or shameful events. For an interesting discussion, see Rivera's (2008) analysis of how, at nation level, actors may deal with what she (from Goffman) calls stigma. Rivera makes the point about temporality that strategies for dealing with stigmatic parts of the nation's memory relate to the timing of strategies in relation to the time passed since the stigmatic experience.
2. The use of the vector imagery is inspired by Whitehead, who applies it to describe prehension between actual occasions (or drops of experience) to express energy:'The experience has a vector character, a common measure of intensity, and specific forms of feelings that convey that intensity. If we substitute the term "energy" for the conception of quantitative emotional intensity and the term "form of energy" for the concept of specific form of feeling, and remember that in physics vector means "definite transmission from elsewhere", we see that this metaphysical description of the simplest elements in the constitution of actual entities agrees absolutely with the general principles according to which the notions of modern physics are framed' (Whitehead 1929a: 177). Whitehead, with his ambitions for a grand theoretical scheme, felt it was also important to show the parallel with physics, and particularly biology, but the intention here is to use the vector imagery in a more metaphorical sense.

3. It may also apply to certain principles of management that are seen as particularly 'infectious' (Røvik 2011).
4. Sutton and Hargadon's account of brainstorming in the presence of material artefacts illustrates particularly well how combinations of articulatory modes may provide powerful temporal agency: 'The design solutions acquired, recalled, and developed in brainstorms are stored mostly in three locations. First, they are stored in the minds of designers who attend and hear about a brainstorm. Second, products and prototypes acquired for, brought to, and built in brainstorms are kept and then used to design future products. Designers collect old products and prototypes, display them in their offices (which don't have doors, or have doors that are usually left open), talk about them, and loan them to one another because, an informant asserted, they are "solidified intellect, not an object, but rather a collection of ideas." One engineer's office had a chrome-plated plastic nameplate from an Isuzu Trooper, a 1950s Hamilton Beach blender, moulded rubber ears from a past project on headsets, the final headset and several early prototypes, toy cars that contained flywheels, a butane torch that runs on a cigarette lighter, an oversized computer trackball for kids, the prototype for that product made of machined aluminum and electrical components, several surgical products he had designed, and a toy dartgun. Many of these objects were first acquired for brainstorms and were often brought to brainstorms. Third, ideas developed in brainstorms are archived in reports and, occasionally, in videotapes. We saw one designer ask another for a brainstorming report about flexible surgical tubing to get ideas about designing a personal appliance. Another designer said that he sometimes watches old videotapes of especially fruitful brainstorms so that he doesn't forget the "cool" ideas he learned' (Sutton and Hargadon 1996: 699).

Chapter 9

1. 'Any social unit that has some kind of shared history will have evolved a culture, with the strength of that culture dependent on the length of its existence, the stability of the group's membership, and the emotional intensity of the actual historical experiences they have shared' (Schein 1985: 17).
2. Bergson (1922: 5) makes the point as follows, 'And as the past grows without ceasing, so also there is no limit to its preservation. Memory, as we have tried to prove, is not a faculty of putting away recollections in a drawer, or of inscribing them in a register. There is no register, no drawer; there is not even, properly speaking, a faculty, for a faculty works intermittently, when it will or when it can, while piling up of the past upon the past goes on without relaxation'.
3. Evidently these are categories that do not exist in a pure state; it would be useful to investigate the dynamics between them. Garfinkel (1967: 173) offers an interesting observation in this respect, pointing to the 'procedural basis' (my term) for declarative processes, 'In the conduct of his everyday affairs in order for the person to treat rationally the one-tenth of this situation that, like an iceberg appears above the water, he must be able to treat the nine-tenths that lies below as an unquestioned and, perhaps even more interestingly, as an unquestionable background of matters that are demonstrably relevant to his calculation, but which appear without even being noticed'.
4. The account is taken from Aune (1992).
5. In fact, Whitehead borrows the expression from William James, who, in a letter to his brother Henry James, wrote, 'I have to forge every sentence in the teeth of irreducible and stubborn facts' (Whitehead 1925: 3).

Chapter 11

1. The finitude of the mind in relation to the infinitude of possibilities was a concern of Whitehead, who was quoted by Price (1954: 160) as saying, 'This relationship between the finite and the infinite is what I was coming to. Our minds are finite, and yet even in these circumstances of finitude we are surrounded by possibilities that are infinite, and the purpose of human life is to grasp as much as we can out of that infinitude. I wish I could convey this sense I have of the infinity of the possibilities that confront humanity—the limitless variations of choice, the possibility of novel and untried combinations, the happy turns of experiment, the endless horizons opening out.'

REFERENCES

Abbott, Andrew (2001) *Time matters: On theory and method*. Chicago: University of Chicago Press.

Albert, Stuart and David A. Whetten (1985) Organizational identity. *Research on Organizational Behavior* 7: 263–295.

Aldrich, Howard (1999) *Organizations evolving*. Thousand Oaks, CA: Sage Publishers Ltd.

Alvesson, Mats and Dan Kärreman (2007) Constructing mystery: Empirical matters in theory development. *Academy of Management Review* 32(4): 1265–1281.

Antonacopoulou, Elena and Zachary Scheaffer (2013) Learning in crisis: Rethinking the relationship between organizational learning and crisis management. *Journal of Management Inquiry* 23(1): 5–21.

Aune, Tormod (1992) *Mayday fra St Svithun*. Namsos: Højem.

Austin, John L. (1955) *How to do things with words*. Oxford: Oxford University Press.

Bachrach, Peter and Morton S. Baratz (1962) Two faces of power. *The American Political Science Review* 56(4): 947–952.

Bakken, Tore (2014) George Spencer-Brown. In J. Helin, T. Hernes, D. Hjorth, and R. Holt (Eds.) *The Oxford handbook of process philosophy and organization studies*. New York: Oxford University Press.

—— and Tor Hernes (2006) Organizing is both a noun and a verb: Weick meets Whitehead. *Organization Studies* 27(11): 1599–1616.

—— and Eric Wiik (2009) An autopoietic understanding of 'innovative organization'. In R. Magalhes and R. Sanchez (Eds.) *Autopoiesis in organization theory and practice* (pp. 169–184). Bingley: Emerald.

Bakken, Tore, Robin Holt, and Mike Zundel (2013) Time and play in management practice: An investigation through the philosophies of McTaggart and Heidegger. *Scandinavian Journal of Management* 19(1):13–22.

Barbalet, Jack (2014) The Daodejing of Laozi. In J. Helin, T. Hernes, D. Hjorth, and R. Holt (Eds.) *The Oxford handbook of process philosophy and organization studies*. New York: Oxford University Press.

Barley, Stephen R. (1983) Semiotics and the study of occupational and organizational cultures. *Administrative Science Quarterly* 28: 393-413.

Bateson, Gregory (1972) *Steps to an ecology of mind*. Northwhale, NJ: Jason Aronson.

Baum, Joel A. C. (Ed.) (2005) *The Blackwell companion to organizations*. Oxford: Blackwell Wiley.

Bechky, Beth A. (2003) Sharing meaning across occupational communities: The transformation of understanding on a production floor. *Organization Science* 14(3): 312–330.

Beckert, Jens (2010) How do fields change? The interrelations of institutions, networks, and cognition in the dynamics of markets. *Organization Studies* 31(5): 605–627.

Bengtsson, Marie (2008) The art of replication. PhD thesis. Linköping: Linköping University, Faculty of Arts and Sciences.

Bergson, Henri (1910) *Time and free will: An essay on the immediate data of consciousness*. London: George Allen and Unwin.

—— (1911) *Matter and memory*. New York: Zone Books.

—— (1922) *Creative evolution*. London: Macmillan.

—— (1999) *An introduction to metaphysics*. City: Hackett Publishing Company.

—— (2007) *The creative mind*. New York: Dover Publications.

Bernstein, Richard J. (1983) *Beyond objectivism and relativism: Science, hermeneutics, and praxis*. Philadelphia: University of Pennsylvania Press.

Birnholtz, Jeremy P., Michael D. Cohen, and Susannah V. Hoch (2007) Organizational character: On the regeneration of camp poplar grove. *Organization Science* 18(2): 315–332.

Bittner, Egon (1965) The concept of organization. *Social Research* 32(3): 239–255.

Blow, Charles M. (2013) History in real time. *New York Times* published online 27.03.13.

Bluedorn, Allen C. (2002) *The human organization of time: Temporal realities and experience*. Stanford: Stanford University Press.

Blumer, Herbert (1969) *Symbolic interactionism: Perspective and method*. London: University of California Press.

Boden, Deirdre (1994) *The business of talk: Organizations in action*. Cambridge: Polity Press.

Boje, David. M. (1991) The storytelling organization. A study of story performance in an office-supply firm. *Administrative Science Quarterly* 36(1): 106–126.

Bourdieu, Pierre (1977) *Outline of a theory of practice*. Cambridge: Cambridge University Press.

—— and Yvonne Delsaut (1975) Le couturier et sa griffe: contribution à une théorie de la magie. *Actes de la Recherche en Sciences Sociales* 1(1): 7–36.

Brunsson, Nils and Hans Winberg (1990) Implementing reforms. In N. Brunsson and J. P. Olsen (Eds.) *The reforming organization* (pp. 109–126). London: Routledge.

Butler, Judith (2011) *Bodies that matter*. New York: Routledge.

Callon, Michel (1986) Some elements of a sociology of translation: Domestication of the scallops and the fishermen of St Brieuc Bay. In J. Law (Ed.) *Power, action and belief. A new sociology of knowledge?* (pp. 196–233). London: Routledge & Kegan Paul.

—— (1998) An essay on framing and overflowing: Economic externalities revisited by sociology. In M. Callon (Ed.) *The laws of the markets* (pp. 244–269). Oxford: Blackwell Publishers.

Capa, Robert. Photo. London. June–July, 1941. Home Guard warden and woman share tea in an air-raid shelter (see http://www.magnumphotos.com/Catalogue/Robert-Capa/1941/UK-London-WWII-NN138971.html, accessed 6 January 2014).

Carlile, Paul R. (2002) A pragmatic view of knowledge and boundaries: Boundary objects in new product development. *Organization Science* 13(4): 442–455.

Carlisle, Clare (2005) *Kierkegaard's philosophy of becoming*. New York: State University of New York Press.

Castells, Manuel (1996) *The rise of the network society*. Oxford: Blackwell Publishers.

Chambers dictionary of etymology (1988) New York: Chambers.

Chandler, Alfred (1962) *Strategy and structure—chapters in the history of the industrial enterprise*. Cambridge, MASS: MIT Press.

Chen, Katherine K. (2009) *Enabling creative chaos*. Chicago: The University of Chicago Press.

Chia, Robert (1996) The problem of reflexivity in organizational research: Towards a postmodern science of organization. *Organization* 3: 31–59.

—— (1999) A 'Rhizomic' model of organizational change and transformation: Perspective from a metaphysics of change. *British Journal of Management* 10: 209–227.

—— (2003) Ontology: Organization as 'world-making'. In R. Westwood and S. Clegg (Eds.) *Debating organization* (pp. 98–113). Malden, MA: Blackwell.

—— and Robin Holt (2009) *Strategy without design*. Cambridge: Cambridge University Press.

—— and Ian W. King (1998) The organizational structuring of novelty. *Organization* 5(4): 461–478.

—— and Ann Langley (2005) Call for papers for the 1st Organization Studies Summer Workshop on Theorizing Process in Organizational Research, 12–13 June, Santorini, Greece.

Clark, Peter (1985) A review of theories of time and structure for organizational sociology. *Research in the Sociology of Organizations* 4: 35–79.

—— (1990) Chronological codes and organizational analysis. In J. Hassard and D. Pym (Eds.) *The theory and philosophy of organizations: Critical issues and new perspectives* (pp. 137–166). London: Routledge.

Clegg, Stewart R., Cynthia Hardy, and Walter R. Nord (2006) (Eds.). *Sage handbook of organization studies*. London: Sage Publications Ltd.

Cohen, Michael D. (1991) Individual learning and organizational routine: Emerging connections. *Organization Science* 2(1): 135–139.

—— James G. March, and Johan P. Olsen (1972) A garbage can model of organizational choice. *Administrative Science Quarterly* 17(1): 1–25.

Cooper, Robert (1976) The open field. *Human Relations* 29(11): 999–1017.

—— (2005a) Relationality. *Organization Studies* 26(11): 1689–1710.

—— (2005b) Making present: Autopoiesis as human production. *Organization* 13(1): 59–81.

—— (2014) Process and reality. In J. Helin, T. Hernes, D. Hjorth, and R. Holt (Eds.) *The Oxford handbook of process philosophy and organization studies*. New York: Oxford University Press.

—— and John Law (1995) Organization: Distal and proximal views. *Research in the Sociology of Organizations* 13: 237–274.

Cooren, Francois (2004) Textual agency: How texts do things in organizational settings. *Organization* 11(3): 373–393.

Corley, Kevin G. and Dennis A. Gioia (2004) Identity ambiguity and change in the wake of a corporate spin-off. *Administrative Science Quarterly* 49(2): 173–208.

Cunliffe, Ann, Jenny Helin, and Thomas Luhman (2014) Mikhail Bakhtin. In J. Helin, T. Hernes, D. Hjorth, and R. Holt (Eds.) *The Oxford handbook of process philosophy and organization studies*. New York: Oxford University Press.

Cunliffe, Ann L., John T. Luhman, and David M. Boje (2004) Narrative temporality: Implications for organizational research. *Organization Studies* 25(2): 261–286.

Cyert, Richard M. and James G. March [1963](1992) *A behavioural theory of the firm*. 2nd ed. Oxford: Blackwell Publishers.

Czarniawska, Barbara (1997) *Narrating the organization: Dramas of institutional identity*. Chicago: The University of Chicago Press.

—— (2004) On time, space, and action nets. *Organization* 11(6): 773–791.

—— (2009) STS meets MOS. *Organization* 16(1): 155–160.

—— and Tor Hernes (2005) Constructing macro actors according to ANT. In B. Czarniawska and T. Hernes (Eds.) *Actor-network theory and organizing* (pp. 7–13). Copenhagen: Copenhagen Business School Press.

Dahlberg, Karin (2006) The essence of essences: The search for meaning structures in phenomenological analysis of lifeworld phenomena. *International Journal of Qualitative Studies on Health and Well-Being* 1: 11–19.

De laet, Marianne and Anne Marie Mol (2000) The Zimbabwe bush pump: Mechanics of a fluid technology. *Social Studies of Science* 30(2): 225–263.

Deleuze, Gilles (1996) L'actuel et le virtuel (1995). *Dialogues*. Paris: Flammarion.

—— (2004) *Difference and repetition*. London: Continuum.

—— and Félix Guattari, F. (2004) *A thousand plateaus*. London: Continuum.

Dewey, John (1938/1993) *Logic: The theory of inquiry*. New York: Henry Holt. Re-edited in J. A. Boydston (Ed.), *John Dewey: The later works, 1925–1953. Volume 12: 1938*. Carbondale: Southern Illinois University Press.

Dille, Therese and Jonas Söderlund (2011) Managing inter-institutional projects: The significance of isochronism, timing norms and temporal misfits. *International Journal of Project Management* 29(2011): 480–490.

DiMaggio, Paul J. and Walter W. Powell (1983) The iron cage revisited: Institutional isomorphism and collective rationality in organizational fields. *American Sociological Review* 48: 147–160.

—— (Eds.) (1991) *The new institutionalism in organizational analysis*. Chicago: The Chicago University Press.

Dodd, Sarah Drakopoulou, Alistair R. Anderson, and Sarah L. Jack (2013) Being in time, and the family owned firm. *Scandinavian Journal of Management* 19(1): 35–47.

Douglas, Mary (1966) *Purity and danger*. London: Routledge.

—— (1986) *How institutions think*. London: Routledge and Kegan Paul.

Du Gay, Paul (2006) The values of bureaucracy: An introduction. In P. du Gay (Ed.) *The values of bureaucracy* (pp. 1–16). Oxford: Oxford University Press.

DuPuis, Melanie (2002) *Nature's perfect food: How milk became America's drink*. New York: New York University Press.

Dutton, Jane M. and Janet E. Dukerich (1991) Keeping an eye on the mirror: Image and identity in organizational adaptation. *Academy of Management Journal* 34: 517–554.

Eddington, Arthur Stanley (1928) *The nature of the physical world*. Ann Arbor: University of Michigan Press.

Elias, Norbert (1978) *What is sociology?* London: Hutchinson.

—— (1992) *An essay on time*. Dublin: University College Dublin Press.

Emery, Fred E. and Eric L. Trist (1965) The causal texture of organizational environments. *Human Relations* 18: 21–32.

Emirbayer, Mustafa (1997) Manifesto for a relational sociology. *American Journal of Sociology*, 103(2): 281–317.

—— and Ann Mische (1998) What is agency? *American Journal of Sociology* 103(4): 962–1023.

Erdem, Derya Sarac and Morten Eilertsen (2013) How micro-interactions produce learning. MSc thesis, Copenhagen Business School.

Feldman, Martha S. (2000) Organizational routines as a source of continuous change. *Organization Science* 11(6): 611–629.

—— and Brian Pentland (2003) Reconceptualizing organizational routines as a source of flexibility and change. *Administrative Science Quarterly* 48: 94–118.

—— (2005) Organizational routines and the macro-actor. In B. Czarniawska and T. Hernes (Eds.) *Actor-network theory and organizing* (pp. 105–131). Stockholm: Liber.

Field, Richard W. (1983) William James and the epochal theory of time. *Process Studies* 13(4): 260–274.

Fiol, Marlena (1995) Thought worlds colliding: The role of contradiction in corporate innovation processes. *Entrepreneurship and Practice* 19(3): 71–98.

Flaherty, Michael G. (2002) Making time: Agency and the construction of temporal experience. *Symbolic Interaction* 25(3): 379–388.

—— (2003) Time work: Customizing temporal experience. *Social Psychology Quarterly* 66(1): 17–33.

Fleck, Ludwik ([1935] 1979) *The genesis and development of a scientific fact*. Chicago: University of Chicago Press.

Fligstein, Neil (1985) The spread of the multidivisional form among large firms, 1919-1979. *American Sociological Review* 50: 377–391.

Foerster, Heinz von (1991) *Observing systems*. Seaside, CA: Intersystems Publications.

Follett, Mary P. (1924) *Creative experience*. New York: Longmans Green.

—— (1927/2003) The psychology of control. In H.C. Metcalf and L. Urwick (Eds), *Dynamic administration: The collected papers of Mary Parker Follett* (pp. 183–209). New York: Routledge.

Foucault, Michel (1972) *The archeology of knowledge*. London: Tavistock.

—— (1973) *The birth of the clinic*. London: Tavistock Publications.

—— (1994) *The order of things—an archeology of the human sciences*. New York: Vintage Books.

Friedberg, Erhard (1993) *Le pouvoir et la règle*. Paris: Le Seuil.

Friedman, Thomas (2005) *The world is flat*. London: Allen Lane.

—— (2010) Just do it. *New York Times* 17.04.10.

Garfinkel, Harold (1967) *Studies in ethnomethodology*. Cambridge: Polity Press.

Garsten, Christina (2008) *Workplace vagabonds: Career and community in changing worlds of work*. Basingstoke: Palgrave Macmillan.

—— and Tor Hernes (Eds.) (2008) *Ethical dilemmas in management*. London: Routledge.

Garud, Raghu, Arun Kumaraswamy, and Peter Karnoe (2010) Path dependence or path creation? *Journal of Management Studies* 47(4): 760–774.

Geertz, C. (1973) *The interpretation of cultures*. New York: Basic Books.

Gell, Alfred (1992) *The anthropology of time: Cultural constructions of temporal maps and images*. Oxford: Berg.

Gephart, Robert P. (1978) Status degradation and organizational succession: An ethnomethodological approach. *Administrative Science Quarterly* 23: 553–581.

Gephart, Robert P, Jr. (1984) Making sense of organizationally based environmental disasters. *Journal of Management* 10(2): 205–225.

Gerson, Elihu M. and Susan Leigh Star (1986) Analyzing due process in the workplace: *ACM Transactions on Office Information Systems* 4(3): 257–270.

Gherardi, Silvia (2000) Practice-based theorizing on learning and knowing in organizations. *Organization* 7(2): 211–223.

—— and Davide Nicolini (2005) Actor-networks: Ecology and entrepreneurs. In B. Czarniawska and T. Hernes (Eds.) *Actor-network theory and organizing* (pp. 348–375). Stockholm: Liber.

Gherardi, Silvia and Antonio Strati (1988) The temporal dimension in organizational studies. *Organization Studies* 9(2): 149–164.

Giddens, Anthony (1979) *Central problems in social theory: Action, structure and contradiction in social analysis*. London: Macmillan.

—— (1984) *The constitution of society*. Cambridge: Polity Press.

Gioia, Dennis A., Majken Schultz, and Kevin G. Corley (2000) Organizational identity, image, and adaptive instability. *Academy of Management Review* 25(1): 63–81.

Gouldner, Alvin (1954) *Patterns of industrial bureaucracy*. New York: Free Press.

Granovetter, Michael (1985) Economic action and social structure: The problem of embeddedness. *American Journal of Sociology* 91(3): 481–510.

Greimas, Algirdas Julien and Joseph Courtés (1982) *Semiotics and language: An analytical dictionary*. Bloomington, IN: Indiana University Press.

Hannan, Michael T. and John Freeman (1989) *Organizational ecology*. Cambridge, MA: Harvard University Press.

Hartshorne, Charles (1987) *Wisdom as moderation. A philosophy of the middle way*. New York: SUNY Press.

—— (1998) The development of process philosophy. In D. Browning and W. T. Myers (Eds.) *Philosophers of process* (pp. 391–407). New York: Fordham University Press.

Harvey, David (1990) *The condition of postmodernity*. Oxford: Blackwell Publishers.

Hassard, John (2002) *Essai*: Organizational time: Modern, symbolic and postmodern reflections. *Organization Studies* 23(6): 885–892.

Hatch, Mary Jo (1999) Exploring the empty spaces of organizing: How improvisational jazz helps re-describe organizational structure. *Organization Studies* 20(1): 75–100.

—— and Majken Schultz (paper in progress) Historicizing in organizations: How organizational actors use history to reach across time.

Heidegger, Martin (1927) *Being and time*. Oxford: Blackwell Publishers.

—— (2000) *Introduction to metaphysics*. New Haven: Yale University Press.

Helin, Jenny (2011) Living moments in family meetings. A process study in the family business context. PhD dissertation. Jönköping: Jönköping International Business School.

—— Tor Hernes, Daniel Hjorth, and Robin Holt (Eds.) (2014) Process is how process does. *The Oxford handbook of process philosophy and organization studies*. New York: Oxford University Press.

Hendry, John and David Seidl (2003) The structure and significance of strategic episodes: Social systems theory and the routine practices of strategic change. *Journal of Management Studies* 40(1): 175–196.

Hernes, Tor (2004) *The spatial construction of organization*. Amsterdam: John Benjamin.

—— (2005) The organization as nexus of macro-actors: Tugs of war around a personnel case. In B. Czarniawska and T. Hernes (Eds.) *Actor-network theory and organizing* (pp. 112–128). Stockholm: Liber and Copenhagen Business School Press.

—— (2008) *Understanding organization as process: Theory for a tangled world*. London: Routledge.

—— (2010) The importance of Callon's scallops for organization studies, and why they deserve to be looked at again in the light of process thinking. In T. Hernes and S. Maitlis (Eds.) *Process, sensemaking and organizing* (Perspectives on process organization studies series) (pp. 161–184). Oxford: Oxford University Press.

—— (2014) Alfred North Whitehead. In J. Helin, T. Hernes, D. Hjorth, and R. Holt (Eds.) *The Oxford handbook of process philosophy and organization studies*. New York: Oxford University Press.

—— and Geertz, C. (1973) *The interpretation of cultures*. New York: Basic Books.

Hernes, Tor and Eirik Irgens (2013) Keeping things mindfully on track: Organizational learning under continuity. *Management Learning* 44(3): 253–266.

Hernes, Tor, Juha Laurila, Anni Paalumäki, Ida Danneskiold-Samsoe, and Ansgar Odegård (2013) Novelty in the flow of time: Taking a view from nowhere in an on-going present. A paper presented at the EGOS 2013 Colloquium, July 4–6, Montreal, Canada.

Hernes, Tor and Elke Weik (2007) Organization as process: Drawing a line between endogenous and exogenous views. *Scandinavian Journal of Management* 23(3): 251–264.

Hoffman, Piotr (2005) Dasein and 'its' time. In H. L. Dreyfus and M. A. Wrathall (Eds.) *A companion to Heidegger* (pp. 325–335). Malden, MA: Blackwell Publishers.

Holt, Robin and Frank Mueller (2011) Wittgenstein, Heidegger and drawing lines in organization studies. *Organization Studies* 32(1): 67–84.

Hosinski, Thomas E. (1993) *Stubborn fact and creative advance: An introduction to the metaphysics of Alfred North Whitehead*. Lanham, MD: Rowman & Littlefield.

Huff, Anne S. (1988) Politics and argument as a means of coping with ambiguity and change. In L. R. Pondy, R. J. Boland, and H. Thomas (Eds.) *Managing ambiguity and change* (pp. 79–90). New York: John Wiley.

Husserl, Edmund (1991) *On the phenomenology of the consciousness of internal time (1893–1917)*. Dordrecht: Kluwer.

Hutchins, Edwin (1995) *Cognition in the wild*. Cambridge, MA: MIT Press.

Huy, Quy Nguyen (2001) Time temporal capability, and planned change. *Academy of Management Review* 26(4): 601–623.

Hylland Eriksen, Thomas (2007) Stacking and continuity: On temporal regimes in popular culture. In R. Hassan and R. E. Purser (Eds.) *24/7 Time and temporality in the network society* (pp. 141–160). Stanford: Stanford University Press.

Irgens, Eirik J. (2011) *Pluralism in management: Organizational theory, management education, and Ernst Cassirer*. London: Routledge.

Isabella, Lynn A. (1990) Evolving interpretations as a change unfolds: How managers construe key organizational events. *Academy of Management Journal* 33(1): 7–41.

Isaacson, Walter (2013) *Steve Jobs: The exclusive biography*. Simon & Schuster.

James, William (1890) *The principles of psychology*. London: Macmillan.

—— (1904) *What is pragmatism? From William James, Writings 1902–1920*, New York: The Library of America.

—— (1909/1996) *A pluralistic universe*. Lincoln, NE: University of Nebraska Press.

Jansen, Bernard J., Mimi Zhang, Kate Sobel, and Abdur Chowdury (2009) Twitter power: Tweets as electronic word of mouth. *Journal of the American Society for Information Science and Technology* 60(11): 2169–2188.

Jarzabkowski, Paula and David Seidl (2008) The role of meetings in the social practice of strategy. *Organization Studies* 29(11): 1391–1426.

Jarzabkowski, Paula and Andreas P. Spee (2009) Strategy-as-practice. A review and future directions for the field. *International Journal of Management Reviews* 11(1): 69–95.

Joas, Hans (1997a) *G.H. Mead: Contemporary re-examination of his thought*. Cambridge, MA: MIT Press.

—— (1997b) *The creativity of actions*. Chicago: University of Chicago Press.

Jones, Candace, Massimo Maoret, Felipe Massa, and Silviya Svejenova (2013) Rebels with a cause: Formation, contestation and expansion of the *de novo* category 'modern architecture', 1870–1975. *Organization Science* 23(6): 1523–1545.

Keller, Jared (2010) Evaluating Iran's Twitter revolution, URL (retrieved September 2012). Available at <http://www.theatlantic.com/technology/archive/2010/06/evaluating-irans-twitter-revolution/58337/>.

Kelly, E. Robert (1882) *The alternative. A study in psychology*. London: Macmillan and Co.

Kline, George L. (1986) Past, present and future as categorical terms and the fallacy of the actual future. *The Review of Metaphysics* 40(2): 215–235.

Knorr-Cetina, Karin (1999) *Epistemic cultures: How the sciences make knowledge*. Cambridge, MA: Harvard University Press.

—— and Urs Bruegger (2002) Global microstructures: The virtual societies of financial markets. *American Journal of Sociology* 107(4): 905–950.

Kogut, Bruce and Udo Zander (1992) Knowledge of the firm, combinative capabilities, and the replication of technology. *Organization Science* 3(3): 383–397.

Kreiner, Kristian and Majken Schultz (1995) Soft cultures: The symbolism of cross-border organizing. *Studies in Cultures, Organizations and Societies* 1(1): 63–81.

Krogstad, Trine and Silia Unneland (2012) Evoking organizational memory. Master thesis, Copenhagen Business School.

Kubler, George (2008) *The shape of time: Remarks on the history of things*. New Haven: Yale University Press.

Kunda, Gideon (1992) *Engineering culture: Control and commitment in a high-tech corporation*. Philadelphia: Temple University Press.

Laclau, Ernest and Chantal Mouffe (1985) *Hegemony and socialist strategy*. London: Verso.

Langley, Ann (1999) Strategies for theorizing from process data. *Academy of Management Review* 24: 691–710.

—— Clive Smallman, Haridimos Tsoukas, and Andrew H. Van de Ven (2013) Process studies of change in organization and management: Unveiling temporality, activity, and flow. *Academy of Management Journal* 58(1): 1–13.

Langley, Ann and Haridimos Tsoukas (2010) Introducing 'perspectives on process organization studies'. In T. Hernes and S. Maitlis (Eds.) *Process, sensemaking and organizing* (pp. 1–26). Oxford: Oxford University Press.

Lanzara, Giovan F. (1983) Ephemeral organizations in extreme environments: Emergence, strategy, extinction. *Journal of Management Studies*, 20(1): 70–95.

—— and Michele Morner (2005) Artefacts' rule: How organizing happens in open source software projects. In B. Czarniawska and T. Hernes (Eds.) *Actor-network theory and organizing* (pp. 75–104). Stockholm: Liber Ekonomi.

Larson, Erik (2004) *The devil in the white city*. New York, London: Bantam.

Larsson, Anders Olof, and Hallvard Moe (2011) Studying political microblogging: Twitter users in the 2010 Swedish election campaign. *New Media & Society* 14(5): 729–747.

Latour, Bruno (1986) The powers of association. In John Law (Ed.) *Power, action and belief. A new sociology of knowledge?* (pp. 264–280). London: Routledge & Kegan Paul.

—— (1987) *Science in action*. Cambridge, MA: Harvard University Press.

—— (1993) *We have never been modern*. Cambridge, MA: Harvard University Press.

—— (1994) Les objets ont-ils une histoire? Rencontre de Pasteur et de Whitehead dans un bain d'acide lactique. In Isabelle Stengers (Ed.) *L'Effet Whitehead* (pp. 197–217). Paris: Vrin.

—— (1996) On interobjectivity. *Mind, culture, and activity* 3: 228–245.

—— (1999) *Pandora's hope: Essays on the reality of science studies.* Cambridge, MA: Harvard University Press.

—— (2005) *Reassembling the social: An introduction to actor-network-theory.* Oxford: Oxford University Press.

—— and Steve Woolgar (1979) *Laboratory life: The social construction of scientific facts.* Los Angeles: Sage Publications Ltd.

Laurila, Juha, Anni Paalumäki, and Tor Hernes (2013) Continuity, discontinuity and uniqueness. A spatio-temporal view of organizational identity. Unpublished paper.

Law, John (1994) *Organizing modernity.* Oxford: Blackwell Publishers.

—— (2004) *After method: Mess in social science research.* Oxford: Routledge.

Lawrence, Thomas B., Roy Suddaby, and Bernard Leca (2011) Institutional work: Refocusing institutional studies of organization. *Journal of Management Inquiry* 20(1): 52–58.

Levitt, Barbara and James G. March (1988) Organizational learning. *Annual Review of Sociology* 14: 319–340.

Lindahl, Marcus (2005) The little engine that could: On the 'managing' qualities of technology. In B. Czarniawska and T. Hernes (Eds.) *Actor-Network theory and organizing* (pp. 50–66). Stockholm: Liber and CBS Press.

Lindsay, Greg (2013) Engineering serendipity. *New York Times.* Published online 5.4.2013.

Lorino, Philippe (2014) Charles Sanders Peirce. In J. Helin, T. Hernes, D. Hjorth, and R. Holt (Eds.) *The Oxford handbook of process philosophy and organization studies.* New York: Oxford University Press.

—— and Damien Mourey (2013) The experience of time in the inter-organizing inquiry. A present thickened by dialog and situations. *Scandinavian Journal of Management* 19(1): 48–62.

Luhmann, Niklas (1990) *Essays on self-reference.* New York: Columbia University Press.

—— (1995) *Social systems.* Stanford: Stanford University Press.

MacKay, R. Bradley, and Peter McKiernan (2004) The role of hindsight in foresight: Refining strategic reasoning. *Futures* 36: 161–179.

McKean, Erin (Ed.) (2005) *New Oxford American dictionary.* Oxford: Oxford University Press.

McTaggart, John (1908) The unreality of time. *Mind* 17(68): 457–474.

Mantere, Saku, Henri A. Schildt, and John A. Sillince (2012) Reversal of strategic change. *Academy of Management Journal* 55(1): 172–196.

March, James G. (1987) Ambiguity and accounting: The elusive link between information and decision making. *Accounting, Organizations and Society* 12: 153–168.

—— (1988) *Decisions and organizations.* Oxford: Blackwell Publishers.

—— (1991) Exploration and exploitation in organizational learning. *Organization Science* 2(1): 71–87.

—— (1994) *A primer on decision making: How decisions happen.* New York: The Free Press.

—— (1995) The future, disposable organizations, and the rigidities of imagination. *Organization* 2: 427–440.

—— (1999a) Research on organizations: Hopes for the past and lessons from the future. *Nordiske Organisasjonsstudier* 1(1): 69–83.

—— (1999b) *The pursuit of organizational intelligence: Decisions and learning in organizations*. Cambridge, MA: Blackwell Publishers.

—— and Johan P. Olsen (1975) The uncertainty of the past: Organizational learning under ambiguity. *The European Journal of Political Research* 3: 147–171.

—— (1976) *Ambiguity and choice in organizations*. Bergen: Universitetsforlaget.

—— (1989) *Rediscovering institutions*. New York: The Free Press.

—— and Herbert A. Simon (1958) *Organizations*. New York: John Wiley.

Martin, Joanne (2002) *Organizational culture: Mapping the terrain*. Thousand Oaks, CA: Sage Publishers Ltd.

—— Martha S. Feldman, Mary Jo Hatch, and Sim B. Sitkin (1983) The uniqueness paradox in organizational stories. *Administrative Science Quarterly* 28(3): 438–453.

—— Kathleen Knopoff, and Christine Beckman (1998) An alternative to bureaucratic impersonality and emotional labour: Bounded emotionality at The Body Shop. *Administrative Science Quarterly* 43(2): 429–469.

Mathiesen, Marie (2013) *Making strategy work: An organizational ethnography*. PhD thesis. Copenhagen: Copenhagen Business School.

Mead, George Herbert (1929) The nature of the past. In John Coss (Ed.), *Essays in Honor of John Dewey* (pp. 235–242). New York: Henry Holt & Co.

—— (1932) *The philosophy of the present*. Amherst, NY: Prometheus.

—— (1934) *Mind, self, and society*. Chicago: The University of Chicago Press.

—— (1938) *The philosophy of the act*. Chicago: The University of Chicago Press.

Mendelsohn, Daniel (2008) *The lost*. London: HarperPress.

Merleau-Ponty, Maurice (1995) *Phenomenology of perception*. London: Routledge.

—— and Elinor G. Barber (2006) *The travels and adventures of serendipity. A study in sociological semantics and the sociology of science*. Princeton, NJ: Princeton University Press.

Meyer, Renate and Marcus Höllerer (2010) Meaning structures in a contested issue field. A topographic map of shareholder value in Austria. *Academy of Management Journal* 53(6): 1241–1262.

Mintzberg, Henry, Bruce W. Ahlstrand, and Joseph Lampel (1998) *Strategy safari. A guided tour through the wilds of strategic management*. Harlow: Prentice Hall.

Moeran, Brian and Jesper Strandgaard Pedersen (2011) Introduction. In B. Moeran and J. Strandgaard Pedersen (Eds.) *Negotiating values in creative industries: Fairs, festivals and competitive events* (pp. 1–35). Cambridge: Cambridge University Press.

Mohr, John W. (1998) Measuring meaning structures. *Annual Review of Sociology* 24: 345–370.

Moorman, Christine and Anne S. Miner (1997) The impact of organizational memory on new product performance and creativity. *Journal of Marketing Research* 34(1): 91–106.

—— (1998) Organizational improvisation and organizational memory. *Academy of Management Review* 23(4): 698–723.

Morgan, Glenn, Richard Whitley, and Eli Moen (Eds.) (2005) *Changing capitalisms? Internationalization, institutional change, and systems of economic organization*. Oxford: Oxford University Press.

—— Peer Hull Kristensen, and Richard Whitley (Eds.) (2001) *The multinational firm: Organizing across institutional and national divides*. Oxford: Oxford University Press.

Muzzetto, Luigi (2006) Time and meaning in Alfred Schütz. *Time & Society* 15(1): 5–31.

Nair, Anup Karath, George Burt, and Robert Chia (unpublished manuscript) Researching process and organization: '*In situ reflexive probing*' as a process methodology.

Nayak, Ajit and Robert Chia (2011) Thinking becoming and emergence: Process philosophy and organization studies. *Research in the Sociology of Organizations* 32: 281–309.

Nelson, Richard R. and Sidney G. Winter (1982) *An evolutionary theory of economic change.* Cambridge, MA: Harvard University Press.

Nippert-Eng, Kristena (1996) *Home and work: Negotiating boundaries through everyday life.* Chicago: The University of Chicago Press.

Nonaka, Ikujiro and Hirotaka Takeuchi (1995) *The knowledge-creating company.* New York: Oxford University Press.

Orlikowski, Wanda J. (1996) Improvising organizational transformation over time. A situated change perspective. *Information Systems Research* 7: 63–92.

—— (2006) Material knowing: The scaffolding of human knowledgeability. *European Information Systems* 15(5): 460–466.

—— (2010) The sociomateriality of organisational life: Considering technology in management research. *Cambridge Journal of Economics* 34: 125–141.

—— and Joanne Yates (2002) It's about time: Temporal structuring in organizations. *Organization Science* 13(6): 684–700.

Orr, Julian (1990) Sharing knowledge, celebrating identity. In D. Middleton and D. Edwards (Eds.) *Collective remembering* (pp. 169–189). Newbury Park, CA: Sage Publications Ltd.

—— (1998) Images of work. *Science, Technology, & Human Values* 43(4): 439–455.

Paalumäki, Anni (2000) Time and organizational identity: Discourses of the past and the future as the constructors of the organizational self. Paper presented at the 4th International Conference on Organizational Discourse: Word-views, Work-views and World-views, The Management Centre, King's College, University of London, London, UK.

Palmer, Donald, Brian Dick, and Nathaniel Freiburger (2009) Rigor and relevance in organization studies. *Journal of Management Inquiry* 18(4): 265–272.

Pascale Richard T. and Anthony G. Athos (1981) *The art of Japanese management.* London: Penguin.

Peirce, Charles S. (1878) How to make our ideas clear. *Popular Science Monthly* 12: 286–302.

—— (1998) *The essential writings.* New York: Prometheus Books.

Perrow, Charles (1986) *Complex organizations. A critical essay.* New York: McGraw-Hill.

Pettigrew, Andrew (1997) What is processual analysis? *Scandinavian Journal of Management* 13(4): 337–348.

—— R. W. Woodman, and K. S. Cameron (2001) Studying organizational change and development: Challenges for future research. *Academy of Management Journal* 44(4): 697–713.

Pfeffer, Jeffrey and Gerald R. Salancik (1978) *The external control of organizations. A resource dependence perspective.* New York: Harper and Row.

Pickering, Andrew (1984) *Constructing quarks. A sociological history of particle physics.* Chicago: University of Chicago Press.

—— (1995a) *The mangle of practice.* Chicago: The University of Chicago Press.

—— (1995b) The temporality of practice and the historicity of knowledge. In J. Z. Buchwald (Ed.) *Scientific practice: Theories and stories of physics* (pp. 42–55). Chicago: The University of Chicago Press.

Pinheiro-Croisel, Rebecca (2013) Pilotage du processus de conception d'un objet évolutif: émergence d'objets, rôles et outils pour les projets urbains durables. PhD thesis, l' École Nationale Supérieure des Mines de Paris.

Polanyi, Karl (1957) The economy as instituted process. In K. Polanyi, C. Arensberg, and H. Pearson (Eds.) *Trade and market in the early empires* (pp. 243–270). Chicago: Henry Regnery Co.

Polanyi, Michael (1967) Sense-giving and sense-reading. *Philosophy* 42(162): 301–325.

Polkinghorne, David (1988) *Narrative knowing and the human sciences*. New York: State University of New York Press.

Power, Michael (1996) Making things auditable. *Accounting, Organizations & Society* 21(2/3): 289–315.

—— (2003) Auditing and the production of legitimacy. *Accounting, Organizations and Society* 28: 379–394.

Price, Lucien (1954) *Dialogues with Alfred North Whitehead*. New Hampshire: Reinhardt.

Prigogine, Ilya and Isabelle Stengers (1984) *Order out of chaos: Man's new dialogue with nature*. New York: Bantam.

Putnam, Linda and Susanne Boys (2006) Revisiting metaphors of organizational communication. In S. Clegg, C. Hardy, T. B. Lawrence, and W. R. Nord (Eds.) *Handbook of organization studies* (pp. 541–576). Oxford: Sage Publications Ltd.

Putnam, Linda L. and François Cooren (2004) Alternative perspectives on the role of text and agency in constituting organizations. *Organization* 11(3): 323–333.

Ranson, Stewart, Bob Hinings, and Royston Greenwood (1980) The structuring of organizational structures. *Administrative Science Quarterly* 20: 1–17.

Ravasi, Davide and Majken Schultz (2006) Responding to organizational identity threats: Exploring the role of organizational culture. *Academy of Management Journal* 49(3): 433–458.

Rescher, Nicholas (1996) *Process metaphysics: An introduction to process philosophy*. New York: State University of New York Press.

—— (2003) The promise of process philosophy. In G. Shields (Ed.) *Process and analysis: Whitehead, Hartshorne, and the analytic tradition* (pp. 49–66) (SUNY series) New York: State University of New York Press.

Ricoeur, Paul (1984) *Time and narrative, vol. 1*. Chicago: University of Chicago Press.

Rivera, Lauren A. (2008) Managing 'spoiled' national identity: War, tourism, and memory in Croatia. *American Sociological Review* 73: 613–634.

Roethlisberger, F. G. and Dickson, W. J. (1939) *Management and the worker*. Cambridge, MA: Harvard University Press.

Rothschild-Whitt, Joyce (1979) The collectivist organization: An alternative to rational–bureaucratic models. *American Sociological Review* 44: 509–527.

Røvik, Kjell Arne (2011) From fashion to virus: An alternative theory of organizations' handling of management ideas. *Organization Studies* 32(5): 631–653.

Rubino, Carl A. (2002) The consolations of uncertainty: Time, change, and complexity. *Emergence* 4(1/2): 200–206.

Rüling, Charles-Clemens (2011) Event institutionalization and maintenance: The Annecy animation festival 1960–2010. In B. Moeran and J. Strandgaard Pedersen (Eds.) *Negotiating values in creative industries—fairs, festivals and competitive events* (pp. 197–223). Cambridge: Cambridge University Press.

Sabel, Charles F. (1993) Studied trust: Building a new form of cooperation in a volatile economy. *Human Relations* 46(9): 1133–1170.

Saussure, Ferdinand de (1986) *Course in general linguistics*. Chicago: Open Court Publishing Company.

Scarbrough, Harry, Jacky Swan, Stéphane Laurent, Mike Bresnen, Linda Edelman, and Sue Newell (2004) Project-based learning and the role of learning boundaries. *Organization Studies* 25(9): 1579–1600.

Schäffner, Birgitte and Edda Sonne Hendrup (2012) *Sensing the momentum*. A change process in Novozymes. Master thesis, Copenhagen Business School.

Scharg, Calvin O. (1970) Heidegger on repetition and historical understanding. *Philosophy East and West* 20(3): 287–295.

Schatzki, Theodore R. (2006) On organizations as they happen. *Organization Studies* 27(12): 1863–1873.

—— (2010) *The timespace of human activity*. Lanham, MD: Lexington Books.

—— Karin Knorr-Cetina, and Eike von Savigny (Eds.) (2001) *The practice turn in contemporary theory*. New York: Routledge.

Schein, Edgar (1985) *Organizational culture and leadership. A dynamic view*. San Francisco: Jossey Bass.

Schmidt, Kjeld and Liam Bannon (1992) Taking CSCW seriously: Supporting articulation work. *Computer Supported Cooperative Work (CSCW): An International Journal* 1(1): 7–40.

Schoeneborn, Dennis (2013) The pervasive power of PowerPoint: How a genre of professional communication permeates organizational communication. *Organization Studies* (online first version).

Schrag, Calvin O. (1970) Heidegger on repetition and historical understanding. *Philosophy East and West* 20(3): 287–295.

Schultz, Majken and Tor Hernes (2013) A temporal perspective on organizational identity. *Organization Science* 24(1): 1–21.

Schütz, Alfred (1953) Common-sense and scientific interpretation of human action. *Philosophy and Phenomenological Research* 14(1): 1–38.

—— (1959) Tiresias, or our knowledge of future events. *Social Research* 26(1): 71–89.

—— (1964) *Collected papers II: Studies in social theory*. Edited and introduced by Arvid Broodersen. The Hague: Nijhoff.

—— (1967) *The phenomenology of the social world*. London: Heinemann Educational Books.

—— and Thomas Luckmann (1973) *The structures of the life-world (vol. 1)*. Evanston: Northwestern University Press.

Sewell, William H. (1996) Historical events as transformations of structures: Inventing revolution at the Bastille. *Theory and Society* 25: 841–881.

—— (2008) The temporalities of capitalism. *Socio-Economic Review* 6: 517–537.

Sheets-Johnstone, Maxine (2008) *The primacy of movement*. Amsterdam: John Benjamins.

Sherburne, Donald W. (1966) *A key to Whitehead's Process and Reality*. New York: Macmillan.

Shotter, John (2006) Understanding process from within: An argument for 'withness'—thinking. *Organization Studies* 27(4): 585–604.

Simpson, Barbara (2009) Pragmatism, Mead and the practice turn. *Organization Studies* 30(12): 1329–1347.

Singley, Mark and John R. Anderson (1989) *The transfer of cognitive skill*. Cambridge, MA: Harvard University Press.

Skærbæk, Peter (2009) Public sector auditor identities in making efficiency auditable: The National Audit Office of Denmark as independent auditor and modernizer. *Accounting, Organizations and Society* 34: 971–987.

—— and Kjell Tryggestad (2010) The role of accounting devices in performing corporate strategy. *Accounting, Organizations and Society* 35(1): 108–124.

Smircich, Linda and Charles Stubbart (1985) Strategic management in an enacted world. *Academy of Management Review* 10(4): 724–736.

Smith, Dorothy E. (2001) Texts and the ontology of organizations and institutions. *Studies in Cultures, Organizations and Societies* 7(2): 159–198.

Sonenshein, Scott (2010) We're changing—or are we? Untangling the role of progressive, regressive, and stability narratives during strategic change implementation. *Academy of Management Journal* 53(3): 477–512.

Sorokin, Pitirim and Robert K. Merton (1937) Social time. A methodological and functional analysis. *American Journal of Sociology* 42(5): 615–629.

Soros, George (1994) *The alchemy of finance*. New York: Wiley & Sons.

Stacey, Ralph D. (2001) *Complex responsive processes in organizations*. London: Routledge.

Star, Susan Leigh (2010) This is not a boundary object: Reflections on the origin of a concept. *Science Technology Human Values* 35(5): 601–617.

—— and James R. Griesemer (1989) Institutional ecology, 'translations', and boundary objects: Amateurs and professionals in Berkeley's Museum of Vertebrate Zoology 1907–1939. *Social Studies of Science* 19: 387–420.

Stengers, Isabelle (2008) A constructivist reading of process and reality. *Theory, Culture & Society* 25(4): 91–110.

—— (2011) *Thinking with Whitehead. A free and wild creation of concepts*. Cambridge, MA: Harvard University Press.

Strauss, Anselm (1988) The articulation of project work: An organizational process. *The Sociological Quarterly* 29(2): 163–178.

—— Shizuko Y. Fagerhaugh, Barbara Suczek, and Carolyn Wiener (1985) *Social organization of medical work*. Chicago: The University of Chicago Press.

Strum, Shirley S. and Bruno Latour (1987) Redefining the social link: From baboons to humans. *Social Science Information* 26(4): 783–802.

Suchman, Lucy A. (2006) *Human–machine reconfigurations: Plans and situated actions*. 2nd ed. Cambridge: University of Cambridge Press.

Sutton, Robert I. (1987) The process of organizational death: Disbanding and reconnecting. *Administrative Science Quarterly* 32: 542–569.

—— and Andrew Hargadon (1996) Brainstorming groups in context: Effectiveness in a product design firm. *Administrative Science Quarterly* 41: 685–718.

Sydow, Jörg and Udo Staber (2002) The institutional embeddedness of project networks: The case of content production in German television. *Regional Studies* 36(3): 215–227.

Taylor, Fredrick W. (1911) *The principles of scientific management*. New York: Harper and Brothers.

Teece, David J. (2012) Dynamic capabilities: Routines versus entrepreneurial action. *Journal of Management Studies* 49(8): 1396–1401.

Thompson, James D. (1967) *Organizations in action*. New York: McGraw-Hill.

Trice, Harrison M. and Janice M. Beyer (1984) Studying organizational cultures through rites and ceremonials. *Academy of Management Review* 9(4): 653–669.

Tryggestad, Kjell, Lise Justesen, and Jan Mouritsen (2013) Project temporalities: How frogs can become stakeholders. *International Journal of Managing Projects in Business* 6(1): 69–87.

Tsoukas, Haridimos (2005) *Complex knowledge: Studies in organizational epistemology*. Oxford: Oxford University Press.

—— (2009) A dialogical approach to the creation of new knowledge in organizations. *Organization Science* 20(6): 941–957.

—— and Robert Chia (2002) On organizational becoming: Rethinking organizational change. *Organization Science* 13(5): 567–582.

—— and Mary Jo Hatch (2001) Complex thinking, complex practice: The case for a narrative approach to organizational complexity. *Human Relations* 54(8): 979–1013.

—— and Christian Knudsen (Eds.) (2005) *The Oxford handbook of organization theory: Meta-theoretical perspectives*. Oxford: Oxford University Press.

Tunby Gulbrandsen, Ib (2012) This page is not meant for a US audience. PhD thesis, Copenhagen Business School.

Varela, Francisco J., Evan Thompson, and Eleanor Rosch (1991) *The embodied mind: Cognitive science and human experience*. Cambridge, MA: MIT Press.

Van de Ven, Andrew H. (1992) Suggestions for studying strategy process. A research note. *Strategic Management Journal* 13: 169–188.

—— Douglas Polley, Raghu Garud, and Sankaran Venkatamaran (1999) *The innovation journey*. New York: Oxford University Press.

—— and Marshall Scott Poole (2005) Alternative approaches for studying organizational change. *Organization Studies* 26(9): 1377–1404.

Vangkilde, Kasper Tang (2012) Branding Hugo Boss: An anthropology of creativity in fashion. PhD thesis, University of Copenhagen.

Verzelloni, Luca (2009) Knowing in an institution: The role of the judicial fascicules in the Italian Courts of Justice. Paper presented at the 25th EGOS Colloquium, Barcelona, 2–4 July.

Vickers, Geoffrey (1983) *Human systems are different*. London: Harper and Row.

Wallack, Florence Bradford (1980) *The epochal nature of process in Whitehead's metaphysics*. State University of New York Press.

Walsh, James P. and Gerardo Rivera Ungson (1991) Organizational memory. *Academy of Management Review* 16(1): 57–91.

Weber, Max (1968) *Economy and society: An outline of interpretive sociology*. G. Roth and C. Wittich (Eds.). Berkeley: University of California Press.

Wegner, Daniel M. (1986) Transactive memory. A contemporary analysis of the group mind. In B Mullen and G. R. Goethals (Eds.) *Theories of group behavior* (pp. 185–208). New York: Springer Verlag.

Weick, Karl E. (1974) Amendments to organizational theorizing. *Academy of Management Journal* 17(3): 487–502.

—— (1976) Educational organizations as loosely coupled systems. *Administrative Science Quarterly* 21: 1–18.

—— (1979) *The social psychology of organizing*. 2nd ed. New York: Random House.

—— (1984) Managerial thought in the context of action. In S. Srivastva and Associates (Eds.) *The executive mind* (pp. 221–242). San Francisco: Jossey-Bass.

—— (1993) The collapse of sensemaking in organizations: The Mann Gulch disaster. *Administrative Science Quarterly* 38: 628–652.

—— (1995) *Sensemaking in organizations*. Thousand Oaks, CA: Sage Publications Ltd.

—— (2001) *Making sense of the organization*. Wiley: Blackwell Publishers.

—— (2005) Organizing and failures of imagination. *International Public Management Journal* 8(3): 425–438.

—— (2006) Faith, evidence, and action: Better guesses in an unknowable world. *Organization Studies* 27(11): 1723–1736.

—— (2011) Reflections: Change agents as change poets: On reconnecting flux and hunches. *Journal of Change Management* 11(1): 7–20.

—— and Karlene H. Roberts (1993) Collective mind in organizations: Heedful interrelating on flight decks. *Administrative Science Quarterly* 38: 357–381.

—— and Robert Quinn (1999) Organizational change and development. *Annual Review of Psychology* 50: 361–386.

—— Kathleen M. Sutcliffe, and David Obstfeld (2005) Organizing and the process of sensemaking. *Organization Science* 16(4): 409–421s.

Whipp, Richard (1994) A time to be concerned. A position paper on time and management. *Time and Society* 3(1): 99–116.

—— Barbara Adam, and Ida Sabelis (2002) Choreographing time and management: Traditions, developments, and opportunities. In R. Whipp, B. Adam, and I. Sabelis (Eds.) *Making time: Time and management in modern organizations* (pp. 1–28). Oxford: Oxford University Press.

Whitehead, Alfred North (1911) *An introduction to mathematics*. London: Williams and Norgate.

—— (1920) *The concept of nature*. Cambridge: Cambridge University Press. (Page numbering refers to 2004 version published by Prometheus Books.)

—— (1925a) *Science and the modern world*. London: Free Association Books.

—— (1925b) *An enquiry concerning the principles of natural knowledge*. Cambridge: Cambridge University Press.

—— (1929a) *Process and reality*. New York: The Free Press.

—— (1929b) *The aims of education*. New York: The Free Press.

—— ([1933]1967) *Adventures of ideas*. New York: The Free Press.

—— (1938) *Modes of thought*. New York: The Free Press.

Williams, James (2003) *Gilles Deleuze's difference and repetition*. Edinburgh: Edinburgh University Press.

Willmott, Hugh (1981) The structuring of organizational structure. A note. *Administrative Science Quarterly* 26: 470–474.

Wittgenstein, Ludwig (1983) *Philosophical investigations*. Oxford: Oxford University Press.

Wouters, Paul, Lina Helsten, and Loet Leydesdorff (2004) Internet time and the reliability of search engines. *First Monday* 9(10): 1–10. <http://firstmonday.org/htbin/cgiwrap/bin/ojs/index.php/fm/article/view/1177/1097> (accessed 21 November 2013).

Zerubavel, Eviatar (1993) *The fine line: Making distinctions in everyday life*. Chicago: The University of Chicago Press.

NAME INDEX

Abbott, Andrew 144
Adam, Barbara 33
Ahlstrand, Bruce W. 186
Albert, Stuart 174–5
Aldrich, Howard 17
Alvesson, Mats 182
Anderson, Alistair R. 120
Anderson, John R. 173
Antonacopoulou, Elena 215n.20
Aristotle 66
Austin, John L. 111, 209n.6

Bachrach, Peter 165
Bakken, Tore 14–15, 18–19, 45, 103–4, 191n.2/4, 198–9n.1
Baratz, Morton S. 165
Barbalet, Jack 184
Barley, Stephen R. 195n.15
Bateson, Gregory 100, 156, 158
Baum, Joel A. C. 19
Bechky, Beth A. 25
Beckman, Christine 54, 193n.5
Bengtsson, Marie 34, 37
Bergson, Henri 5–6, 24, 30, 37, 41, 55, 68–9, 83, 87–9, 90, 120, 156, 172, 192n.6, 196n.22, 201n.16, 202n.25, 205–6n.11–12, 217n.2
Bernstein, Richard J. 187
Beyer, Janice M. 132
Birnholtz, Jeremy P. 112
Bittner, Egon 28, 104
Blow, Charles M. 94, 208n.26, 214n.13
Blumer, Herbert 131–2
Boden, Deirdre 78, 81, 134, 205n.6, 214n.8
Boje, David M. 132, 180
Bourdieu, Pierre 134, 197n.31, 211n.19
Boys, Susanne 132, 141
Brown, George Spencer 15, 26
Bruegger, Urs 81–3, 125–7, 193n.4, 202n.23, 213n.3
Brunsson, Nils 131
Burnham, Daniel 146
Butler, Judith 110, 115

Callon, Michel 61, 141, 184, 194–5n.14, 202–3n.29
Cameron, K. S. 17

Capa, Robert 46
Carlile, Paul R. 137
Castells, Manuel 197n.32
Chandler, Alfred 27
Chen, Katherine K. 112–13
Chia, Robert 1, 3, 16–17, 21, 27, 28, 30–1, 40, 42, 55, 62–3, 90, 103, 157–8, 160, 182, 191n.2, 193n.4
Churchill, Winston 75
Clark, Peter 196n.28, 334
Clegg, Stewart R. 19
Cohen, Michael D. 78, 112, 173
Cooper, Robert 65, 67, 77, 114, 126, 141, 184, 196n.24
Cooren, Francois 37, 140–2, 213n.4
Corley, Kevin G. 36–7, 173–4
Courtés, Joseph 213n.1
Cunliffe, Ann 94, 132, 134, 180, 206–7n.16
Cyert, Richard 54
Czarniawska, Barbara 23, 37, 54, 57, 107, 131–2, 203n.30, 210n.11

Dahlberg, Karin 209n.6
De laet, Marianne 138
Deleuze, Gilles 4–5, 19, 45, 68–9, 80, 83–4, 90, 116, 172, 193n.8, 201n.16, 203–4n.33, 208n.22
Dewey, John 205–6n.11, 210n.10
Dickson, W. J. 54
DiMaggio, Paul J. 17
Dodd, Sarah Drakopoulou 120
Douglas, Mary 187, 195–6n.20
Du Gay, Paul 27
Dukerich, Janet E. 36
Dutton, Jane M. 36

Eilertsen, Morten 46
Elias, Norbert 40, 92
Emery, Fred E. 18
Emirbayer, Mustafa 40, 95, 135, 198n.38, 205n.9
Erdem, Derya Sarac 46

Feldman, Martha S. 44, 114, 116, 132, 211n.16
Field, Richard W. 209n.31
Fiol, Marlena 195–6n.20
Firth, Colin 131

Flaherty, Michael G. 196n.25
Fleck, Ludwig 195–6n.20
Fligstein, Neil 196n.21
Foerster, Heinz von 175, 198–9n.1
Follett, Mary P. 210n.10
Foreman, George 90–1
Foucault, Michel 116, 209n.2
Freeman, John 17
Friedman, Thomas viii, 15, 191n.1

Garfinkel, Harold 2, 129–30, 133, 194–5n.14, 207n.18, 216n.2, 217n.3
Garsten, Christina 27
Garud, Raghu 28–9, 114, 165
Gell, Alfred 43, 196n.27, 197n.36
Gephart, Robert P, Jr. 94–5, 104
Gherardi, Silvia 111, 134
Giddens, Anthony 34, 48, 69–70, 134, 201n.14, 211n.17
Gioia, Dennis A. 36–7, 173–4
Gouldner, Alvin 197n.30
Granovetter, Michael 194–5n.14
Greenwood, Royston 31, 69
Greimas, Algirdas Julien 195n.15, 209n.7, 213n.1
Griesemer, James R. 137
Gualtieri, Giuseppe 23
Guattari, Félix F. 116

Hannan, Michael T. 17
Hargadon, Andrew 168, 217n.4
Hartshorne, Charles 157–8, 198–9n.1, 205–6n.11
Harvey, David 197n.29, 345
Hatch, Mary Jo 132, 147–8, 186, 214n.7, 215n.18
Heidegger, Martin 1–2, 5–6, 37–8, 42, 67, 69, 95, 104, 107–9, 114, 116–19, 124, 129, 132, 135, 163, 186, 192n.6, 199n.5, 202n.22, 205n.7, 206n.15, 208n.24, 209n.6, 211n.18, 212n.23–4, 213n.28
Helin, Jenny 58, 70, 94, 134, 184, 206–7n.16
Helsten, Lina 214–15n.15
Hendrup, Edda Sonne 195n.17
Hendry, John 89
Heraclites 120
Hernes, Tor 4, 5, 18–19, 27, 36, 45, 47, 51, 59, 75, 79, 102, 103–4, 104, 109, 114, 117, 145, 158, 172, 175, 178, 181, 184, 191n.2, 193n.4, 198–9n, 214n.12, 216n.3
Hinings, Bob 31, 69
Hjorth, Daniel 184
Hoch, Susannah V. 112

Holt, Robin 45, 55, 184
Hosinski, Thomas E. 178
Huff, Anne S. 207n.19
Hull Kristensen, Peer 27
Husserl, Edmund 19, 55, 121, 202n.24, 204n.34, 213n.29
Hutchins, Edwin 209n.4
Huy, Quy Nguyen 34
Hylland Eriksen, Thomas 33

Irgens, Eirik 5, 117, 145, 198n.38
Isabella, Lynn A. 37–8
Ive, Jonathan 110

Jack, Sarah L. 120
Jacobsen, Carl 186
James, William 54, 87, 107, 121, 197n.33, 201n.16, 205–6n.10–11, 208n.29, 210n.9, 213n.20
Jarzabkowski, Paula 38, 55, 89
Joas, Hans 200n.12
Jobs, Steve 40, 110, 145
Jones, Candace 149, 166, 209n.1
Justesen, Lise 199n.7

Karnøe, Peter 165
Kärreman, Dan 182
Keller, Jared 143–4
Kelly, E. Robert 80
King, Ian W. 27
King, Martin Luther 168–9
Kline, George L. 80, 91
Knopoff, Kathleen 54, 193n.5
Knorr-Cetina, Karin 81–3, 125–7, 193n.4, 202n.23, 210n.8, 213n.3
Kogut, Bruce 211n.14
Kreiner, Kristian 28
Kristiansen, Ole Kirk 79
Krogstad, Trine 164
Kumaraswamy, Arun 165
Kunda, Gideon 132

Laclau, Ernest 114, 116–17, 124, 213–14n.5
Lampel, Joseph 186
Langley, Ann ix, 35, 191n.2
Lanzara, Giovan F. 113, 114, 115, 192–3n.1
Laozi 184
Larson, Erik 146
Latour, Bruno 1, 24, 52–3, 61–2, 82, 101, 104, 111, 116, 129, 138, 200n.11, 201n.14, 202n.28, 216n.7
Laurila, Juha 175
Law, John 14, 63, 65, 138, 196n.24, 203n.30

NAME INDEX

Lawrence, Thomas B. 12
Leca, Bernard 12, 177
Levitt, Barbara 46, 51, 121
Leydesdorff, Loet 214–15n.15
Lindahl, Marcus 22, 138
Lindsay, Greg 208n.25
Little, Omar 48
Lorino, Philippe 31, 135, 210n.10, 213n.27
Luckmann, Thomas 58, 119
Luhman, Thomas 94, 132, 134, 180, 206–7n.16
Luhmann, Niklas 3, 17, 89, 109, 124, 193n.9, 195n.19, 201n.13, 204n.36, 212n.25

MacKay, R. Bradley 197n.35
McKean, Erin 116
McKiernan, Peter 197n.35
McTaggart, John 37, 198n.36
Mantere, Saku 71
Maoret, Massimo 149, 166, 209n.1
March, James G. ix, 12, 19, 22, 41, 45–6, 47–8, 51, 54, 75, 78, 100, 116, 121, 145, 158, 185, 193n.9, 200n.9, 210n.8, 214n.9
Martin, Joanne 54, 132, 193n.5
Massa, Felipe 149, 166, 209n.1
Mathiesen, Marie 139–40
Mead, George Herbert 4, 5–6, 31, 41, 46, 48, 60–1, 68, 71, 80, 85–8, 90–1, 107, 114, 124, 127, 131–2, 156, 159–60, 192n.3, 193n.3, 195n.18, 198n.39, 200n.12, 202n.27, 207–8n.21, 212n.24
Merleau-Ponty, Maurice 107, 209n.6
Merton, Robert K. 33, 182, 196n.27
Miner, Anne S. 116, 173
Mintzberg, Henry 185
Mische, Ann 95, 135, 198n.38, 205n.9
Moen, Eli 17
Moeran, Brian 125, 213n.2
Mohammed Ali 90–1
Mohr, John W. 209n.6
Mol, Anne Marie 138
Moorman, Christine 116, 173
Morgan, Glenn 17
Morner, Michele 113–15
Mouffe, Chantal 114, 116–17, 124, 213–14n.5
Mourey, Damien 31, 210n.10
Mouritsen, Jan 199n.7
Muzzetto, Luigi 58

Nayak, Ajit 28, 90
Necker, Jacques 77
Nicolini, Davide 111, 134

Nippert-Eng, Kristena 27
Nonaka, Ikujiro 145

Obstfeld, David 56, 131
Ødegård, Ansgar 165
Olsen, Johan P. 17, 46, 47–8, 54, 78, 193n.9
Orlikowski, Wanda J. 33–5, 138
Orr, Julian 134–5

Paalumäki, Anni 175
Peirce, Charles S. 115–16, 116, 135, 201n.16, 205–6n.11, 209n.6
Pentland, Brian 211n.16
Perrow, Charles 12
Pettigrew, Andrew 17, 200n.10
Pfeffer, Jeffrey 17
Pickering, Andrew 49–51, 111, 135, 171
Pinheiro-Croisel, Rebecca 67
Polanyi, Karl 194–5n.14
Polanyi, Michael 15, 109, 131, 145, 211n.15
Polkinghorne, David 192n.6
Polley, Douglas 28–9
Powell, Walter W. 17
Power, Michael 115, 142
Prigogine, Ilya 191n3
Provenzano, Bernardo 23
Putnam, Linda 37, 132, 141

Quinn, Robert 157

Ranson, Stewart 31, 69
Rescher, Nicholas 40, 191n.2
Rivera, Lauren A. 216n.1
Roethlisberger, F. G. 54
Rosch, Eleanor 187
Rothschild-Whitt, Joyce 142
Rüling, Charles-Clemens 150

Sabel, Charles F. 120
Sabelis, Ida 33
Salancik, Gerald R. 17
Saussure, Ferdinand de 127, 140
Schäffner, Birgitte 195n.17
Schatzki, Theodore R. 54, 61, 83, 135, 201n.17, 211n.20
Scheaffer, Elena and Zachary 215n.20
Schein, Edgar 54, 171, 217n.1
Schildt, Henri A. 71
Schoeneborn, Dennis 212n.22
Schultz, Majken 4, 28, 36–7, 45, 51, 79, 114, 156, 158, 174, 181, 186, 216n.3

Schütz, Alfred 5–6, 19, 31, 55–9, 69, 75, 80, 83, 88, 119, 121, 123–4, 127, 132, 139, 172, 195n.15, 201n.20–1, 202n.23, 208n.24
Seidl, David 38, 89
Sewell, William H. 77
Sheets-Johnstone, Maxine 85
Shotter, John 35, 121, 145, 182, 198n.41
Sillince, John A. 71
Simon, Herbert A. 12, 54, 116
Simpson, Barbara 194n.10
Singley, Mark 173
Sitkin, Sim B. 132
Skærbæk, Peter 55, 142
Smallman, Clive 35
Smircich, Linda 22, 201n.15
Smith, Dorothy E. 144, 194n.12
Söderlund, Jonas 34
Sonenshein, Scott 181
Sorokin, Pitirim 33, 196n.27
Spee, Andreas P. 55
Staber, Udo 214n.10
Stacey, Ralph D. 193n.3
Star, Susan Leigh 137–8, 194n.13
Stengers, Isabelle 191n3, 209n.3, 214n11
Strandgaard Pedersen, Jesper 125, 213n.2
Strauss, Anselm 212n.21
Strum, Shirley S. 24, 111
Stubbart, Charles 22, 201n.15
Suchman, Lucy A. 132
Suddaby, Roy 12, 177
Sutcliffe, Kathleen M. 56, 131
Sutton, Robert I. 95, 168, 217n.4
Svejenova, Silviya 149, 166, 209n.1
Sydow, Jörg 214n.10

Takeuchi, Hirotaka 145
Taylor, Fredrick W. 54, 197n.29
Teece, David J. 145
Thompson, Evan 187
Thompson, James D. 12
Trice, Harrison M. 132
Trist, Eric L. 18
Tryggestad, Kjell 55, 199n.7
Tsoukas, Haridimos 19, 21, 30, 35, 42, 62–3, 132, 157–8, 191n.2, 211n.15, 214n.7

Ulstein, Idar 108, 163–4
Ungson, Gerardo Rivera 120
Unneland, Silia 164

Van de Ven, Andrew H. 28–9, 35, 191n.2, 200n.10
Vangkilde, Kasper Tang 146, 215n.16
Varela, Francisco J. 187
Venkatamaran, Sankaran 28
Verzelloni, Luca 20
Vickers, Geoffrey 31

Wallack, Florence Bradford 14
Walsh, James P. 120
Weber, Max 55–6, 127, 201n.20
Weick, Karl E. 4, 11–12, 21, 22, 24–6, 47, 49, 51, 56–7, 62, 92–3, 102–3, 127–8, 131, 148, 157, 164, 185, 192n.4, 194n.11, 195n.18, 198–9n.1, 205–6n.11, 208n.24, 212–13n.26, 215n.17/19
Weik, Elke 47
Whetten, David A. 174–5
Whipp, Richard 33
Whitehead, Alfred North vii, 1, 3, 5–7, 20, 28, 30, 36, 42, 45–6, 62, 65–6, 78, 80, 82, 90–4, 95–7, 101–4, 105, 114, 118–19, 128–30, 150–1, 157, 159, 166–8, 178, 185, 187, 193n.6, 194n.12, 195n.16, 196n.26, 199–200n, 201n.16, 205–6n.11/13, 207–8n.21, 208n.29, 209n, 214n.11, 215n.21–2, 216n.2, 217n.5
Whitley, Richard 17, 27
Wiik, Eric 18–19
Williams, James 193n.8
Willmott, Hugh 69–70
Winberg, Hans 131
Wittgenstein, Ludwig 193n.7
Woodman, R. W. 17
Woolgar, Steve 52–3, 61, 185
Wouters, Paul 214–15n.15

Yates, Joanne 33–5

Zander, Udo 211n.14
Zeno 30–1, 36
Zerubavel, Eviatar 174
Zundel, Mike 45

SUBJECT INDEX

Absence 117; as opposed to nothingness 183; in articulation of meaning structures 117, 126
Abstractions 20–21
Achilles and the tortoise 30, 156, 157
Actors 60, 62; heterogeneity of viii, 23, 94, 113
Actor-Network theory 23, 61–62, 82, 102
Acts 25, 55; and inter-acts 25; and articulation 111, 114, 117
Agency of the present 4; and collectivities 61
'Agnes' 129, 132–133
Analysis; levels of 20, 24, 55, 93, 110; and ethno-methodology 104
AOC (appellation d'origine controlée) 106
Apple 40, 106, 110, 166, 174
the Arctic 137
Arrow of time 84
Articulation 78, 103, 105, 109, 110, 114, 115–117; etymological roots of 116; as projection of possibilities 117
Articulatory modes 123–149
Atomism x, 95
Auditing 115, 142–143
Autopoiesis 89
Awareness 109; subsidiary awareness 109, 145; focal awareness 145

Becoming 39–44, 66, 120
Boxing 91
Burning Man event 112–113

Categories 100
Causality 91
Change 29–31, 42, 157–158; and temporality 32; vectors of 167
Collective versus individual distinction 24; texts as 141–142
Communities 25
Complex unity 101
Connecting processes 13, 62, 102; and connectivity 102, 126; and surplus of connections 126; texts as 141, 142
Consciousness; stream of 29
Contingencies 106, 144–145
Continuity 31, 124, 155–163, 185; as different from stability 185
Co-presence 58

Correspondence view of organizations 17; and temporality 19
Culture 50–51

Dance improvisation 85
Dualisms 62–63

Episodes 89
Ethno-methodology 104
Entities 57; as event-objects 99–100; categories of 100–101; and entification 102
Eventness 94, 134, 180
Events 52, 53; agency of 32, 128–130; linear progression of 31, 37; trigger events 38, 94; and evocation 58; trajectory of 90, 95, 113, 114; and closure 84; and atomism 95; and organizational meaning structures 112; and feeling 128; prehension of 75, 95, 159; mirroring of 91, 94, 97–98, 150; density of and change 168
Event formations 94, 97, 160, 165; as manifold 95–96; and vectors 166–167; direction and intensity of 66–67, 169; and meaning structures 181
Event-objects 99–101, 105–106, 151
Evocation 58, 101; and materiality 137; vividness of 76, 127, 132, 134, 137

Fashion 146
Finance traders 81–82, 125–126
Flat world viii, 15
Framing and overflowing 141, 184
French Revolution 77

Gestures 83, 86, 131–132

Habit 134
Habitus 134
Heterogeneity vii, x, 13, 26, 60, 101, 105, 107
Historicity 49, 101, 114, 129
Historicizing 38, 129–130, 181, 186–187,
History; as counterfeit 41; re-interpretation of 46
Homogeneity 21–26
Hugo Boss 146

Human Resource (HR) policies 116; as articulation 116

Identity; materiality and individual identity 23, 106
Institutions 20–21, 176–178; as stubborn facts 78, 177–178; and organizational politics 178
Intersubjective articulation 130–134, 168–169
Intersubjectivity 60, 82, 83, 86, 87, 90, 130–134
Intuition 29, 109, 110
Iranian 'Twitter Revolution' 144
Isochronism 34

Jazz 147–148

Kristiansen, Ole Kirk 168

Leadership 163–170; and articulatory modes 168
LEGO 79–80, 156–157, 159
Living present 82–85, 103, 119; contraction in 84; passive synthesis in 84; temporal float in 86; closure of 86; materiality at 103
Living experience 21, 103
Luther King, Martin 168

Mafia 23
Material articulation 136–139
Materiality 20, 22, 23–24, 60, 76, 97, 101, 103, 105, 106, 112, 116, 128, 138
Meaning 99, 107; as structure 111; as 'upon-which' 117
Memory 51–52, 164, 172–173, 172; forms of 172, 181; procedural and declarative 173
Microsoft 174
Misplaced concreteness 19–21,
Mohammed Ali 90
Movement 5, 30, 103, 156; and Zeno's paradox 30, 156; and spatial representation 103; and meaning structures 126
Mysteries and organizational research 183–188

Narratives 132
Naskapi Indians 127–128
Newspapers 141
Nike 106
Novo Nordisk 150

Ongoing temporality 44–47
Open source software development 113–114, 115
Organization studies; and timelessness 32; and memory 120
Organizational boundaries 28,
Organizational culture 54, 171–173
Organizational death 95
Organizational identity 25, 36–37, 173–176; and distinction drawing operations 175; temporal and spatial distinctions 175–176
Organizational life viii
Organizational meaning structures 99–122; articulation of 115–122; definition of 105; and becoming 109; performativity of 110; as organizations 111; and events 112; connectedness and 126; surplus of connections and 126; absence in 126; event formations and 181
Organizational memory 120; and an on-going view of temporality 120; as projective memory 120
Organizational structure 76
Organizations; as nouns 21, 57 102, 103, 115; as verbs 103; as flux 21, homogeneity assumptions about 21–26; materiality of 23; circumscription assumptions about 26–29; proximity assumptions about 26–29; as bounded systems 27; and inert temporalities assumptions 31–32; as connecting 62, 102; as relational wholes 107, 111
Organizing; as connecting 23, 41, 59–65, 102, 141; example at Ulstein 107–108; temporal stretch of 114; Particle physics 49–51

Passage of nature 1, 42, 78
Performativity 56, 110–111
Periodic temporality 35, 44
Philosophy, and social science 5–6,
Plot 108–109
Polysemy 117
Potentiality 3, 65–67, 148; and correspondence view 18
PowerPoint presentations 117, 149, 151
Practical articulation 134–136, 168–169, 173
Practice 135
Pragmatism 53–54
Prehension 75, 95, 159
Present 80–86; specious present 80; organizational present 81; co-presence in 81; simultaneity 81, 128;

closure of 84, 85; 'pure present' 90; mirroring of 91, 94, 97–98, 150; and feeling 128; Process; endogenous view of 47–53; 119; exogenous view of 47; and structure 67–72, 157
Process thinking vii, 39–40; and interpretive sociology 55; and potentiality 66; and sensemaking 56; and relationality 65
Proposition 102

Reflection 83, 85
Repetition 19, 30, 33, 42, 68, 120, 135, 168, 185
Rituals 42, 43; and timing 46
Roles 101–102
Running shoes 106; as organizers 106

School 107
Sense-making 25; and acts 25; interpretation 25; and commitment 25; and institutions 25; and temporality 56; and events 93
Serendipity 182
Shepherding 63–64
Social media 143–144
Social construction 26
Socio-materiality 12–13, 15, 61
Sharedness 22; shared assumptions 22; sharing of knowledge 26; Spatial view of organizations 16, 2
Spatio-temporality 61, 76, 85, 89
St Svithun 176–177
Stability 29–31
Stories 132, 180
Strategy 55, 79, 108, 114–115, 139–140, 159, 175
Strategy-as-practice 54–55
Structure and process 67–72, 115–116, 181
Studying process 179–182; and serendipities 182

Tacit articulation 15, 127, 134, 145–149
Tacitness 145
Temporal agency 38, 93, 95, 167; and texts 140, 142
Temporal logics 32–35; meaning and identity 35
Temporal present 61
Temporal reach 33, 151
Temporal structures 34
Temporary work 34
Texts 141–143; 'read-only' 143
Textual articulation 139–144
Time; experienced 33; clock time 33, 45; ongoing view of 44–47; periodic view of 36; and mattering vii, 31, 32; social construction of 32–35; and organization studies 35; sequential view of 36–37, 150; and organizational identity 36; as discrete 'nows' 37; as evanescence 45–46, 168; and perishability 45–46; Timing 43, 165; and politics 165
Twitter 143–144

Ulstein Group 96–97, 107–108, 109
Urban development 67

Vectors 157, 166–168; and leadership 168

We-ness 58, 83
Wholeness 108
Wink of an eye 88
World on the move 1, 11–16, 26, 39–44

X-BOW 97, 107, 109, 111, 149, 150–151, 179–180

Zeitgeist 146
Zeno 30–31, 36, 156
Zimbabwe bush pump 138